TOM MANN'S MEMOIRS

SOCIALIST CLASSICS

Available from Spokesman

A History of British Socialism
Max Beer

Cromwell and Communism
Eduard Bernstein

The Levellers and the English Revolution
H. N. Brailsford

Readings and Witnesses for Workers' Control
Ken Coates & Tony Topham

A Radical Reader
Christopher Hampton

Studies in Socialism
Jean Jaurès

Social and Economic Writings
Tom Mann

Roads to Freedom
Bertrand Russell

Pig's Meat
Thomas Spence

The Attack
R. H. Tawney

The Industrial Syndicalist 1910-1911

The Syndicalist 1912-1914

Tom Mann's Memoirs

Introduced by
Ken Coates

SPOKESMAN

First published in 1923
Reprinted in 1967 by MacGibbon & Kee in the Fitzroy Edition.
This edition published in 2008 by
Spokesman
Russell House
Bulwell Lane, Nottingham NG6 0BT, England
Phone 0115 9708318
Fax 0115 9420433
e-mail elfeuro@compuserve.com
www.spokesmanbooks.com

ISBN13: 978 0 85124 758 8

A CIP Catalogue record is available from the British Library

Printed by the Russell Press Ltd
(phone 0115 9784505 www.russellpress.com)

CONTENTS

Preface by Ken Coates		vi
Postscript 2008		xv
Further Reading		xxiii

EUROPE

I	Childhood and Apprenticeship	3
II	Early Jobs and Workmates	12
III	First Socialist Activities	24
IV	The Fight for an Eight hour Day	42
V	The Dock Strike of 1889	60
VI	After the Dockers' Strike	70
VII	The Labour Movement and the Churches	85
VIII	Secretaryship of the Independent Labour Party	98
IX	International Labour Organization	106
X	Organization of General Workers	118

SOUTHERN SKIES

XI	New Zealand	129
XII	First Years in Australia	142
XIII	Socialist Workers, Writers, and Poets	157
XIV	Free-speech Fight	168
XV	New South Wales; New Zealand Revisited	177
XVI	The Broken Hill Dispute	185
XVII	South Africa	197

HOME AGAIN

XVIII	Industrial Solidarity	203
XIX	Police Brutality	214
XX	The 'Don't Shoot' Leaflet	230
XXI	Trial for Incitement to Mutiny	250
XXII	Conclusion and Farewell	263
Index		274

PREFACE

THE FIRST secretary of the Independent Labour Party, the President of the dockers' union, the first General Secretary of the Amalgamated Engineering Union: a mere roster of the positions he held in the Labour Movement, of which this is a tiny fraction, would establish Tom Mann as a Pioneer. In his time he was editor or director of a whole plethora of Labour and Trade Union journals. He operated in four continents. He founded the British Section of the Red International of Labour Unions. He became the chairman of the Minority Movement, the left-wing Trade Union ginger group which *might* have transformed the General Strike from object lesson in defeat into signpost for a new society. But impressive though the catalogue of his formal positions undoubtedly is, Tom Mann's real significance can easily be underestimated. What he *did* was always far more impressive than the positions from which he did it. He was an initiator, a catalyst, a goad to action. He was also a man of huge generosity, of sympathy and insight. In an important sense it is perhaps true to say that he was often too broad, too big for many of the situations with which he had to cope. Yet whenever a real crisis came, his stature found its true proportions, and again and again Tom Mann became a pivot for the actions of downtrodden people, a focus for grinding but fragmented discontent, a legend revived. Throughout his lifetime as a militant socialist, whatever the stages of the evolution of his thought, he invariably displayed a gift for finding himself at the centre of every major struggle of his time. For this reason it is important that these Memoirs should again become available, if only because there is still no comprehensive biography of a key figure.[1]

Everyone knows of Tom Mann's role in the great dock strike of 1889, which so excited the elderly Chartist leader, George Julian Harney, that he wrote:

---

[1] The first volume of a biography by Dona Torr (with some chapters written up from her notes by Christopher Hill) was published in 1956 by Lawrence and Wishart. It is useful, but concludes with an account of the dock strike of 1889. A second volume was promised, bringing the story to 1910, but it has not yet apperred. A pamphlet by Dona Torr was published in 1936 and reprinted in 1944 with a preface consisting of Harry Pollitt's funeral tribute. It is heavily dependent on these Memoirs, and has only one page of information on events subsequent to those covered in this book. In 1941 the Communist Party published a memorial pamphlet which contained a brief chronology of Mann's life.

'all strikes, turnouts and lockouts of the past must pale their ineffectual fires in presence of the great revolt at the East End of London ... Not since the high and palmy days of Chartism have I witnessed any movement corresponding in importance to the great strike ...'[2]

Mann controlling the distribution of strike funds, stripped to the waist and sweating, blocking the doorway of the office with his back to one jamb and his boot to the other, and at one moment bludgeoning and consoling the unruly dockers, creating discipline where once was a mob, sharing the relief moneys and inspiring solidarity at the same time: this picture has become an image of the meaning of the New Unionism which reached down from the craftsmen to the dispossessed and forgotten unskilled workers, at a time when one third of London's population lived in abject poverty.[3] Less known, but perhaps more important, was Mann's activity immediately before and after those dramatic events. It was his shrewd and unremitting campaign for shorter working hours, culminating in the demand for a legal eight-hour day, which was the trigger not only for trade union struggles, but for a deepening political awareness: by causing the established politicians to reveal their limitations, exposing the difference between their interests and those of their workpeople, it played a major part in creating the dawning but persistently brightening conviction among workers that they needed independent political representation.[4] It was Tom Mann, pursuing this goal, who proposed the first Mayday demonstration to the London Trades Council.[5] At the same time, in a short phase of alignment, albeit at a distance, with the moderates, it was Tom Mann who both sat as a member of the Royal Commission on Labour alongside the Duke of Devonshire, Professor Marshall, Mr Mundella and Mr Plimsoll, and also harangued his dignified colleagues about the justice of the eight-hour day.

The socialist movement of the eighteen nineties was fiercely divided into warring factions: and when, in alliance with Keir Hardie, he became the secretary of the Independent Labour Party, Mann made numerous attempts to link the fractious groupings. The fabians were not very interested:[6] but the tetchy Hyndman could see some advantages

[2] Quoted from the *Labour Elector*, 28 September, 1889, by E. J. Hobsbawm, *Labour's Turning Point*; Lawrence and Wishart, 1948, p. 85–6.
[3] Llewellyn-Smith and Nash: *Story of the Dockers' Strike*: 1889, p. 94.
[4] Dona Torr, op. cit., Volume 1, pp. 214–25.
[5] *The London Trades Council; a History; 1860–1950*: Lawrence and Wishart, 1950, pp. 75–6.
[6] Cf Bernard Shaw's letter to Walter Crane: *Collected Letters*, Reinhard, 1965, p. 578.

in trying. However, he reacted very sharply from Mann's renewed interest in religion. Privately, he described the philosophy of the ILP as

> 'that queer jumble of Asiatic mysticism and supernatural juggling which we call Christianity, put forward by Keir Hardie and Tom Mann as the basis of a social and economic propaganda.'[7]

This side of Mann's thought has not been emphasised in subsequent writing about him: but the description he gives in these Memoirs should be understood in the light of the things he preached at the time: he addressed himself directly to the churchgoers, and if he made himself unpopular with his atheistic socialist co-thinkers, there is no reason to imagine that he became universally popular among the pious, as he stridently flayed their consciences:

> 'O preachers! who turn up at your church or chapel service and follow you in praying "Thy kingdom come; Thy will be done; as in heaven, so upon the earth". Can they, do you think believe there is anything in heaven corresponding to the wretched slumdwellers of Whitechapel or Spitalfields? Are there any in heaven corresponding to these Christian rent-takers, who wax fat at the expense of the downtrodden? What are you ministers and plutocratic members of the rich churches and chapels doing to make earth like heaven? ... Some of us, when we say the Lord's prayer, do indeed mean it, amongst whom I am glad to be one. I am not willing to be included with those cowards who say it is impossible of realisation.'[8]

The rumours that he was considering entering the Church were discounted by Mann: but in these pages it is fairly clear that his rejection of the idea was by no means so categorical, or so whole-hearted, as subsequent generations have often thought. But he did not take the vow: instead he became the President of the International of Ship, Dock and River Workers, formed with the help of Havelock Wilson, who was at that time almost as much of a firebrand as he later became of an obscurantist reactionary. Intensive international action, both on the Trade Union and Socialist fronts, increasingly widened his horizons.

During his first phase of activity in England, Tom Mann made a mixed impression on the circle of Frederick Engels. In 1899, Engels wrote with very guarded warmth of the new agitator:

[7] Letter from Hyndman to Ely, 28 September, 1894, cited Tsuzuki; *Hyndman and British Socialism:* OUP, 1961, p. 101.

[8] *A Socialist's View of Religion and the Churches:* Tom Mann: Clarion Pamphlet, 1896, pp. 4-13.

'The most repulsive thing here is the bourgeois "respectability" bred into the bones of the workers. The social division of society into innumerable gradations, each recognised without question, each with its own pride but also its inborn respect for its "betters"... is so old and firmly established that the bourgeois still find it pretty easy to get their bait accepted. I am not at all sure, for instance, that John Burns is not secretly prouder of his popularity with Cardinal Manning, the Lord Mayor and the bourgeoisie in general than of his popularity with his own class... And Champion – an ex-lieutenant – intrigued years ago with bourgeois, and especially with conservative, elements, preached socialism at the parsons' Church Congress, etc. Even Tom Mann, whom I regard as the best of them, is fond of mentioning that he will be lunching with the Lord Mayor. If one compares this with the French, one can see what a revolution is good for, after all."[9]

Two years later, Engels wrote to Marx's daughter Laura in far more derisory terms:

'There is a regular crop of "labour" papers: the *Trade Unionist*, by Tom Mann – soft like Mann himself, who for a Mann, has one n too much in English and one too little in German: nice sincere fellow as he otherwise is, as far as a man without backbone can be so.'[10]

By 1896, Eleanor Marx was describing Mann as the 'henchman' of Keir Hardie.[11] Hardie and Mann had both voted to seat the anarchist 'free communists', who were anti-parliamentarian, at the Congress of the Second International. 'It might be alleged,' said Hardie,

'that if they supported these people's claims they were supporting the anarchists. For his part, he was more afraid of doing an unfair thing towards a body of socialists with whom he did not see eye to eye, than he was of being called an anarchist.'[12]

This indictment of 'softness' can be seen to compound two distinct elements, which should be separated even if they are often, in fact,

---

[9] Engels, letter to Sorge, 7 December, 1889. In Marx-Engels on Britain, Moscow FLPH, 1953, pp. 522–3. This letter was several times quoted by Lenin.
[10] Engels, letter to Laura Lafargue, 13 June, 1891; Engels-Lafargue *Correspondence*, Volume III; Moscow FLPH, 1963, p. 77.
[11] Cf Tsuzuki, op. cit., p. 121.
[12] W. Stewart: *J. Keir Hardie;* ILP, 1921, p. 123.

connected. There is the softness which consists in toleration of other socialist views, which is not surprising in a generation which did not directly experience the great rumpus between Marx and Bakunin in the first International: and there is the far more serious charge of softness towards oppositional representatives of a hostile social class. It is pointless to speculate about Engels' ability as a judge of character: but he was an experienced politician, and no hysteric. What is clear is that whether Engels was right or wrong about Tom Mann in the nineties, his assessments have no validity whatever for Mann's second and lasting stay in England. There was no tougher, more unflinching opponent of capital in England than Tom Mann, when he returned from his prolonged stay in New Zealand and Australia. He lost nothing in tolerance of other socialist views: but in the face of the employers he was a man of iron. It would be interesting to explore in detail the effect that emigration had in all this: in Australia, at the age of fifty, he went to prison for the first time in his life, in the course of a campaign for free speech. Did the sharper confrontation of classes, in a continental social structure bereft of 'innumerable gradations', transform Mann's outlook? Certainly, when he returned to Britain, and voyaged almost immediately with Bowman to France to study syndicalism, he showed every sign of having come to 'see what a revolution is good for'. Five years after his jail sentence he was tearing round England, leading and inciting the new syndicalist movement, preaching with extraordinary fire and verve the gospel of 'workers' control', from which he was never again to waver, and directing the great Liverpool strike in which he became 'dictator' of the city, while the Government hastened to police the Mersey with gunboats. Immediately afterwards he was in prison again, for incitement to mutiny, as a result of the publication of the famous 'don't shoot!' appeal to the soldiers. Insistently campaigning, through 'amalgamation committees', and direct appeals, for trade union unity, solidarity and militant workshop organisation, he dominated Labour's prewar years. 'Tom Mann was the voice ... and a very different voice from the MacDonalds and Snowdens', wrote Maurice Reckitt, many years later.[13]

In 1917, he spoke at the Leeds Convention which greeted the February Revolution in Russia.[14] A huge excitement was in the air, and the wartime militants, formed in the 'great unrest', but uninhibited by their wartime experiences, in which shop steward organisation in the factories went from strength to strength, watched every move in

[13] *As It Happened;* Dent; 1941, p. 106.
[14] *Archives in Trade Union History:* CSE, Nottingham; No. 4, 1966, p. 8.

Russia with tense attention. But in 1918 *Justice*, the social-democratic organ, reported that Tom Mann was going to retire, to take up farming.

> 'A sum of money is being raised' it said, 'to help him forward in his new enterprise ... And yet, somehow, we cannot imagine to ourselves our friend settling down as a poultry farmer, or market gardener, when things are stirring all around. It will surely be pain and grief to him to dig and to plant, to prune and to hoe, to trim and to gather, when the battle is joined between the workers and the shirkers, between the people who toil, and the parasites who spend ... Mann unfortunately had the defects of his qualities. He could not keep upon one line. He has tried all sorts of nostrums. One thing, however, he never did try: he never sold out to the capitalist enemy. That is why we all respect him ...'[15]

Of course, he did not retire. Indeed, it would almost be fair to say, he started all over again, were it not for the fact that he had not stopped. He became an early member of the new Communist Party. In 1919, he became the first general secretary of the AEU, newly amalgamated; and it was at the Engineers' offices in Peckham Road that, three years later, he granted an interview to Harry Pollitt, who persuaded him on the spot to go to Moscow to help to launch the Red International of Labour Unions.[16] As chairman of this body's British section, he helped to launch the Minority Movement, which extended its influence out from the mineworkers to embrace metal and transport workers, and declared as its aims at a founding conference in 1924:

> 'We are not out to disrupt the unions, or to encourage any new unions. Our sole object is to unite the workers in the factories by encouraging the formation of factory committees; to work for the formation of one union for each industry; to strengthen the local Trades Councils ... We stand for a General Council that shall have the power to direct, unite and co-ordinate ... in order to secure, not only our immediate demands, but to win complete workers' control of industry.'[17]

The next year this programme was largely adopted at the TUC, but by then Mann was warning about the imperative need for urgent preparatory measures for the forthcoming General Strike. His warnings did not reach a wide enough audience to take effect, and soon Beatrice Webb was writing in her diary, after the defeat of the Strike, that it signalled the

---

[15] Lee and Archbold: *Social-Democracy in Britain;* SDF, 1935, p. 243.
[16] Harry Pollitt: *Serving my Time;* Lawrence and Wishart, 1940, p. 130.
[17] Pollitt's speech, quoted Allen Hutt: *The Postwar History of the British Working Class;* Gollancz, 1937, pp. 93-4.

'death gasp of that pernicious doctrine of "workers' control" of public affairs through the trade unions, and by the method of direct action... This absurd doctrine was introduced into British working-class life by Tom Mann ... Popular disgust with the loss and inconvenience of a General Strike will considerably check the growth of the Labour Party in this country, but will lead to a rehabilitation of political methods and strengthen JRM's leadership within the party itself.'[18]

Immediately after the defeat, the TUC began a gadarene rush to the right: in late 1927 Walter Citrine launched an attack on disrupters which provoked a forthright rebuttal from Mann: in this, he not only defended the militants, but reasserted their goals: 'We aim', he wrote, 'at applying the principle of workers' control in the shops, factories, mills, mines, ships and railroads until we get complete control.'[19] But the TUC was not in a mood to accept such goals, and it quickly slid through a variety of postures about 'participation' into abject quiescence. Neither was Beatrice Webb's hero more hopeful: and indeed, Sidney was to wake up one morning to find that he had been abruptly dumped by MacDonald, who was terminating the second Labour Government in order to form a National administration, and retrench. The retrenchment, which involved sharp attacks on the already baleful standards of the unemployed, provoked riots all over the country. In Belfast, in October 1932, riots escalated into a pitched battle with the police, in which fifty people were wounded and two died. Tom Mann went to speak at the funeral. He was arrested the moment it was over, and instantly deported.[20] In December 1932 he was again imprisoned for three months, under a form of preventative arrest which involved the invocation of an Act of the reign of Edward III and the Seditious Meetings Act of 1817.[21] During the frightful distress of the years which followed, the Labour Movement was at a very low ebb, and the struggles of the unemployed became increasingly desperate. In 1934, when he was seventy-eight years old, Mann was placed on trial, alongside Harry Pollitt, for sedition. The Swansea magistrates acquitted the pair of them.[22]

During his last years, Tom Mann maintained his travels. He went to China for the RILU in 1927, where he met Chen Tu-Hsui, the then leader of the Chinese Communist Party. By 1933 Chen, along with Peng

[18] Beatrice Webb: *Diaries, 1924-32* (ed. M. Cole); Longmans, pp. 92-3.
[19] Article in *Sunday Worker*, 11 December, 1927.
[20] Hutt: op. cit., pp. 225-6.
[21] Ibid, p. 237.
[22] Ibid, p. 253.

Shu-tse, had become in turn leaders of the breakaway Trotskyist movement: and in that year they were arrested by Chiang Kai Shek. Mann immediately signed an appeal for protests against their imprisonment, even though this was, to say the least of it, by then an unconventional thing for a leading communist to do.[23] In the early thirties he was deported from Canada. As late as 1938 he went to Stockholm to help in the election campaign of the Swedish Communist Party.[24] Throughout the thirties he was consistently a member of the presidium at successive congresses of the British Communist Party. He died on 13 March, 1941. During the last ten years of his life, socialist politics both in England and internationally had become increasingly harassed, anguished and apprehensive. It had been a decade of defeat and retreat. But Tom Mann's last message was to the young people:

> 'The young people will have a lot to go through, but they will succeed in the end', it concluded.[25]

If they are to do so, they will need to look very carefully at the experience of his life, particularly during the upsurge of syndicalism and the immediate postwar struggles. The struggle for workers' control, in which Tom Mann never hesitated, is now finding increasing support among a new generation of trade unionists. If they search through the mistakes, both theoretical and practical, of those years, they will find there, amongst them, a golden thread of dedication without which they cannot hope to succeed.

Back in 1895, J. L. Garvin described a meeting at which Tom Mann spoke:

> 'To the usual fierceness of his swarthy face, to the habitual menace of his facial gesture, he was led on this occasion to add the airs of a mountebank – shrugging his shoulders, spreading his arms, distorting his mouth and exciting roars of laughter by his whining parody of the Liberal workman. He laid himself out to split the ears of the groundlings ... and then he played to the passions of the gallery. He spoke here with terrible method and terrible intention. He knows all the hardship of a labouring life; he knows the discontents and resentments that Labour broods over most sullenly; he knows how frequently workmen hate the very idea of "having a master"; and in this knowledge he deliberately touched his hearers on the raw, until

---

[23] Constant Reader (Brian Pearce): *The Newsletter*, 24 October, 1959, p. 302.
[24] Torr; pamphlet, p. 48.
[25] Communist Party: Memorial pamphlet: *Tom Mann*, 1941, p. 8.

they bayed with rage ... But Mr Tom Mann's incendiary invective gradually passed into finer thought and not less effectual appeal. In rapid and dark lines he sketched the intolerable fate of an Elswick labourer, whom he called "a 17s and 10d a week man with a small wife and a large family." He denounced that, he denounced all life on such terms. He called upon his audience to dare to be men; and "Now young chaps", he trumpeted, flinging up to the crowded galleries and side elevations an excitant gesture. "Now young chaps, what are *you* going to live for?" The young chaps were electrified.'[26]

There is still a message like that which can electrify the young. It is, naturally, still unpopular in high places. For this reason, unfortunately, we still sorely need men like Tom Mann.

KEN COATES

[26] *Fortnightly Review;* September 1895, cited Hobsbawm, op. cit., p. 146.

POSTSCRIPT 2008

Tom Mann's Memoirs were originally published in 1923 by the Labour Publishing Company, and they were reissued in 1967 by MacGibbon and Kee as part of their series of Fitzroy Reprints. I was asked to contribute an introduction to the *Memoirs*, standing in for E. P. Thompson.

At the time, research into the life and works of Tom Mann was somewhat rudimentary. A biography had been begun by Dona Torr, an accomplished scholar whose work was never completed. The first volume did appear, and is noted in my preface. But the sequels, taking the story beyond the great dock strike, never saw the light of day.

MacGibbon and Kee's interest in these Memoirs was accompanied by their decision to publish the book of readings on *Workers' Control*, which I edited with Tony Topham, and which contributed to the revival of a serious movement on industrial democracy, which not unnaturally fostered great interest in Tom Mann and his works. So we were able to reprint some of his scattered articles and papers on syndicalism.

In 1988, John Laurent collected Tom Mann's early writings, which we published in the Spokesman imprint under the title *Social and Economic Writings*. But it was not until 1991 that the first full-scale biography, by Joseph White, was published by the Manchester University Press. In the same year, Chushichi Tsuzuki published his biography with the Clarendon Press in Oxford. Both these books devoted serious attention to Tom Mann's 'missing years' during the First World War.

Tony Topham and I had actually been working on this question in the course of preparing the first volume of our *History of the Transport and General Workers' Union*. We were able to inform Dr. Tsuzuki of our findings, although we did not learn of the existence of Joseph White's project until it appeared after our book was already in print. To cut a long story short, Tom Mann did not agitate against the First World War, and it might be thought that this was one of the problems encountered by Communist historians in presenting his among the lives of the Saints. Tsuzuki's judgement seems fair. 'A Responsible Patriot' he entitles the relevant chapter of his book. We presented the evidence quite fully in Chapter 16 of our own book, *The Making of the Labour Movement*. The Socialist trade unionists took a very sharp position in opposition to the bloodbath. Here is the view of Robert Williams, writing in the Transport Workers' Federation's *Weekly Record* on the first week of the hostilities.

> 'We know full well that the German working men hate war as much as we do ourselves ... Let us who can, be calm during the next few weeks. Let us rigorously suppress the blood lust in ourselves, and among those whom we can influence ... These myriads of Russia, France, Austria, Germany, – what quarrel can they have amongst one another? What sympathy has the French peasant and the French industrial worker with Russia that in order to support a tottering despotism, they shall attempt to butcher other German workers, who are divided from them by an imaginary line called a frontier? Why are hundreds of British transport workers torn from their occupations and their little homes to join the naval reserves ... in anticipation of a naval engagement the carnage of which will blacken our reputation for centuries? This German fleet may easily contain reservists from the German working class who contributed £5,000 to the London Transport Workers when they were fighting the "patriotic" London Employers ...'

Ben Tillett, by contrast, spent his time during those early days visiting Lord Kitchener at the War Office. The super-patriots in the transport union field were led by Havelock Wilson, the Seamen's leader, with whom Tom Mann maintained close and friendly relations in spite of their political differences. The war, of course, widened political schisms everywhere, not least among trade unionists. To recapture something of the context of those arguments, I will quote a short passage from our book. The transport workers are debating their responses to the introduction of conscription.

'In 1916 military conscription was introduced amidst a storm of protest from trade unionists, and the direct militarization of munitions and transport workers was threatened.

The Western Front had devoured so many volunteers that the army, by late 1915, feared that it might become unable to maintain the slaughter. A scheme was initiated by Lord Derby, inviting men to register for military service so that they could be enrolled and trained when they were needed. Thus, they would remain 'volunteers'. Notwithstanding fervid attempts to intimidate them, with white feathers and charges of cowardice, young men were increasingly reluctant to offer themselves. Word was getting round. The popular press launched an attack on professional footballers who declined to volunteer, and wanted to know why the fans were not in the trenches as well. This campaign failed. In January 1916 conscription was introduced for single men. By 21st March Sir William Robertson was telling the Cabinet that, of 193,891 called up under the new scheme, 57,416 had failed to appear.

Compulsion was accordingly applied more widely, and on 25th May married men of military age were included in the call-up. The unions had been strongly opposed to this measure, partly because it was a blow against the civil freedom of those pressed into service, but also because they feared the militarization of industrial life.

In Hugh Clegg's words, "the labour movement was in a turmoil" when, on 5th January 1916, the government presented its Military Service Bill. Lord Derby's attempts to avoid conscription had provided for men to "attest" that they were willing to serve. Lists of reserve occupations were drawn up, and the scheme was controlled under a National Registration Act to standardize the process of granting exemption from the moral obligation to enlist, and to conserve essential civilian labour supply. The whole Labour movement had seized on the Derby Scheme as an escape from conscription, but it failed the test. It was announced by the authorities that over one million unmarried men had not "attested", and the prospect of calling up married men who had offered themselves was too much for the government to accept. Compulsion for single men, it was judged, had to follow. An immediate wave of official Labour Party and TUC protest was met with Asquith's promise that conscription would for ever be limited to single men and that it would end immediately after the war.

A meeting of the TUC and the Labour Party had resoundingly declared its opposition to the Bill the day after its introduction, and called on Labour's ministers to resign. Asquith's promise, however, was enough to save the ministers' faces and, more important, to keep their bottoms on the front bench. They remained in office, and the Labour Party conference on 27th January confined its opposition to a protest vote. There would be no Labour campaign against conscription. In April, Asquith's pledge was withdrawn; the Bill to extend conscription to married men was introduced, and the TUC advised the unions to support it.

On 8th and 9th June the National Transport Workers' Federation Annual General Council took place in Glasgow. Harry Gosling, in his presidential address, conceded that whilst "we are carefully watching every tendency in the direction of industrial conscription, military conscription has been reluctantly agreed to". Samuel March moved, on behalf of the National Union of Vehicle Workers, the London and Provincial Union and the National Amalgamated Labourers' Union, that the NTWF

> "views with deep misgivings the introduction of compulsory military service into Great Britain. This country has been regarded as the chief stronghold against tyranny and oppression of every kind, and should lose no single opportunity of re-establishing individual liberty and the right voluntarily to refrain from organised destruction. It therefore calls upon the EC to press for the repeal of all Acts of Parliament imposing compulsion, especially in view of the very definite promise of the Government that it would be limited to single men, and this Conference pledges itself to oppose Conscription with all its power until it is coupled with the conscription of the wealth of the country. We particularly protest against the compulsory retention of time-expired men. We ask all Affiliated Societies supporting this resolution to press for a national conference to support these demands."

Conscription had not come about from military necessity, he began. (About this he was not wrong. There were more men in the army than it could equip.) The capitalists wanted conscription, he said, because they did not like the way trade unionism was growing, and because workers were demanding more of the wealth they produced: "They were more afraid of the worker getting his rights than they were of losing the war." The forceful organizer of the London and Provincial Union of Licensed Vehicle Workers, Ben Smith, seconded, with a strong call for the conscription of wealth. The workers were "giving their all", their lives. The wealthy were simply enriching themselves:

> They lent their money at huge interest, the Government spent it with the people who lent it, and they made a further profit out of that. The result of this was that the wealthy class sacrificed nothing; they got their money back, they got their interest and they got huge profits as well. It

had to be remembered that money would be dearer after the war, and that this would lead to unemployment for the workers, but he had hopes that this would eventually lead to the repudiation of the debt altogether.

After George Grisly (general secretary of the Cranemen and Enginemen's Union of London) had spoken in opposition, on grounds of patriotism, Ernest Bevin intervened. His was a swingeing contribution, forthright in the extreme. First, he impeached the Labour Party for reneging on its clear mandate:

> Reference had been made to the conduct of the Labour Party in dealing with the Government in connection with the passing of the Act. It would be remembered that when the first Act was before the country a national conference was called, which declared against the Act. He would respectfully suggest that those who conducted the negotiations had been jockeyed into undoing the work of the conference. The second Act was introduced, and he had heard suggestions that in secret conclave representatives of the Labour movement met the Government and agreed that a second conference should not be held.
> Mr. Sexton: That is not true.
> Mr. Bevin: If it is not rue, it should be contradicted. I have made the suggestion that it was true in more than one place, and I have never had a contradiction.

Then he rounded on the general staff of the army:

> He had to suggest that the higher command of the British Army had not been all that it might be. He objected to the right of the military authorities to continue to call upon the country for more men while men were sacrificed through the bad strategy of the Staff. The closer they got to grips with the enemy, the more their strategy seemed to consist of sacrificing lives, and he had yet to learn that those who had been responsible for disasters where thousand of lives had been sacrificed had been punished or seriously dealt with at all.

Moreover, there was another reason to oppose conscription:

> The people who advocated conscription were doing it with the intention of leading up to industrial conscription, and before the Act had been in operation three months they would find that the Northcliffe Press and their tools would be clamouring for the extension of the Act to industry, and they would find Labour men agreeing with it on the ground of military necessity. He wished that these Labour men had to come down amongst the men themselves and settle the troubles that

arose. He believed that if there was not a lead given on this question there would arise a kind of blind action of the part of the men themselves which would disorganise the Labour movement. They had a conflict of evidence on the part of the Government. At one moment it was munitions that was wanted, at another men. At another time the difficulty was shortage of transport labour, and incidentally it was drunkenness – he was sure that whatever Grisley's opinion on other subjects, he was opposed to the compulsory powers of the Liquor Control Board – they were never sure what it was. There was a doubt in his mind whether the Government had any co-ordinated policy on the war at all: there were the differences between the Army Council and the Munitions Ministry. Again he had to express surprise at the action of the Labour men. One Liberal politician had told him that he could not understand why the Labour men had allowed themselves to be so easily twisted to suit the whims of the Government.

James Sexton opposed the motion:

He was never fond of militarism; on the contrary, he had opposed it always. If anyone had told him before the war that he would be advocating a big army and a big navy, that he would be advocating war to the finish, he would have told them, quite politely, that they were liars. What had happened to change his opinion? What had happened to change Tillett's? Nobody could accuse Tillett of being in favour of the capitalist class. What had changed the president's opinion? Nobody could accuse the President of being in favour of militarism; all his thoughts and inclinations had been in the opposite direction. The thing that had changed their opinions was the unmistakable fact that Germany had been deliberately preparing for this war for thirty or forty years.

Then Tom Mann intervened. He favoured the resolution, because it was neither a pacifist nor an anti-war declaration. Sexton erred to see in it a pronouncement on the merits of the war. What were the national duties in the conflict? There were three:

We had to provide men, munitions, and money. They were told they must maintain on behalf of themselves and their Allies the magnificent Fleet which had swept the seas. They had to supply the Allies with munitions. They had to maintain the trade of the country in order to finance the Allies. That meant that men had to remain at home to produce the wealth to cover the expenses not only of ourselves but of our Allies. Could that be done while they depleted the country of wealth-producers? They declared that the men could not be got. A call was made for three millions of men. Three millions came forward. A call was made for more, and more came forward. The question was not one of men. Their Allies had millions of men. Russia had its millions of men who wanted arms and equipment, who wanted big guns, and who wanted finance. There was France, which had its millions of men, who also wanted arms, equipment, and guns. It was our duty to provide the arms, the equipment, and the money, and he repeated that there was no military necessity for the conscription of men in this country while the Allies were possessed of millions of men whose chief requisites were the arms and the money that this country alone could provide. And he was there to declare that Lord Kitchener could not, and no man could, make out a case for conscription. Russia's man-power was nineteen million men of military age. France's man-power was five and a half millions. Britain had six millions, and, with the dominions, eight millions. Did that look like deficiency of men? Italy had five millions. Was that a reason for taking a few hundred thousand more men from the trades essential to the financing of the Allies? It amounted to this: that Russia alone had as large a man-power as the whole of the enemy countries. The plea of military necessity could not be substantiated. The one thing that animated the conscriptionists was the fear of organised Labour. Immediately the Triple Alliance came into being the press was full of articles demanding that it should be controlled in the interests of the country. Conscription was the gateway to industrial compulsion. Sexton had quoted Lord Kitchener, but how many times had Lord Kitchener said that he thought voluntaryism would fill the bill. He [Tom Mann] said that this country must win the war; he would declare that to the conference, but he was also one who said that he was in favour of a settlement by negotiation as early as possible.

At this point, Ben Tillett had the last word. He had been at the front. The nearer he got to the front line, the more the soldiers supported conscription:

> Mistakes had been made, that was true, but was there a man there who had not made a mistake? Was there ever a strike conducted in which blunders had not been made? And in a strike they were conscriptionists; they were more than conscriptionists, they were coercionists, and God help the conscientious objectors. Let them all realise that this was something more than a strike; it was a world-war, and although he could feel and endorse the anti-compulsionist point of view, he did not want the country to get the impression that the transport workers were pacifists and anti-warites.

A card-vote followed. The vehicle workers lost their motion by 100,000 to 81,000. This was some measure of the movement of opinion; but it was more. By far the most radical statement had come from Ernest Bevin. Around him were crystallizing the hopes of the younger men, the idealists and the radicals. More and more "mistakes" by the generals were, alas, guaranteed. But now there were men who were unafraid to challenge them.'

All these are complex matters, in which yesterday's heroes may easily become today's villains, and vice versa. Seamless consistency is not always found among Labour leaders, even those we number among the best.

Ken Coates

FURTHER READING

The Industrial Syndicalist, monthly July 1910 to May 1911, introduced by Geoff Brown, Spokesman Books, 1974.

The Syndicalist, 1912-1914, reproduced in facsimile, with an introduction by Geoff Brown, Spokesman Books, 1975.

Tom Mann's Social and Economic Writings, a pre-Syndicalist selection edited and with an introduction by John Laurent, Spokesman Books, 1988. It includes:
The 8-Hour Day (1886)
Preachers and Churches (1894)
The Socialists' Programme (1896)
Socialism (1905)
The War of the Classes (1905)
The Way to Win (1909)

Chushichi Tsuzuki: *Tom Mann 1856-1941 – The Challenges of Labour*, Clarendon Press, Oxford 1991.

Joseph White: *Tom Mann*, Manchester University Press, 1991.

Europe

CHAPTER I

CHILDHOOD AND APPRENTICESHIP
1856 to 1880

I WAS born at Foleshill, Coventry, Warwickshire, on 15 April, 1856. I fix upon 1880, when I was twenty-four years of age, as a suitable opening date for what follows, because in this year I first began to realize that the faults of individuals, and the evils in the community, the existence of which I deplored, were not to be eliminated or cured by urging individuals of every class and station to live 'godly, righteous, and sober lives'.

I must explain that I had only a very short time at school as a boy, less than three years all told; about a year and a half at Foleshill Old Church Day School, and about a year at Little Heath School, Foleshill. As by this time I was nine years of age I was considered old enough to start work. My mother had died when I was two and a half years old. My father was a clerk at the Victoria Colliery; so it was counted fitting that I should make a start as a boy on the colliery farm. A year as an ordinary kiddie doing odd jobs in the fields, bird-scaring, leading the horse at the plough, stone-picking, harvesting, and so on, and I was ready to tackle a job down the mine.

I started work down the mine in the air courses. A number of men and boys were always at this work: the duties were to make and keep in order small roads or 'courses' to convey the air to the respective workings in the mines. These air courses were only three feet high and wide, and my work was to take away the 'mullock', coal, or dirt that the man would require taken from him as he worked away at 'heading' a new road, or repairing an existing one. For this removal there were boxes known down the mine as 'dans', about two feet six inches long and eighteen inches wide and of a similar depth, with an iron ring strongly fixed at each end. I had to draw the box along, not on rails; it was built sledge-like, and each boy had a belt and chain. A piece of stout material was fitted on the boy around the waist. To this there was a chain attached, and the boy would hook the chain to the box, and crawling on all fours, the chain between his legs, would drag the box along and take it to the 'gob' where it would be emptied. Donkey work it certainly was. The boys were stripped to the waist, and as there were only candles enough for one each, and these could not be carried, but had to be fixed at the end of the stages, the boy had to crawl on hands and toes dragging his load along in worse than Egyptian darkness. Many a time did I actually lie down groaning as a consequence of the heavy strain on the loins, especially when the road was wet and 'clayey' causing much resistance to the load being dragged.

The work is now rarely done in this way. More generally a larger road is made, rails are laid, and horses do the pulling; but it must be remembered that I am writing of a period before the Mines Regulation Act of 1872, and four years before the Education Act of 1870.

I had been working at the mine about four years when a spontaneous fire broke out, and proved to be of such a serious nature that it could not be extinguished. Several attempts were made to restart work; but every time fresh air was admitted the fire burst forth anew. At length the mine was closed altogether, and thus it remains to this day – 1922.

Our family, like the rest, had to leave the district. We settled in Birmingham, and I became apprenticed to a tool-making firm. This was in 1870, the year the Elementary Education Act was passed. Its operation was too late to be helpful to me, as I was already in my fifteenth year when it became law, and had been at work five years. By degrees it dawned on me that I had missed something in the educational line; I realized that all boys under fourteen were now required to attend school. I, like other boys, very frequently had to work overtime, so the only school I could attend was Sunday School, to which I went regularly, and I became a regular churchgoer as well – at St Thomas', Holloway Head, Birmingham.

The working hours at the factory were sixty a week, but, as I have said, frequently we were called upon to work overtime, usually two hours of an evening, thus leaving at eight o'clock instead of six o'clock, and as we started punctually at six in the morning, it made a long day of it.

At this time I knew nothing at all about trade unionism, but occasionally one or other of the men would be pointed out to me as 'belonging to the Society'. I had no clear idea as to what this signified, until, when I was sixteen, I became conscious of some kind of activity amongst the men, particularly the 'Society men', which neither I nor my boy workmates would make much of. As the weeks passed, we overheard mention of the *Beehive*, the trade-union paper, which, however, I have no recollection of having seen at that time. Then we heard of meetings being held. We youngsters had not so far been counted of sufficient importance to be consulted, or even informed, till we learned that the men were negotiating with the firm about the Nine-Hour Day. The next bit of news was indeed exciting. We learned that every person in the firm, men and boys, was summoned to a meeting. This was the first meeting of the kind I had ever attended. The proceedings did not last long. The business consisted of a report from the committee that had been negotiating with the firm for the nine-hour day, or fifty-four hour week, instead of the ten-hour day and the sixty-hour week. It was proposed that all should continue to start work at six in the morning, and leave at five in the evening instead of six; also that there must be 'penalization of overtime'. This, I gathered, meant that the men would refuse to work overtime unless there was more than the ordinary time rate for it. All the proposals being endorsed, negotiations were continued and completed, the firm granting the conditions. How truly pleased I was I need not trouble to add, and how thoroughly all enjoyed the dinner held to celebrate the event requires no further comment! I did not know at the time that there was a general move throughout the country establishing the nine-hour day in all engineering works; but so it was, and I had good reason to be glad of it.

The reduction of working hours to nine a day, coupled with the stoppage of overtime, had a very important bearing on my life. The firm having agreed to pay extra for overtime, very astutely gave orders immediately for a considerable extension of the factory, sufficient to accommodate an additional hundred men and boys. This was exactly what the men had aimed at, and I believe all were delighted at the diminution of overtime. For myself, I very rarely worked any overtime after this during the additional five years I remained there to complete my apprenticeship.

Fortunately for those of my age, others who had sorely felt the need of education, had already – in co-operation with influential persons – taken action to establish evening classes in the town. Thus, at the Midland Institute, at the Severn Street Institute, and elsewhere, classes on many subjects were available at very reasonable rates. Three evenings a week for five years I attended classes in connection with the Science and Art Department, South Kensington.

In addition I attended a Bible class one evening a week, and found it very helpful. I shall refer to this later. Also, I went on one evening a week to the meeting of a temperance society of which I was a member. Every Sunday evening, along with a young religious enthusiast, I attended a church or religious service of some kind, and became familiar with all varieties, not only of forms of worship and doctrine, but also of preachers and their styles. This left one evening only out of seven for ordinary purposes during the winter months.

I think I was particularly fortunate in most of the teachers I came into contact with. Three in particular I am quite sure had much to do in giving to me and strengthening any characteristics I may have worth referring to.

My Sunday School teacher, Mr Watts, in whose class I was twice each Sunday during four successive years (till I consented to take a class myself), was a man of great religious fervour. As soon as the scriptural lesson was read, he addressed the class, tactfully attending to each member of it with a warmth and zeal that riveted interest and stimulated enthusiasm for a devotional life. At Severn Street, where I studied machine construction and design, the teacher, Mr E. Shorthouse, a Quaker, was no ordinary man. He was dignified and refined and gave personal attention to each student. His quiet, forceful manner, his kindly but pointed comments, his helpful suggestions on the subject of one's efforts, with an occasional personal inquiry as to one's welfare, commanded not only our admiration, but our genuine love.

Although I was connected with the Anglican Church, the Bible class I attended and liked so much was conducted by Mr Edmund Laundy of the Society of Friends. Mr Laundy was a public accountant, a precise speaker, a splendid teacher. He taught me much, and helped me in the matter of correct pronunciation, clear articulation, and insistence upon knowing the root origin of words, with a proper care in the use of the right words to convey ideas. He encouraged the class systematically to use a good dictionary, and ever to have the same handy. Following his valuable advice I have always been grateful that I was privileged to attend his class. He has gone: it is forty-five years since I left Birmingham, and, therefore, left the class; but I have never been unmindful of the value of the lessons that fine old man gave us.

During the period I spent in Birmingham, Mr John Bright was one of the three Members of Parliament for the borough. I frequently heard him in the Birmingham Town Hall. I have heard many prominent speakers in that hall, and in many other places, but never one comparable to John Bright. The plainness of his language, the unaffected simplicity of his illustrations, his power to drive home the points of his speech, in conjunction with the mellifluous vocalization of which he was a master, made one feel that it was a great privilege to listen to such oratory, and to observe the orator.

During this same period Mr Joseph Chamberlain was on the Municipal Council, and filled the position of mayor of the borough for three years in succession. Municipal politics in Birmingham were then of a rather high standard, the reconstruction scheme in particular being, for that date, a bold undertaking. Joseph Chamberlain was full of energy, and exhibited great capacity. I well remember the meeting in the Town Hall on the occasion of his becoming the MP in place of either Muntz or Dixon, who resigned to make room for him. Chamberlain's maiden speech in Parliament was in favour of the Gothenburg system. As a wholesouled advocate of total abstinence, I was an ardent supporter of Chamberlain in his efforts to introduce the Gothenburg scheme into Britain. I continued to think highly of this scheme until years after, when I visited Gothenburg and Scandinavia generally; then I lost my enthusiasm for it.

National politics at this period were not very enlivening. No one was as yet advocating Socialism; to preach Radicalism or Republicanism was as far as any public speaker went; but Secularism was well to the front. Charles Bradlaugh, G. W. Foote, Annie

Besant, and others, were exceedingly active. George Jacob Holyoake was also a strong advocate of Secularism. What was known as the Free-thought movement not only had numerous adherents, but many of the best speakers in the country were identified with the movement, and the National Secular Society had a very large membership. G. J. Holyoake, himself a Birmingham man, was a highly-cultured and most refined speaker. I heard him occasionally at the Baskerville Hall, Birmingham, and always admired his transparent sincerity and broad-mindedness.

The first time I heard Mrs Besant was in Birmingham, about 1875. The only women speakers I had heard before this were of mediocre quality. Mrs Besant transfixed me; her superb control of voice, her whole-souled devotion to the cause she was advocating, her love of the down-trodden, and her appeal on behalf of a sound education for all children, created such an impression upon me, that I quietly, but firmly, resolved that I would ascertain more correctly the why and wherefore of her creed.

Charles Bradlaugh was at this period, and I think for fully fifteen years, the foremost platform man in Britain.

When championing an unpopular cause, it is of advantage to have a powerful physique. Bradlaugh had this; he had also the courage equal to any requirement, a command of language and power of denunciation superior to any other man of his time. On matters that he held to be right none could make a better case and few so good. He was a thorough-going Republican. Of course, in theological affairs, he was the iconoclast, the breaker of images. He had never been a trade unionist, but the trade unionists of the north, particularly of Northumberland and Durham, regularly invited him to their annual galas, and looked upon him as the most valiant helper they could secure.

I am not concerned to take sides as regards the respective principles championed by those to whom I refer in these Memoirs. My purpose in directing attention to the personalities I mention is to enable the reader to size up the situation at the date referred to.

One of the most prominent figures in trade-union activity at this period was Joseph Arch. He was an agricultural labourer of Barford, Warwickshire. During the seventies he devoted himself to organizing the farm workers, and on a number of occasions they received the hearty support of the trade-union movement in general. The bitterness shown by the farmers and in many cases by the clergy, particularly those of the Church of England, was of a tyrannical and persecuting order. It was the bitterness of those who have issued proclamations in favour of liberty, but who fiercely oppose all attempts towards emancipation that are made by persons living in their own immediate neighbourhood. As with all other sections of workers, substantial successes, and at other times, failures, were experienced by the farm workers, but beyond any question the Agricultural Labourers' Union did more than all other agencies put together to improve the farm workers' status, and to give them an insight into the possibilities of a better future.

By the time I was twenty-one, in April 1877, any knowledge I had of trade unionism, co-operation, politics, or other forms of activity, sank into nothingness in comparison with my then dominant conviction that everything was subservient to the 'one thing needful', the 'salvation of the soul'. All social distress, according to this view, is the direct outcome of neglecting the soul's salvation. With missionary zeal I worked in the temperance movement, as an adjunct to church work, believing in the orthodox way that a vicious environment was mainly responsible for keeping human beings in the 'wide road that leads to destruction'. I realized, however, that I ought to try and change that environment by social activities.

Had I had the guidance at this stage, to teach me how far environment is really responsible for character, and to show me the respective values of social institutions, undoubtedly I should have changed my attitude; but I had no grounding in sociology or in economics. The teachers I had revered knew nothing of such subjects; their outlook upon life, and, therefore, mine at this time, was conditioned by the orthodox interpretation of the Christian religion, which in its turn was mainly conditioned (but this I did not know) by economic determinism.

It was of great value to me that there was a fine Public Library at Birmingham, easily get-at-able, and available to all. I read considerably, but not systematically. I knew nothing of Shelley; Ruskin only very superficially; and nothing whatever of Malthus or Marx. Still, I was groping my way, if not directly, towards the light. At least I was becoming conscious of mental darkness. Giving attention to physiology, stimulated thereto by the statements made by temperance advocates as to the poisonous effects of alcohol on the human system, I grew convinced that excessive and improper drinking habits were largely engendered by unwise eating. The effect of this study was to cause me to become a vegetarian, and an enthusiastic food reformer.

From two directions I received a tilt towards the region of economics. Mr W. Hoyle's book on temperance first led me to connect the problem of the working day with the social problem in general. Mr Hoyle contended that, if temperance habits universally prevailed, the hours of labour need not be more than four per day. In food-reform literature I read, not only of the waste of material in the consumption of malt, etc., in the making of liquor, but also of the enormously extravagant custom of living upon animal food when, the same land cultivated to supply humans with foodstuffs direct, would maintain several times as many people as was possible when animals were maintained on the land, and the humans fed on the animals. I am not here concerned with physiological or humanitarian reasons for a non-flesh diet. I merely refer to my first realization that acreage of land and the produce therefrom had, or might have, a direct bearing upon population and the standard of life.

Young men of the present generation may be disposed to smile at the lack of economic knowledge possessed by young men at the period I am writing of. In this connection it should be remembered that no propagandist meetings advocating Socialism were held in those days. No Socialist society existed. Although Karl Marx had written the first volume of his great work *Capital*, in London, and it had been published in Germany in 1867, the English translation of this volume did not appear until 1886.

There was no general activity amongst trade unionists. The trade unionists whose names were before the public at this period were Henry Broadhurst, George Howell, George Odger, Randall Cremer, Robert Applegarth, and George Shipton. The furthest they had reached in matters political in 1874 was to run Labour candidates under the auspices of the Labour Representation League. Two (the first ever elected in Britain) were returned in

1874; Thomas Burt for Morpeth, and Alexander Macdonald for Stafford. All the above-named were nothing more than liberal Labourites; they merely claimed full legal recognition of the right to organize trade unions, with safeguarding of trade-union funds. A number of them, and notably Charles Bradlaugh (whose name was included in the list of candidates), were Land Reformers, not Land Nationalizers.

In the autumn of 1877, having completed my seven years' apprenticeship, and being now twenty-one years and six months old, I left Birmingham for London. The engineering trade was experiencing a very slack time. I had a spell of 'out of work', and rather than remain idle I obtained a situation as dock clerk at Swan & Edgar's, Piccadilly Circus. I continued my interest in food reform, and joined in propagandist efforts with a group of similar-minded enthusiasts, finding considerable satisfaction in the advocacy and practise of the same. I continued rigidly on these lines for three years.

CHAPTER II

EARLY JOBS AND WORKMATES
1880 to 1884

I NOW come to 1880. I was working as an engineer at the Westinghouse Company, Canal Road, King's Cross, London. This was the first works established by Westinghouse in Europe, for the manufacture of the Westinghouse Automatic Brake, and I found the work of the air brake particularly interesting. A number of the staff and some of the mechanics were from the United States, and Mr George Westinghouse himself was frequently there. Most of the machinery was from America. The atmosphere of the works was that of America, and it suited me well. Notwithstanding the fact that the brake was wonderfully efficient, experiments were always being carried on with a view to greater efficiency, and large sums were spent in this direction. George Westinghouse, the inventor, was a very big man physically, as well as otherwise, and to all appearances took the keenest delight not only in the designs, but in the mechanical finish. He seemed to take great interest in comparing English workmanship with American. Many yarns were told about Mr Westinghouse's early experiences in the States. One – and I believe it was quite true – was as follows: Mr Westinghouse had invented the brake and was ready to get to business, but was in need of the capital to start a factory. He was advised to go to New York and get in touch with the moneyed men who are always ready to invest in a sound proposition. Westinghouse left his models at Pittsburg and made for New York, ultimately securing an appointment with a millionaire – Pierpont Morgan, I believe it was. Westinghouse explained the invention, describing how he 'would put two small cylinders on the side of the locomotive boiler, one of which would be operated by steam from the boiler, and this would operate its companion cylinder, pumping air into the pipes that were connected with the cylinders under each vehicle, and the release of the air would operate the brake blocks that would stop the train'. The millionaire chimed in at this stage: 'Do I understand that your invention is to stop railroad engines and trains by blowing wind at them?' – 'Well, by pumping the air to a pressure of ninety pounds per inch and then releasing it.' The millionaire here cut the conversation short by jumping up and opening the door, directing Westinghouse out, and saying: 'That'll do, young man, I've no time to spend on damn fool propositions'; and thus ended the interview. The money difficulty was, however, overcome, and rapid development followed.

At this time I was mainly interested in two subjects apart from workshop affairs – social problems and astronomy. What turned my attention to the study of astronomy was the fact that, before starting with the Westinghouse Company, I had been employed in Cubitt's engineering works, in Grays Inn Road. I was working as a turner on a chuck lathe. The British Museum authorities had received a large meteorite weighing some seventy or eighty pounds, and they wanted to have it cut into approximately three equal pieces, for exhibition in different museums. The Museum people sent it to Cubitt's for this purpose. It so happened that the lathe I was working on was the most suitable on which to do the job, so it came to me. I remember I spent about two days on this, and naturally it gave me a good stimulus to thought, as to where it came from; as to what it consisted of I had ample evidence in sawing it through twice, to make three portions as required. It consisted of metal that seemed to me exactly like Bessemer steel. This, however, was not continuous but interspersed all through the mass in pieces about an inch and a quarter in diameter; the rest of the meteorite resembled slag from a blast furnace, and was very hard. While I was at work on this, I was questioned by other workmen who passed me as to what it was. I soon realized my ignorance, and resolved to lose no time in getting some knowledge from reliable sources. Hence I became keen upon a number of things astronomical, and this science has ever since been my chief standby as a recreative study.

At this time also I was much attracted by the Malthusian theory of population. My additional experience and study in the field of practical social-reform convinced me that persistent attention given to individuals might, and often did, result in the developing on their part of qualities of self-reliance and self-respect, thus temporarily, and sometimes permanently, changing their characters for the better; but it was plain that into the quagmire from which these individuals had been rescued, others had been forced by the pressure of their surroundings. It was impossible to take comfort in 'plucking brands from the burning' if the rescues thus effected merely added to the pressure which would force others into a similar position.

It was clear that there was a mighty force of some kind counteracting and nullifying the efforts of well-disposed reformers. With altruistic enthusiasm, such persons worked in and through religious institutions, temperance and food-reform agencies, people's concerts, organ recitals, penny readings, Christian Endeavour societies, and Young Men and Young Women's Christian Associations. These, and all the other benevolent and kindly efforts made by the comfortably placed on behalf of the miserable, failed to reduce the totality of misery, or to minimize the sum of human suffering.

I was in contact with large numbers of workmates in conditions where serious fluctuations of employment prevailed. I was myself one of those liable to summary discharge, and to considerable spells of unemployment, quite irrespective of personal habits. Since the most intelligent and virtuous were affected equally with the others, it became nauseous to listen to statements from the temperance platform as to how careless individuals who had neglected their homes, etc., had become total abstainers, had regained regular employment, were able to keep at work in consequence of their reliability, and so on. This line of argument had such marked limitations that it was impossible to tolerate it. In view of the effort expended and the numbers enrolled in the various bodies, making due allowance for the excellent work done, the observer who computed the percentage of the physically unfit, the number of badly housed and insufficiently fed (what General Booth of the Salvation Army called the 'submerged tenth'), perceived that the army of the wretched remained just as large as before all these efforts had been made.

Something more far-reaching must be found, or the prospect was indeed a gloomy one. I was in this stage of development when I was confronted with the doctrine of Malthus. Thomas Robert Malthus wrote his *Essay on Population* in 1798 in reply to William

Godwin's book *Enquiry concerning Political Justice*. The Malthusian contention is that population always treads on the limits of subsistence. The population under free conditions tends to double itself every twenty-five years. The means of subsistence under the most favourable conditions cannot be made to increase so fast, hence the growth of population is checked by the want of food. Malthus claimed that population increased in a geometrical ratio, and the means of subsistence in an arithmetical ratio.

He stated the case as follows:

> Let us call the population of this island eleven millions; and suppose the present produce equal to the easy support of such a number. In the first twenty-five years the population would be twenty-two millions, and the food being also doubled the means of subsistence would be equal to this increase. In the next twenty-five years, the population would be forty-four millions, and the means of subsistence only equal to the support of thirty-three millions. In the next period the population would be eighty-eight millions, and the means of subsistence just equal to the support of half that number... Taking the whole earth, instead of this island, emigration would of course be excluded; and supposing the present population equal to a thousand millions, the human species would increase as the numbers 1, 2, 4, 8, 16, 32, 64, 128, 256, and subsistence as 1, 2, 3, 4, 5, 6, 7, 8, 9. In two centuries the population would be to the means of subsistence as 256 to 9; in three centuries, as 4,096 to 13, and in two thousand years the difference would be almost incalculable.

This result is not to be witnessed because no more people can live than there is subsistence for. Malthus' conclusion is that the tendency of population to indefinite increase must be held back by moral restraint of the reproductive faculty. In default of this, Nature steps in with positive checks to the population, including 'all unwholesome occupations, severe labour and exposure to the seasons, extreme poverty', resulting in early deaths, with a percentage of the people always below even the poverty line, and ready to die at the next touch of economic pressure. This theory destroys all hope of curing poverty and the evils arising from poverty by attempts to uplift the mass through changing the environment, or in any other way than by regulating the number of children that may be born, and by adapting that number to the possible maximum production of life's necessaries. It declares that the production of these necessaries cannot by any possibility be made to keep pace with the unregulated natural increase in population. The illustrations given by Malthus, more particularly as regards America during the eighteenth century, seemed to give strong support to the theory. Although the author's endeavours to apply the principle to various countries and to show that everywhere population tended to increase in a geometrical ratio, whereas the means of subsistence could increase only in arithmetical ratio, were obviously fanciful, still, in the main, the Malthusian theory seemed to be supported by fundamental facts.

The Malthusian League was very active in these days, and in 1877 public attention had been directed to the population question by the prosecution of Mr Bradlaugh and Mrs Annie Besant for publishing and circulating the pamphlet known as *The Fruits of Philosophy*, written by Dr Knowlton of America. The League spread considerable literature on the population question, and everyone really concerned about social reform was sooner or later brought into contact with this question.

For myself, I did not feel equal to meeting the many arguments advanced by the Malthusians, nor could I convince myself that they were right. While in this unsettled state of mind I went to work at Thorneycroft's, the torpedo-boat builders, at Chiswick. Here, in 1881, I read Henry George's book, *Progress and Poverty*. This was a big event for me; it impressed me as by far the most valuable book I had so far read, and, to my agreeable surprise at the time, it seemed to give an effective answer to Malthus. I was greatly interested in the book. It enabled me to see more clearly the vastness of the social problem, to realize that every country was confronted with it, and the capable and comprehensive analysis of the population question supplied me with what I had not then found in any book in this country before. I must again give a reminder that Socialism was known only to a very few persons, and that no Socialist organization existed at this time.

Henry George's cure for economic troubles, as advocated in *Progress and Poverty* is the Single Tax. I could not accept all George's claims on behalf of his proposal, though for lack of economic knowledge I was unable to refute these claims. I am not wishful, however, to pass any criticisms upon Henry George; I

Early Jobs and Workmates

wish, rather, to express my indebtedness to him. His book was a fine stimulus to me, full of incentive to noble endeavour, imparting much valuable information, throwing light on many questions of real importance, and giving me what I wanted – a glorious hope for the future of humanity, a firm conviction that the social problem could and would be solved. Although it was not till 1884 that I acquired a real grasp of social economics, the study of Henry George's book was of untold value, and never since I gave it careful attention have I had one hour of doubt but that the destiny of the human race is assured, and that the workers will, in due time, come to occupy their rightful position.

I must revert to the Westinghouse firm, for while here I took part in a strike. The firm, knowing the prejudice against piece-work on the part of Englishmen in the trade, had not at first attempted to introduce it; but the time came when they insisted upon its being resorted to. They submitted proposals of a special character, and offered high prices which, the men admitted would pay well; but this was a policy experienced men had knowledge of. On one floor, the men were practically all non-union men, and here, piece-work was in operation. The firm claimed the right to apply the same principle on another floor. The attitude of the men was, on advice of the union (the Amalgamated Society of Engineers), that to start piece-work on a floor where hitherto day-work had obtained, was, from the union standpoint, an attempt to start it in a new shop. Consequently, all members of the ASE left work. In a few days I restarted at Cubitt's. This was the first time I had actually participated in a strike. Since then I have been identified with many hundreds of them.

Working on the next lathe to myself at Cubitt's was a quite unusual type of Scotsman. He was a tall, dignified person, never indulging in frivol, but absolutely obsessed by the continuous study of Shakespeare. His one and only recreation was to read Shakespeare, and books that dealt with Shakespeare, plus seeing every Shakespearian piece performed, so that, naturally, he became a critic of no mean ability. His enthusiasm for Shakespeare infected me, and I, too, became a student of the great bard. As a Warwickshire man myself, and not a stranger to the Birmingham library, I had turned over the pages of the Stratford-on-Avon giant; but the devotion of my fellow-workman impelled me to carefully read, mark, and learn. I derived benefit accordingly, and from that time I was never lonely so long as a volume of Shakespeare was available. As I write these lines and think of my old workmate, whom I have not seen for very many years, I recall the only occasion when he looked at me with an unfriendly glare, and I probably deserved it. On the last day of March I had put many questions to my friend Jeffries on Shakespeare, and he had been equal to them all. It occurred to me to try the April-fool trick on him; so I made up a doggerel kind of question, and said I thought it occurred somewhere in the tragedies, as follows: 'Oh, what a numskull to turn over the page and not to see that he's had.' Of course, he 'could not recall such a sentence, but would look for it.' Next morning, he expressed regret and astonishment at his 'inability to trace it; he had spent several hours trying to do so.' I then reminded him that it was April 1st, and he gave me the look referred to. No wonder!

The engines that propel the Whitehead torpedo were made by the inventor of the engine, Peter Brotherhood, whose firm was then in Compton Street, Clerkenwell. I left Cubitt's to go to Brotherhood's, to turn forty sets of pistons for that number of engines then ordered by the Admiralty. The atmosphere at Brotherhood's was quite different from that of previous shops I had been at – more cosmopolitan, varied, and essentially engineering and nothing but engineering. The foreman was a fine, intelligent man, broadminded and tolerant; but there seemed to be nothing to talk about at meal times or on any odd occasion but work, Government orders, and who had them, patents just launched or expected, prospects of greater trade for engineers, the mechanical progress of the world as it affected engineers. No talk here of social problems; but every man was in the ASE and seemed to me to possess ability of the highest grade. Nothing could prove insurmountable to them, as mechanics.

From Clerkenwell, where I had been working on torpedo engines, I went to Chiswick to work on the engines for the torpedo boats. This I have already referred to. Amongst workmates here were enthusiastic co-operators; good propagandists they were, and they tactfully tried to interest their workmates in the principles of co-operation. Naturally, the next thing was membership of the store. There were those also who had a scientific turn of mind, and a number attended classes. Science and art classes were held in the neighbourhood, and I made another start by attending them. Here also were some who had a disposition to study systematically. It was decided to form a society. This was done under the name of the Shakespeare Mutual Improvement Society. I became president of this. The meetings were held at the Devonshire Club and Institute in Chiswick High Road. I happen to have a copy of the syllabus from January to July 1884. Shakespearian subjects occupy a good portion of the programme. Amongst others is a lecture on 'Electricity', another on 'The Chemistry of the Sun', another on 'Are other Worlds Habitable?' Both the lectures on Astronomy were given by a Mr G. Wells. Another was on 'The Circulation of the Blood'. One was on 'The Tower of London', and I remember vividly another lecture on 'The River Thames'. This last was given by James Aitken Welch. He was working on the 'surface plate', marking off – a term well understood by engineers. A well-developed man of cosmopolitan interests, he was a workman of the type that exercises a great influence for good over others. He was an ardent co-operator, an enthusiastic trade unionist, and is still active, well on in the eighties, as a trustee of the Amalgamated Engineering Union. My own contribution to the programme of the society in this first session of 1884 was a lecture on 'Progress and Poverty', and another on 'Astronomy'. On Saturday afternoons, visits were arranged to various museums and other public institutions.

At this period Mr Richard A. Proctor, the astronomer, was lecturing at Kensington on, 'The Birth and Death of Worlds', I was a regular reader of Proctor's magazine *Knowledge*, and I had succeeded in interesting two of my workmates in some elementary items of astronomical information, so that they readily agreed to accompany me to the lecture. After a brief explanatory statement the lecturer exhibited a series of very fine pictures showing nebulae and the resultant worlds, their life and decay. I had been engrossed, giving all attention with eyes and ears. After a time, I looked round to my friend Ted on my left hand. He was fast asleep. I turned to Jack on my right hand, and he, too, was fast asleep! The spirit indeed was willing, but the flesh was weak. They were sorry, for they were really interested in the subject.

Whilst working at Chiswick in the year 1882, I made my first trip to Paris, in company with a young workman of London with whom I had been maintaining a correspondence in shorthand, for the purpose of interchanging opinions and gaining a familiarity with Pitman's phonography. My friend was a Swedenborgian, and amongst other matters we talked over was the doctrine of 'uses' as taught by the New Church. We discussed theology, and frequently he would return to his main contention as expressed by Swedenborg, viz.: 'All religion has relation to life, and the life of religion is to do good.' In explaining 'goodness' the contention was that a man was good by the amount of service he rendered to his fellows: therefore, to be of use was to be good. My friend was also a capable violinist, and I, too, gave some little attention to this fine instrument, though I was never equal to a creditable performance thereon. Still, it was a helpful influence. We were both delighted with our week in France. This was the first time either of us had been out of England, and we were eager for new experiences. It was of intense interest to both of us to muddle our way through, with about a half-dozen French phrases of the guide-book order. We watched men at work, and noticed not only how they worked, but took stock of every garment they wore, and every gesture they made. The week did not satisfy me, but we returned, and started work. Yet I could not keep my mind off the desirability of a longer trip and the sampling of some other country. So the following year I resolved upon a visit to New York, determined to take my tools and stay a few months, and get greater satisfaction than I had done from the short time in Paris.

I arrived in New York just as the preparations had been made to celebrate the opening of Brooklyn Bridge. This took place on the second day after my arrival, and that morning I had succeeded in getting a situation as an engineer ('machinist', they term it), to start the next day. So I participated in the opening of the bridge celebrations with zest. There are four very fine bridges across the East River now, but this was the first of them.

I got along all right in the workshop. It was the engineering department at Havermeyer & Elder's Sugar Refinery in Brooklyn. There had been a considerable recent extension of the works, and the engineers were working night and day shifts. My first unsatisfactory experience was that of the working hours. For years past in England we had had a nine-hour day, or fifty-four hour working week, so arranged that we could leave work at one o'clock on Saturdays. In the States a ten-hour day or fifty-nine hour week still prevailed, the men leaving off on Saturdays only one hour earlier than on other days. I was, of course, a member of the Amalgamated Society of Engineers, but not more than a third of the men I was working with belonged to any union. My mate, taking turns about with me on the same lathe (in working the double shifts we changed about, each working a week on nights and a week on days), was a Norwegian. On the next lathe on my right there was a German, working mate with an American; and on my left an Austrian was mated with an Italian. On that one floor, accommodating about one hundred and twenty men, there were a dozen nationalities represented.

I put in four months in New York, working in Brooklyn; and all that time I found only one workman who had any knowledge of Henry George, and he was a Scotsman. This same man came from the Western States, and fixed up for lodgings at what was known as Lafayette Hall, in Delancy Street. I also was staying there. We became friendly, and he recited many of his experiences to me; but he was weak in the chest, the lungs were faulty, he became ill and went to the hospital. On a Sunday morning, quite early, information was sent from the hospital that he had died during the night. Only three persons, including myself, had talked with him at any length. All we knew of him was that he was a member of the Amalgamated Engineers, and that his home was in Scotland, his mother's address being found in his trunk. It was August, the weather was exceedingly hot. As the result of a conference of the three mentioned and the landlord, it was decided that the best thing to do was to accept responsibility for the burial of our departed comrade, and to proceed to make arrangements for the funeral. This was done. We obtained the permit to get the corpse, arranged with the undertaker to take same across the North River to a cemetery on the Jersey Heights; we paid six dollars for a grave; we four and two grave-diggers were the only ones to attend at the graveside. No service of any kind was held, no speech made. We each took a shovel and slowly dribbled earth on to the coffin. Ten minutes later the grave-diggers had filled in the grave. It was now five o'clock in the afternoon, and the man had not been dead more than twenty hours. It seemed to me awfully callous, and yet no proposal I could make was considered any improvement on the course taken.

Returning to London in the autumn, I at once commenced working for the old firm of Thorneycroft's at Chiswick, and engaged actively in the work of the lecture society before referred to.

It was about this time that the late Professor Thorold Rogers published his work *Six Centuries of Work and Wages*. I got hold of this and devoured it, and many parts of it were very helpful. Particularly was I interested in the details that showed the hours of labour and the purchasing power of wages received five or six hundred years ago in this country; and to find that Rogers contended, and gave many documentary proofs in support, that the hours of labour were only eight a day six hundred years ago.

The following extract will serve to show the style, and it can be easily be understood that a student would delve into the mass of facts and figures the Professor's complete edition provided:

> I have protested before against that complacent optimism which concludes, because the health of the upper classes has been greatly improved, because that of the working classes has been bettered, and appliances, unknown before, have become familiar and cheap, that therefore the country in which these improvements have been effected must be considered to have made, for all its people, regular and continuous progress. I contend that from 1563 to 1824, a conspiracy, concocted by the law, and carried out by parties interested in its success, was entered into, to cheat the English workman of his wages, to tie him to the soil, to deprive him of hope, and to degrade him into irremediable poverty.

I had become convinced of the necessity for a reduction in the hours of labour, and made use of any occasion that offered to advocate the eight-hour day. No one that I knew or heard of was doing this, but I felt impelled to take action and did so. One of my earliest attempts was when I introduced the subject to Hammersmith Branch of the Amalgamated Engineers, of which I was a member. There were some seventy or eighty members present, and I submitted a resolution to the effect that the time had arrived when definite action should be taken to secure an eight-hour working day instead of the nine that generally prevailed. On the vote being taken five voted in favour, and the rest against. As far as I can remember no one really opposed in principle, but 'the time was not ripe'. I was the 'young man in a hurry', etc. But the matter did not end here.

CHAPTER III

FIRST SOCIALIST ACTIVITIES
1884 to 1886

THORNEYCROFT'S was slack; a number of men, myself included, were discharged. I remember that it was on the fourth of July we were discharged. I joked about our Independence Day. Trade was dull. I tried many engineering shops with no success: but Tilbury Docks were then in course of construction. Lucas & Aird of Chelsea were the contractors. Another of the discharged men, a fitter, and I went to Tilbury having learned there would be a good prospect. We both obtained work in the engine shop in connection with the docks, and this will help to indicate the kind of change made in a workman's surroundings in London simply by changing his job. My home was in Chiswick, eight miles west of Charing Cross, whilst Tilbury Docks are twenty-two miles east. It was not merely that there was a distance of thirty miles between home and work, but in order to reach Tilbury from Chiswick in early morning the following was the method. To get the first workman's train from Hammersmith, it was necessary to walk the two miles from Chiswick to Hammersmith, then on the Metropolitan to Aldgate, then walk to Fenchurch Street to get the Tilbury train to start a day's work with the rest. The present town of Grays was at that time no more than a few streets to meet the needs of the men engaged on the Docks, and I lodged there getting home at weekends; but also, on the night of the meeting of our lecture society at Chiswick, I used to ask for an hour off, and so leave at four o'clock and get to Chiswick to participate in the meeting and then enjoy the morning journey as already described: and 'enjoy' is correct, for I certainly had much more satisfaction in maintaining my interest in the affairs of the society than I possibly could have had by being in a state of mind that would have counted it too much trouble to bother with.

It was at this time, 1884 and on, that the Social Democratic

Federation was conducting a vigorous propagandist campaign. The social Democratic paper *Justice* had been started, and those who were able to sense the situation recognized that something was buzzing.

I was on the alert for a situation in London so as to be near home, when I learned that Brotherhood's, for whom I had previously worked at their old shop in Clerkenwell, were now in a fine new up-to-date establishment at Belvedere Road, Lambeth. I applied there. I may add that this building occupied part of the site on which the New County Hall has been built, and the firm of Brotherhood's is now located at Peterborough. I started again for this firm, and moved to Battersea to be within easy travelling distance. The Battersea branch of the Social Democratic Federation was a rapidly growing body. It held meetings every Sunday morning in the open air, at Battersea Park gates, on Sunday evenings in Sydney Hall, and at various other places during the week. John Burns was the foremost member of the branch, and had already won renown as a public advocate of the new movement. I at once became a member of the branch and a participant in the work thereof, literature selling and public speaking.

I threw myself into the movement with all the energy at my command. I thoroughly endorsed the principles, and such palliative proposals as I considered to be of a practical character. In any case, full of a desire to help in developing opinion favourable to change in the directions indicated, I found my bearings very quickly on fraternizing with, and listening to the speeches of, John Burns, H. M. Hyndman, H. H. Champion, John Williams, James Macdonald, and many others with whom I came into contact. I became their colleague in the cause. The power of these men to attract and hold an audience, coupled with the wonderful amount of valuable information they imparted in their speeches, plus their glorious fearlessness and absence of apologetic timidity in the presentation of their case, attracted and pleased me immensely. I lost no time in endeavouring to become equally qualified, and as I look back upon that period it affords me satisfaction to recall that there was no time wilfully wasted. Travelling by workman's train from Queen's Road, Battersea, to Waterloo, I was at work in the morning by six o'clock. Every week-end I was busy on propaganda work, usually speaking three times on the Sunday—

twice in the open air and once indoors. Often the round would be near Bricklayers' Arms, Old Kent Road, at 11 a.m., Victoria Park in the East End, 3.30 p.m., and indoors at some branch meeting or other public gathering in the evening, rarely reaching home before 11 p.m., to be up at five o'clock next morning. No payment of any kind was received for this, a fact which I only mention to illustrate the truth of the axiom 'where your treasure is there will your heart be also'.

John Burns and I became close friends and good comrades. He was two years my junior, but looked older than I. We were both members of the Amalgamated Engineers, he of the West London branch, and I of the Battersea branch. He had a splendid voice and a very effective and business-like way of putting a case. He looked well on a platform. He always wore a serge suit, a white shirt, a black tie, and a bowler hat. He looked the engineer all over, and was very easily recognized. When Charles Bradlaugh showed signs of physical weariness, John was in the ascendant. Surprisingly fluent, with a voice that could fill every part of the largest hall or theatre, and, if the wind were favourable, could reach a twenty-thousand audience in the parks, etc., he was undoubtedly the most remarkable propagandist speaker in this country. Close friends and fellow agitators as we were, there were occasions when we differed considerably in our estimates as to what was best in tactics, as I shall have occasion to show later.

Hyndman was a very different personality. In the early days of open-air propaganda – for he took his turn regularly at outdoor gatherings as well as indoor – his essential bourgeois appearance attracted much attention. The tall hat, the frock coat, and the long beard often drew the curious-minded who would not have spent time listening to one in workman's attire. Hyndman always gave the unadulterated Social Democratic doctrine, as propounded by the Social Democratic Federation. He never whittled down his revolutionary principles, or expressed them in sugar-coated phrases. He took the greatest delight in exposing the exploitation carried on by the capitalists, and especially by those who championed Liberal and Radical principles, and were thought highly of by the workmen members of Radical clubs. He cleverly criticized the workmen listening to him for not being able to see through the machinations of those members of the master class, closely associated with the church or politics, or both. At almost every meeting he addressed, Hyndman would cynically thank the audience for so 'generously supporting my class'. Indeed, he brought in 'my class' to an objectionable degree. It seemed to some of us that it would have been better if he could have dropped this reference, but none of us doubted his whole-souled advocacy of Socialism as he conceived it. Hyndman, like many strong personalities, had very pronounced likes and dislikes. To myself, he was ever kind and courteous. I am quite sure he did much valuable work at the particular time when that special work was needed.

It was no small matter to know that in our advocacy of the principles we had learned to love, which on so many occasions brought forth stinging criticisms from the press, Hyndman's ability to state the case comprehensively, logically, and argumentatively, was at our disposal always, and was of very great value indeed. I am convinced, however, that Hyndman's bourgeois mentality made it impossible for him to estimate the worth of industrial organization correctly. For many years he attached no importance whatever to the trade-union movement, and his influence told disastrously on others. This phase it will be necessary to refer to later.

Henry Hyde Champion was about my own age, an ex-artillery officer, a foremost member of the SDF, taking part in all forms of propagandist activity, showing keen sympathy with the unemployed. He had a fine, earnest face, and a serious manner in dealing with the sufferings of the workers. He approved my ardent advocacy of the eight-hour day, and urged me to write a pamphlet on the subject, which he would print. At that time he had a printing business in Paternoster Row. I wrote the pamphlet: it was published in 1886, the first on this subject. Champion, being a man of vigorous individuality, and genuinely devoted to the movement, could not always wait to get his views as to various forms of propagandist activity endorsed by a committee. He would act upon his own initiative, and betimes commit the organization to plans and projects without consultation. Naturally this would give rise to strong expressions of opinion, frequently of an adverse character, arising from the natural human dislike to being pitch-forked into a project, however excellent, without having had reasonable opportunity for consideration. As a result, Champion aroused considerable hostility amongst the members who were not less devoted than himself to the advancement of the cause. My own conclusion with regard to him was that he was profoundly convinced that his judgement was right, that situations arose which necessitated prompt and decisive action, and that he could not endure to wait several days before the committee met. Anyway, he was more sure of his own judgement than of theirs! Later, events, which I shall record in their place, throw light upon this interesting personality. I saw much of him in after years in Australia, and still keep in regular correspondence with him. Indeed, it is largely at his earnest and repeated request that I am writing these reminiscences. Champion is now a literary agent in Melbourne, while his wife runs a very successful book-store there – the Book-lovers' Library.

A very different type of man was John Williams. He was rather below medium height, round-shouldered, with one shoulder higher than the other. He spoke with a strong Cockney accent. On the platform, John was the picture of pugnacity. He had a fine command of language, was well-informed, and full of apt illustrations of the seamy side of a workman's life. He could hold an audience with the best, and was a most effective propagandist. He had a large family, and frequently had long spells out of work, but this never damped his ardour. In work or not, Jack was at his post taking his turn in any part of London, outdoors or in. He knew the East End particularly well, speaking its peculiar tongue, and using its characteristic phrases. Jack has gone to his long rest; he deserves to rest in peace. He, with Burns, Hyndman, and Champion, was tried at the Old Bailey for sedition – but that will come later.

'Jem Macdonald', of the London Tailors' Union, but an Edinburgh man, was one of the finest speakers the SDF ever had. No one possessed a more scientific grasp of vital principles, and few sensed so quickly any attempt at subterfuge or scheming. Since opponents were often disguised as friends, a man of Jem's type was especially valuable when an important discussion was on, and all the better for us if Jem could be kept till last, so as to have nothing sprung on us that would not get handled effectively. In recent years Jem's hearing has proved defective, and it has been a serious barrier to his participation in propagandist work, but he still carries on the secretaryship of his trade union.

The Amalgamated Society of Engineers, with the late John Burnett as general secretary, had become very respectable and

First Socialist Activities

deadly dull. Burnett had rendered exceptionally good service at the time of the nine-hour day agitation in 1871. He had been chairman of the Nine-Hour League in Newcastle. Negotiations were attempted with the employers to obtain the nine hours without a stoppage of work, but unsuccessfully. On 1 June, 1871, began the struggle which won the nine-hour day for the iron trades. It was not till October 6 of the same year that the employers made the concession demanded by the men. At that time William Allan was general secretary of the Engineers, a man of commanding influence over a period of years in the trade-union movement. Allan died in 1874, and in July 1875 Burnett became general secretary. His period of office lasted eleven years, nothing remarkable taking place during that period beyond abnormal fluctuations in trade, and efforts of the society to cope with the same. In 1886, Burnett resigned the secretaryship, becoming Labour Correspondent to the Board of Trade, and Robert Austin of Manchester was elected secretary in his place.

I conceived it to be my duty, in addition to my Socialist propagandist effort, to try and shake up the Engineers. The branches, then, as now, met fortnightly. The branch meeting did not afford sufficient scope to touch upon general topics of an educational character. With others, therefore, I founded the Battersea Progressive League. Its meetings were held fortnightly in the alternate weeks to those of the branch. It was chiefly for branch members, but was open to all trade unionists. By such means general subjects were dealt with in addition to purely ASE affairs, and this served as a feeder to the propagandist efforts at park gates and elsewhere.

The fact that I was working for some time at Tilbury withheld me from close relationship with the leading activities in Socialist circles in 1884. The Social Democratic Federation grew out of the Democratic Federation, formed in London in 1881, amongst the chief promoters of the latter being H. M. Hyndman, Herbert Burrows and Dr G. B. Clark.

William Morris joined the Democratic Federation in 1883. He favoured a distinctively Socialist policy, and this body became the Social Democratic Federation in 1884. Those who are concerned to understand the development of affairs from this most interesting period must be willing to give some attention to detail. It soon became manifest that differences of opinion existed, and no doubt some incompatibility of temperament between members of the SDF. The question of parliamentary action was a bone of contention. William Morris and other members of the executive decided to resign, and to form the Socialist League. The following copy of a manifesto was issued explaining why this action was taken. I am indebted for this to James Tochatti, himself a member of the League throughout the greater part of its existence.

We, the Members of the Council of the Social Democratic Federation who, although a majority, resigned on 27 December [1884], wish to explain our reasons for that retirement, and for our forming a body independent of the Social Democratic Federation.

It is admitted by those who remain on the Council, as well as by ourselves, that there has been for some time past a want of harmony in the Council; we believe that this has been caused by a real difference in opinion as to what should be the aims and tactics of a Socialist propaganda.

Our view is that such a body in the present state of things has no function but to educate the people in the principles of Socialism, and to organize such as it can get hold of to take their due places, when the crisis shall come which will force action on us. We believe that to hold out as baits hopes of amelioration of the condition of the workers, to be wrung out of the necessities of the rival factions of our privileged rulers, is delusive and mischievous. For carrying out our aims of education and organization no over-shadowing and indispensable leader is required, but only a band of instructed men, each of whom can learn to fulfil, as occasion requires it, the simple functions of the leader of a party of principle.

We say that on the other hand there has been in the ranks of the Social Democratic Federation a tendency to political opportunism, which if developed would have involved us in alliances, however temporary, with one or other of the political factions, and would have weakened our propagandist force by driving us into electioneering, and possibly would have deprived us of the due services of some of our most energetic men by sending them to our sham parliament, there to become either nonentities, or perhaps our masters, and it may be our betrayers. We say also that among those who favoured these views of political adventure, there was a tendency towards

National assertion, the persistent foe of Socialism: and it is easy to see how dangerous this might become in times like the present.

Furthermore, these views have led, as they were sure to lead, to attempts at arbitrary rule inside the Federation; for such a policy as the above demands a skilful and shifty leader, to whom all persons and opinions must be subordinated, and who must be supported (if necessary) at the expense of fairness and fraternal openness.

Accordingly, attempts have been made to crush out local freedom in affiliated bodies, and to expel or render unpopular those individual members who have asserted their independence. The organ of the party, also, has been in the hands of an irresponsible editor, who has declared himself determined to resign rather than allow the Federation to have any control over the conduct of the paper.

All this we have found intolerable. It may be asked of us why we did not remain in the body and try to enforce our views by steady opposition to it. We answer, as long as we thought reconciliation possible, we did do so; but the tendencies mentioned were necessarily aggressive, and at last two distinct attacks on individuals showed us that the rent could not be mended.

We felt that thenceforth there must be two opposed parties in the Social Democratic Federation. We did not believe that a propagandist body could do useful work so divided, and we thought that it would not be in the interests of Socialism to carry on the contest further in the Federation; because, however it might end, it would leave a discontented minority, ruled by a majority, whose position would have been both precarious and tyrannical.

On the other hand, our view of duty to the cause of Socialism forbids us to cease spreading its principles or to work as mere individuals. We have therefore set on foot an independent organization, the Socialist League, with no intention of acting in hostility to the Social Democratic Federation, but determined to spread the principles of Socialism, by the only means we deem effectual. 13 January, 1885.

(Signed) Edward Aveling W. J. Clark
Eleanor Marx Aveling Joseph Lane
Robert Banner S. Mainwaring
E. Belfort Bax J. L. Mahon
J. Cooper William Morris

Issued from the offices of the Socialist League, 27, Farringdon Street, London, EC.

One of the signatories to the above document was Sam Mainwaring. He was a member of the Amalgamated Engineers, and one of the very first to understand the significance of the revolutionary movement, and the first, as far as my knowledge goes, to appreciate industrial action as distinct from parliamentary action. He had been, in the late seventies, a member of the East London Labour Emancipation League, and was an early member of the SDF. Then, when the severance took place, he was one of the founders of the Socialist League. Sam Mainwaring was once my foreman, and he showed in the workshop the same quiet, dignified bearing that characterized him at public meetings. He was full-bearded like Morris. After attending propagandist meetings William Morris frequently walked back with Mainwaring, and it was said of them that they looked like the skipper and the first mate of a ship. Mainwaring was a good speaker, and took part in many meetings. As time went on he showed an increasing disposition towards Anarchist Communism, but the members of the League generally called themselves Revolutionary Socialists, to differentiate themselves from Parliamentary Socialists. In 1891, Sam Mainwaring removed to Swansea, and there he started the Swansea Socialist Society. It was about this period that J. Tochatti, a member of the Hammersmith branch of the League, produced the anarchist paper *Liberty*, and Mainwaring identified himself with it. He later settled again in London, and, while actually engaged addressing a meeting on Parliament Hill Fields, he turned faint and died. This was on Sunday, 29 September, 1907.

The Socialist League was formed on 30 December, 1884, and a manifesto was issued setting forth its principles as a revolutionary socialist body, signed by twenty-three supporters. Among the names were William Morris, Belfort Bax, Frank Kitz, Edward Aveling, W. Bridges Adams, Robert Banner (Woolwich), Tom Maguire (Leeds), and Andreas Scheu (Edinburgh). It was decided to start a monthly organ, *The Commonweal*. William Morris became editor, and Dr Aveling, sub-editor. J. L. Mahon was secretary of the League. Now began a friendly rivalry between the League and the Federation as to which should do the most effective propaganda work. The chief importance was attached to open-air meetings, and especially to the Sunday meetings. I first met William Morris in the summer of 1885. The lecture lists were regularly printed for SDF speakers in *Justice*, and for the League speakers in *The Commonweal*. One Sunday afternoon, when I was the appointed speaker for the SDF in Victoria Park, making my way to the rendezvous to take up my position under a large tree, I saw at some two hundred yards distant signs of a gathering meeting under another fine old tree. I was informed that the League was to hold their meeting there, and that William Morris was the appointed speaker. I therefore arranged to speak for only one hour instead of the usual two hours. I left the SDF meeting to be carried on by others, and slipped quietly away to get to Morris's meeting, that I might have the pleasure of seeing and listening to him. Of course, I was well repaid. I had to get close to hear distinctly, but he was a picture on an open-air platform. The day was fine, the branches of the tree under which he was speaking spread far over the speaker. Getting him well in view, the thought came, and has always recurred as I think of that first sight of Morris – 'Bluff King Hal'. I did not give careful attention to what he was saying, for I was chiefly concerned to get the picture of him in my mind, and then to watch the faces of the audience to see how they were impressed. As is often the case at outdoor meetings, nine-tenths were giving careful attention, but on the fringe of the crowd were some who had just accidentally arrived, being out for a walk, and having unwittingly come upon the meeting. These stragglers were making such remarks as: 'Oh, this is the share-and-share-alike crowd'; 'Poverty, eh, he looks all right, don't he?' But the audience were not to be distracted by attempts at ribaldry: and as Morris stepped off the improvized platform, they gave a fine, hearty hand-clapping which showed real appreciation.

In 1885, a general election took place, and the SDF decided to run John Burns as a Socialist candidate for West Nottingham against the sitting member, Colonel Seeley. This meant that Burns must be absent from Battersea for a while, and someone must step in and take up the work of the branch, as chief advocate, etc. I was ready and willing; also I became the treasurer of a John Burns Election Fund to enable John to proceed to the scene of the contest. The activities in Battersea did not slacken, and the movement was recognized as of growing importance. There was no hope of winning the election; no one could gauge with any accuracy what the vote was likely to be. The result was: Colonel Seeley (Lib.), 6,609, E. Cope (Con.), 3,797, John Burns (Soc.), 598. At this stage of affairs I was not much concerned over the relative merits of parliamentary effort. I was chiefly anxious to see something done to arouse the inert mass of workers. With the old religious fervour I kept at the agitation incessantly, and ran risks of getting discharged from employment. One instance was about this time whilst working at Brotherhood's. I was told by the foreman that my 'back time' would be in, which meant the 'sack'. Asking the foreman as to why, he answered: 'You'd better see the manager.' I did, and put the same question to him. He replied kindly but firmly: 'The reason is, Tom, that whilst we admit you are a decent young fellow, we don't keep this shop going to give you opportunities of preaching Socialism.' I was conscious there was some warranty for the observation, so I finished.

My next place was at Pomeroy Street, Peckham. Here they were building the air compressors which would supply the compressed air that gives the Whitehead torpedo the initial impulse when fired. The job suited me well, and I worked along comfortably, being careful to keep regular time, but taking frequent part in outdoor agitation, etc. I made it my special work to urge the necessity for a reduction of hours, on the ground that, owing to the many improvements in machinery from the time the nine-hour day was established, this was a right step to take, irrespective of whether Socialism was approved or not. As the unemployed agitation was general at that time, I argued that a reduction of hours would be the most practical method of coping with the evil. But I declared no less emphatically that shorter hours would not cure unemployment, and that no restriction of the working day, however rigid, would meet the case. It was to be looked upon merely as a palliative, pending the realization of Socialism. I quoted Ruskin and Thorold Rogers more often than any other authorities.

In appealing for independent thought and self-reliance instead of leaning upon capitalist advice and instruction, I quoted John Ruskin's eighty-ninth letter in *Fors Clavigera* – 'Whose Fault is it?' – to the trade unions of England, and especially that portion where Ruskin states that he at one time had confidence in the 'learned and the rich', and adds:

First Socialist Activities

And during seven years I went on appealing to my fellow scholars in words clear enough to them, though not to you, had they chosen to hear; but not one cared nor listened, till I had sign sternly given to me that my message to the learned and the rich was given, and ended.

And now I turn to you, understanding you to be associations of labouring men who have recognized the necessity of binding yourselves by some common law of action, and who are taking earnest council as to the conditions of your lives here in England, and their relations to those of your fellow workers in foreign lands. And I understand you to be, in these associations, disregardant, if not actually defiant, of the persons on whose capital you have been hitherto passively dependent for occupation, and who have always taught you, by the mouths of their appointed Economists, that they and their capital were an eternal part of the Providential arrangements made for this world by its Creator.

In which self-assertion, nevertheless, and attitude of inquiry into the grounds of this statement of theirs, you are unquestionably right....

Trade Unions of England – Trade Armies of Christendom, what's the roll-call of you, and what part or lot have you, hitherto, in this Holy Christian Land of your Fathers?

Is not that inheritance to be claimed, and the Birth Right of it, no less than the Death Right?... What talk you of wages? Whose is the wealth of the world but yours? Whose is the virtue? Do you mean to go on for ever, leaving your wealth to be consumed by the idle and your virtue to be mocked by the vile?

The wealth of the world is yours; even your common rant and rabble of economists tell you that: 'no wealth without industry.' Who robs you of it, then, or beguiles you? Whose fault is it, you cloth-makers, that any English child is in rags? Whose fault is it, you shoe-makers, that the street harlots mince in high-heeled shoes and your own babies paddle bare-foot in the street slime? Whose fault is it you bronzed husbandmen, that through all your furrowed England, children are dying of famine?

Many hundreds of times have I made some portion of the above serve as my text for a speech on *The Condition of England Question*. The last-named work of Carlyle's, itself contains a number of passages that can be used with great effect on the minds of those not wholly weaned from conventionalism.

In dealing with unemployment, for a long time I supported the establishing of Municipal Workshops. Here again I made use of Ruskin, but this time it was *Unto this last*, and especially the preface thereof, where he says:

> Thirdly – that any man, or woman, or boy, or girl, out of employment, should be at once received at the nearest Government School, and set to work as it appeared, on trial, they were fit for, at a fixed rate of wages, determinable every year: that being found incapable of work through ignorance, they should be taught, or being found incapable of work through sickness, should be tended: but that being found objecting to work, they should be set, under compulsion of the strictest nature, to the more painful and degrading forms of necessary toil, especially to that in mines and other places of danger (such danger being, however, diminished to the utmost by careful regulation and discipline), and the due wages of such work be retained, cost of compulsion first abstracted, to be at the Workman's command, so soon as he has come to sounder mind respecting the laws of employment.

This with variations, dealing with the apathy of the trade unions, and urging them to definite action, gave me a good jumping-off ground at open-air meetings.

Thorold Rogers I used largely too. Holding meetings in densely populated areas, such as at the East India Dock gates where it was always easy to obtain a large audience chiefly of waterside workers, many of whom were out of work, and many others on only two or three days' work a week, it was helpful to tell them of the conditions that prevailed five hundred years ago when no machinery existed – and the people were accounted poor then – but as regards food, see what Thorold Rogers the economist said:

> Fortunately for the English people, as I have frequently stated, their habit, even under the adverse circumstances of their existence and the uncleanly ways of their life, was always to subsist on abundant provisions of naturally high quality. They ate wheaten bread, drank barley beer, and had plenty of cheap, though perhaps coarse, meat. Mutton and beef at a farthing a pound, take what multiple you

First Socialist Activities

please, and twelve is a liberal one, were within the reach of far more people than they now are. The grinding, hopeless poverty under which existence may be just continued, but when nothing is won beyond bare existence, did not, I am convinced characterize or even belong to mediaeval life.

As showing the attitude of the Government towards the old guilds, the counterparts or forerunners of the trade unions, the following also from Rogers' *Six Centuries of Work and Wages*, was a good text:

> For nearly five centuries the legislature had declared that labour partnerships, that is, associations of working men formed for the purpose of selling their labour collectively to the best advantage, were under the ban of the law. The motive for this repression was never concealed. It was designed in order to increase and secure rents and profits at the cost of wages.

I followed this up by telling of the action of the employers in the first quarter of the nineteenth century, when workmen again attempted to organize; how that, being unable to dissuade them or terrify them into not doing so, the employers requested Parliament to make it a punishable offence for any two or more workmen to associate together in order to adjust working conditions; and a Bill to this effect became law in 1799, and remained operative until 1824. During that twenty-five years, numbers of English workmen were transported as convicts to Australia and Tasmania for no other offence than that of endeavouring to organize in unions to try and cure some of the evils which Parliament refused to deal with. In 1824, largely as the result of the tactful behaviour of Francis Place the Charing Cross tailor, the obnoxious Combination Laws were repealed; but it required many years of battling to establish the full right to organize. Those who wish for information on this subject cannot do better than turn to the *History of Trade Unionism* by Sidney and Beatrice Webb.

The Fabian Society came into being about the same time as the SDF, but was founded by persons of a very different type. The Fabians soon became very active in the holding of meetings and the issuing of pamphlets. Intellectuals such as Sidney Webb,

Bernard Shaw, Hubert Bland, William Clark, E. R. Pease, Sidney Olivier, and Annie Besant, probably did more work in this separate organization than they would have done had they been members either of the Social Democratic Federation or of the Socialist League. The Fabian Society invited me at the end of 1885 to give an address on 'The Eight-Hour Working Day'. I did so, and a very good discussion took place almost entirely favourable. I remember Mrs Besant taking part in it, and I had a conversation with her at the close. This was the first time I had spoken to Mrs Besant, whose powers and courage I so much admired.

I was now entirely devoted to the advocacy of Socialism. With a temperament easily enthused when favourably impressed, and a strong desire to be identified with efforts for the curing of social distress, I found in Socialism a more complete satisfaction than I had ever before experienced. Enthusiasm I had possessed before, and had put a good deal of energy into the advocacy of teetotalism. When I came to recognize limitations in the temperance movement, I extended my activities to embrace food reform. My first spell as a vegetarian was for a period of three years. For a considerable portion of this time I was more of a fruitarian, as I did not include in my dietary either fish, flesh, fowl, milk, eggs, cheese, or butter. I lived almost exclusively on bread and fruit, and as far as health was concerned the diet suited me well. I never had an hour's illness, or lost time from work. But I must admit it did tire me to be continually asked: Would I not make some departure or other? Was I not likely to suffer if I kept to such a diet? I found myself on so many occasions holding forth on the qualities of food, telling the composition of foodstuffs, explaining the assimilative power of the human organism to draw nourishment from the most varied foodstuffs, that I spent much more time than was pleasant contraverting the stupid views which are all but universally held with regard to this subject. But that which weakened my ardour in this direction was the recognition that however widely food reform might be diffused, it would never prove a cure for the economic evils I deplored. The fact was, I had not yet realized that the social evils I was cognizant of were economic in origin. I did not yet understand the relationship of the working class to the employing class. I did not, therefore, yet realize that the employing class is also the exploiting class, and that it is inevitable under a wage-paying and profit-making system that everything produced by the working class will for a certainty be taken by the profit-receiving class, less the amount necessary for the workers to exist upon, and that the standard of life of the worker is decided, not by the amount he produces, so much as by intelligent association with his fellows in insistence upon a decent standard. At length I came to see that stricter economy in working-class homes did not mean a higher standard in other directions in those homes. Such thrift ultimately furnished increased profits for the master class; for profits always advance proportionately with harder work, greater production, and increasing economies on the part of wage receivers.

I was fully conscious that I had much to learn, and in my own interest I did not miss many opportunities of learning; but I saw clearly enough that the employers as controllers of industry never even attempted to regulate production in the interests of the community; that they had no regard, as employers of labour and controllers of industrial establishments, for the well-being of the people. Indeed, I could see that, as industrial magnates, they were utterly disregardant of the common well-being, and that neither individually nor collectively did they aim at producing a sufficiency of life's necessaries. They never even pretended to have any concern that the wants of the needy should be supplied. Whatever interest in such matters they might show in private life, by identifying themselves with societies for ameliorating the condition of the people, was nullified and swamped every hour of every day by the profit-making system they were identified with as business men.

The presentation of the case admitted of and necessitated such a variety of illustration, and explanation that there was no lack of subject-matter; the danger was, in my case, that, when attempting to deal with main principles exhaustively, I frequently gave too little attention to current events.

Two Social Democratic candidates were run in the metropolitan area in the 1885 election, when John Burns stood for Nottingham. The candidates were John Williams, for Hampstead, and John Fielding, for Kennington. The Socialist vote was insignificant, but the discussions that took place over this on the executive of the SDF were the hottest I had ever up to this time listened to. The controversy brought out the respective qualities of the disputants, and the question of what constituted good and bad tactics was exhaustively thrashed out.

Shortly after this I felt the necessity for a change in attitude on the part of some of the prominent members of the SDF towards the trade-union movement. At an executive meeting (or it may have been a conference) I therefore suggested the desirability of avoiding such strong and hostile criticism of the trade-union movement as was frequently indulged in, and that care should be taken to show that we attached great importance to the trade-union and co-operative movements. I urged my colleagues to bestir themselves and get into line to help in solving the social problem.

This brought Hyndman to his feet. He criticized me severely for my championship of the trade unions. What were these precious unions? By whom were they led? By the most stodgy-brained, dull-witted, and slow-going time-servers in the country. To place reliance upon these, or to go out of our way to conciliate them, would be entirely wrong, and the same applied to the co-operative movement. I summarize from memory, but I am sure that I give the gist correctly. Herbert Burrows followed in the same strain as Hyndman, though less vehemently. I forget what the vote was, but I know that my proposition received little support, and that the meeting endorsed Hyndman's views. I refer to the matter because at this early stage I felt the tactics were not the best. The conviction grew. Now, some thirty-seven years later, I am still of opinion that Hyndman failed to realize what should have been the attitude of himself and the SDF towards the industrial organizations of the time. It was a serious disservice to the cause; this policy antagonized trade unionists without drawing over any considerable percentage to the Socialist position. Herein Hyndman was essentially bourgeois, and lacked perspicacity in that he failed to see the probable development of affairs. Small blame to him; he boasted that he was not of the working class, and neither he nor Champion could be expected to see the position from the industrial standpoint. I venture to believe that had the tactics been different, had it been the recognized and persistent policy to attach what I will call proper importance to the co-operative and trade-union movements, the growth of the SDF would have been far more rapid, and there would have been no necessity for the coming into existence of the Independent Labour Party. But who shall complain of what Fate has decreed?

CHAPTER IV

THE FIGHT FOR AN EIGHT-HOUR DAY
1886 to 1889

ONE of the periodic fluctuations in industry brought on a bad turn of industrial depression in the winter of 1885-6. The Social Democrats habitually directed attention to the root causes of unemployment, and explained the economic remedy therefor; but they also laid stress upon the necessity for immediate provision for those suffering from unemployment, this being one of their palliative proposals. There then existed a Fair Trade League, largely the outcome of Mr Joseph Chamberlain's activities. Three or four men belonging to a group connected with this league usually took a prominent part at open air gatherings. These were Messrs Peters, Kelly, Kenny, and Lemon. On 8 February, 1886, they organized a demonstration in Trafalgar Square, to call for protective tariffs against the increasing importation of foreign goods, for such imports, they alleged, were unfairly depriving the British workers of the opportunity of work, wages, etc. The Social Democrats were present in Trafalgar Square before the arrival of some of the contingents. John Burns was called upon to hold a meeting, and did so. Considerable manoeuvring took place when the organizers of the demonstration appeared, and while the Fair Traders were addressing a portion of the people in the Square, Burns, Champion, Hyndman, and Williams were speaking from the National Gallery side. Finally, at the close of the meeting, it was decided to march to Hyde Park, with a view to another meeting. On the way rioting took place, many windows were broken, and considerable damage was done. This resulted in the four mentioned, viz. Burns, Hyndman, Champion, and Williams being brought to trial at the Old Bailey for sedition. John Burns had carried a red flag in the Square and on the march towards Hyde Park, and he became known as 'the Man with the Red Flag'. The trial attracted much attention;

in the end the four were acquitted. The stone-throwing, etc., on the occasion of the march, led to the immediate opening of a Mansion House Fund to relieve the unemployed, and substantial sums were quickly subscribed. The effect upon business people in London generally was very noticeable, and for a while, whenever the unemployed were about to march in any direction, the utmost concern and caution were manifested. I was working at Peckham at the time. The local unemployed had announced a march during the week in which the riots took place. I remember that the works' gates were strengthened, and that props were fixed ready for barricading purposes should need arise. This, of course, was groundless alarm in the minds of persons unable to gauge the situation accurately.

I continued to concentrate upon the reduction of working hours, believing that this demanded persistent attention until the end should be achieved. The programme of the SDF demanded 'The Nationalization of the Means of Production, Distribution, and Exchange', but also called for palliatives, one of which was the eight-hour day. The Battersea branch of the SDF was in a flourishing condition. Many new members were enrolled every week, and the indoor and outdoor meetings were invariably successful. I was taking my full share of the work of the branch, and, being on the speakers' list, I went wherever appointed by the lecture secretary, but Sydney Hall was the inspiring rendezvous for all Battersea members. On a certain occasion when the hall was full, I took the opportunity to urge upon the branch the desirability of dealing more specifically with the eight-hours question, as whatever else might be done, this would prove of permanent as well as immediate value. I stated that it was the practice for the recognized spokesmen of the SDF to make incidental reference to the reduction of hours, complained that no definite steps were taken to force the matter to the front – and more on similar lines. As I have said, the hall was full, crowded indeed, and John Burns rose immediately I sat down. He at once expressed entire disapproval of what I proposed. He declared the time had passed for such trivial reforms as the eight-hour day, notwithstanding the fact that it was included among the palliative proposals of the SDF. Amid loud cheers he declared that the capitalist system was on its last legs, and that it was our duty to prepare at once to seize the whole of the means of production and wipe out the capitalists altogether. This received thunderous applause. The next speaker was John Ward, the present Colonel John Ward, MP. He followed on lines exactly like Burns, but if possible more revolutionary. He was ready to take action for a physical-force overthrow, and certainly was not prepared to spend time over anything so paltry as an eight-hour day. When the vote was taken, the attitude of Burns and Ward was endorsed by an overwhelming majority. That was thirty-five years ago. Naturally it has been a matter of considerable interest to me to observe events during this period!

As the result of the decision of the SDF branch not to give special attention to the eight-hours question, a group of us who held this to be necessary decided that, while remaining active members of the branch, we would independently form an 'Eight-hours League', and this was done. It was necessary to shape a definite course, and to hold meetings dealing specially with the question of reduction of hours, and to get in touch with the trade-union branches of London. Amongst other prominent personages who became identified with the league was Mr Cunningham Grahame, MP. He had recently been returned as the member for North-West Lanark. His maiden speech in Parliament attracted much attention, and we lost no time in securing his adhesion and his advocacy. Our chief task was to communicate with trade-union branches, offering to send one or more speakers to address the branch on the eight-hour day. This proved a great success, and after many branches had been visited, a conference of London trade unionists was specially convened at Bricklayers' Hall, Southwark Bridge Road, to discuss their attitude towards the eight-hour day. Over ninety per cent of the delegates to this conference voted in favour of the proposal. This was the first time that such a conference had been held, and henceforward the London trade-union movement was correctly classed as favourable to the eight-hour day.

The SDF persistently kept up an agitation on behalf of the unemployed. It was made the chief subject in all the propagandist speeches, much correspondence took place in the press, etc., and, as Lord Mayor's Day approached (9 November, 1886), the SDF

The Fight for an Eight-Hour Day

issued a manifesto calling upon the unemployed to demonstrate in their thousands, and to follow the Lord Mayor's procession through the City. The next day there were enormous posters on the hoardings, directing attention to the doings of the SDF, and declaring that no procession other than the officially recognized Lord Mayor's procession would be allowed on the line of route. The proclamation was signed by Sir Charles Warren, Chief of the Metropolitan Police. At a council meeting of the SDF the subject was discussed at great length, and it was decided to call for a mass meeting of the unemployed instead of a procession. A new manifesto was issued, saying: 'Trafalgar Square not being on the "line of route", we call on the unemployed to assemble there,' etc. This was issued on 8 November, the eve of the great day. During the night Sir Charles Warren had a fresh lot of eight-foot posters put up, forbidding any procession or meeting or display of placards or banners or, speechifying in Trafalgar Square or in any other street or thoroughfare adjacent to the procession.

So matters were really interesting. A rapidly convened meeting of the council was held that morning near Trafalgar Square. A plan of action was decided upon, and various comrades were selected with their own full approval, to participate and to be in readiness for all eventualities. At that time Mr John Ward was a militant member of the SDF, ever ready to take his share of responsibility. It was part of my accepted task to stand quietly as an observer on the west side of Trafalgar Square, and to receive and pass on any important message as to police manoeuvres, etc. The police had by this time entirely surrounded the Square, and on the upper level in front of the National Gallery there was a double row of police. Just as it reached the stage when everything appeared to be passing off very tamely, several SDF men, headed by John Ward, made an attempt to pass through the police ranks. This, of course, caused a diversion. The arrest of John Ward monopolized the attention of the police, and inside of one minute some hundreds of us that were near to the spot walked past the police into the Square, a few of us mounted the plinth of the Nelson Column. Here, Mr George Bateman (for many years now closely connected with the *Daily Chronicle*), acted as chairman, made a short speech, and called on myself. I reviewed the situation, telling why such action was taken, and dealt with the SDF proposals for the relief of unemployment.

After discussing the economic remedy, I recited some verses from Shelley. By this time the Square was filled with a lively but quite orderly mass. Several other speakers followed, and the resolution was duly submitted and carried with the greatest enthusiasm. Then there was a call that the Horse Guards were coming, and a couple of minutes after the resolution had been voted the mounted Guards came along and trotted their horses through and round about the Square to disperse the crowd. But the crowd had already largely responded to a cry of 'Now for Hyde Park', which was shouted out immediately on the resolution having been carried. To Hyde Park the crowd marched, and a meeting was held there. I did not go to the park, but, learning that John Ward had been taken to the King Street Police Station, I made for that spot to see how matters were developing. During the evening, Ward was set free, and we reunited at Battersea. Here, John Ward became a regular drill sergeant, preparing the comrades for possible physical-force eventualities.

About the same time, the SDF organized a very successful demonstration in Trafalgar Square on the occasion of the visit of fourteen trade-union delegates sent to London by the Municipal Council of Paris. In addition to open-air gatherings and indoor meetings, there was given in honour of the French delegation a public banquet as a climax to the visit. The speeches naturally dealt chiefly with the desirability of closer international relationships. For me it was quite an eventful year, and I found scope at the street corners, public parks, and many indoor meetings, for the advocacy of the principles I had come to appreciate with whole-souled fervour.

Early in 1887 I was out of employment, and, as I was becoming somewhat notorious, it was not easy to get a new job. A strike had been entered upon in the coal-field of Northumberland. It was supported by the Northumberland Miners' Union, and affected all the mines in the county. I was asked by the SDF to go to Newcastle-on-Tyne, and to report as to whether the prospect was favourable for educational work. I agreed to go, and went. I reported that there was a grand opportunity for propaganda work amongst the miners, and that I should have no difficulty in getting audiences. I commenced operations, and remained in Northumberland and Durham all that year. Every Sunday evening I addressed large audiences at the Cattle Market, Newcastle; every Wednesday I also had a meeting in Newcastle. On Sunday mornings I addressed meetings at the Quay Side, and on other days of the week in some mining town or village in Northumberland or Durham. The progress of the dispute showed clearly that the methods of organization were unfavourable to the solidarity of the miners. The Northumberland Miners' Association included the miners and others at the pits on the north side of the River Tyne; the Durham Miners' Association catered for the men on the south side of the Tyne; but the utmost goodwill prevailed and friendship existed between the officials and the men of the two unions. While the whole of the Northumberland men were out resisting the employers, the Durham men sent messages of congratulation, and also substantial contributions to the dispute funds; but they did not cease to work to make common cause. They saw nothing wrong in even supplying the customers of the Northumberland men, and thus contributing largely to bring about the latter's ultimate defeat. This taught a lesson. Henceforward it was recognized that a closer relationship must be established between the miners of these two northern counties. Furthermore, efforts were made that later on resulted in the whole of the miners of Britain being incorporated into the Miners' Federation of Great Britain.

It was during this year, 'eighty-seven, that I was requested to visit Dundee, and give a series of addresses there. I did so, and my visit was considered a success.

When the Northumberland men's dispute was over, and I sought to obtain employment at the engine shops on the Tyne, I found the task far from easy. I did start at the North-Eastern Engineering Works, Wallsend. Everything went on all right for about four days, when pay-day came on the Friday. I was then told that 'the whole of my time would be in'. This meaning, 'no time kept in hand' – in a word, discharge. I went to the foreman and asked for a reason. His reply was: 'I am carrying out instructions. When I started you earlier in the week, I didn't know your name, and didn't ask for it, but I was soon told that I had started Tom Mann. It's not my doing that you are stopped. It is from the office.'

I had a similar experience the next week on the south side of the river when I started at Clarke Chapman's, and after three days was stopped in a similar way. Economic pressure was pretty strong at this time. I had a fairly good collection of books, a violin, and a telescope. All had to go to obtain necessaries. It was, however, an intensely interesting experience I had on the Tyne. Many public debates, many outdoor meetings, organizing the unemployed, making demands on their behalf, pressing questions on the Municipal Council to obtain relief measures, etc. As part of the propagandist effort, coupled with an earnest attempt to get something done for the unemployed, we organized a Church Parade on a Sunday morning, and announced we would march from the Quay Side to St Nicholas' Cathedral Church. I was speaking from the base of the big crane prior to the audience lining up four abreast for the march to church. I had a small red flag easily handled, and while I was addressing the crowd, and stating what the arrangements were, describing the route we would take, and so on, I saw the Mayor, Mr Benjamin Browne, of engineering fame – afterwards Sir Benjamin – in company with the Superintendent of Police, walk up to the edge of the crowd, and stand there listening. I thought 'Hello! this looks like forbidding the march'. I ignored them, finished my speech, jumped off the pedestal, lined up the men for marching. As we were about to start the Mayor approached me, and spoke in quite friendly terms, saying that he would walk to church with us if we had no objection; and he did.

Already our proposals for dealing with unemployment were before the council, and apparently the Mayor had decided to see for himself what the unemployed looked like. One of these proposals was the planting of trees around the town moor, which at that time was very plain and bare. At the council meeting a few days later, the Mayor made a very sympathetic speech respecting the necessity for action to provide for the unemployed, and advised that several of the proposals our committee had made should be acted upon, including the one for the planting of trees around the town moor. This was agreed to and carried out. These new trees are now a genuine ornament and valuable asset to Newcastle, with thirty-five years' growth. But the unemployed problem is not yet solved. Unemployment is as rife in 1923 as it was in 1887, when the shipbuilding trades had twenty-five per cent of their members out of work.

The Fight for an Eight-Hour Day

Early in 1888 there was a strike of engineers at several of the principal firms in Bolton, Lancashire. While this was on I was requested to visit Bolton, and did so. Before I left, the Social Democrats of that town requested me to take up my residence there and help on the movement in Lancashire. I did so; and in this, to me new area, I found scope for effective propaganda. I usually spoke from the Bolton Town Hall steps twice a week; and I regularly visited Bury, Rochdale, Blackburn, and Darwen.

One of the active young men of that time, Councillor Chas. A. Glyde, was subsequently a member for many years of the Borough Council of Bradford, Yorkshire, and secretary of the Bradford branch of the National Union of General Workers. In that capacity he issued the 'Socialist Vanguard' for a number of years. Not long before his death, on 25 August, 1923, he published a series of articles entitled 'Thirty Years' Reminiscences in the Socialist Movement'. One of these was devoted to the time I am now dealing with. It is written in his usual racy style. He says:

> Tom Mann was invited by the branch (SDF) to come to Bolton as organizer, and agreed. A shop in one of the main streets was stocked with tobacco, newspapers, etc., and he was installed as manager. Tom drew very large crowds to the Town Hall Square. Street corner and propaganda meetings were held in the surrounding towns and villages. His fiery speeches were marvels of eloquence and power. I was always with him, pushing the literature while he did the speechifying. The authorities got alarmed with the results of his brilliant burning eloquence, and his name was taken by the police authorities with a view to prosecution for creating an obstruction on the Town Hall Square. It was also alleged that the meetings interfered with the clerks in the Town Hall when working overtime.
>
> Tom stoutly stood to his guns, he never flinched, his crowds grew to enormous dimensions, his popularity increased, his name was taken night after night by the police, he never wavered, although he knew that he was hampered by his family of little chicks. He won the right of free speech hands down, the opposition of the police and Corporation collapsed, they dared not prosecute him, he never received a summons; he vindicated and won the right of public meetings on the Town Hall steps, which I believe has not been interfered with since.

He started an economics class of which I was a member, and under his leadership the branch made splendid progress. An agitation sprung up in the town for the Sunday opening of the Public Library and reading room. Tom was one of its foremost supporters. Nearly the whole of the clergy and Nonconformist parsons, and the church and chapel people opposed the proposal. A public meeting was called in the Temperance Hall, the largest meeting place in the town, by those who were opposed to opening. Tom and a small band of SDFers attended for the purpose of moving an amendment. The chairman was a local landowner, named Ainsworth, and when Tom rose to move his amendment on behalf of the Socialists, he was received with howls of derision and jeers by the large crowd of members of chapels and churches, but he stood his ground, and eventually the chairman invited him on to the platform. The principal argument used by those who opposed was that it would cause attendants to be on duty on Sundays, but when Mann pointed out that the coachman for the chairman of the meeting did more work on a Sunday than any other day in the week, the Nonconformists and church people met him with a storm of booing. Our amendment was defeated by an overwhelming majority, and when I raised my hands in favour a young churchman spat on them, a typical example of religious intolerance, bigotry and anti-fair play. However, the following week a very large meeting was held in the same hall in favour of Sunday opening, with the Vicar of Bolton (Canon Atkinson) in the chair, he being the only prominent churchman in favour, and all the chapel people held aloof.

In 1889 the great strike for the dockers' 'tanner' per hour broke out in London, and B. Tillett sent for Tom to assist him and John Burns. The strike was won and the trio became famous everywhere where the English language was spoken.

Tom Mann at the time he was in Bolton was in his prime. He was well grounded in Socialism and economics. He was one of the best speakers I have known. Of medium height, well built, with black hair, and with the first word uttered he gripped his audience and kept them spell-bound until the end. He had a thorough command of language, and he sent forth his arguments in rasp-like incisive sentences which greatly impressed his auditors and carried conviction to their minds. During his stay in Bolton I was his towel carrier, bottle holder, and sponger down, and he has never forgotten his

The Fight for an Eight-Hour Day

humble follower of bygone days. He has made mistakes, let him who has not, cast the first stone, but he has been as true as steel. He has always tried to assist the bottom dog, the unskilled and semi-skilled worker, as is proved by his services to the dock labourer, and his connection with the Workers' Union as one of its founders. He has adopted new methods and new ideas, always with a view to the betterment of his class, and to obtain for them a share of the good things of life. I raise my hat to this great tribune of the workers, who has always followed the dictates of his conscience and brain whatever the consequences. All his talents and abilities have always been at the service of his class.

It was one of the rules of the ASE that members should, as far as practicable, belong to a branch near to where they resided. On leaving Newcastle, therefore, I joined one of the Bolton branches. In November of this year, 1888, an International Conference was called in London, by the Parliamentary Committee of the Trade Union Congress, and I was sent as delegate by the Bolton engineers, with the endorsement of the Social Democrats. It was my first congress of the kind. Substantially it was a congress of trade unionists, though amongst the delegates were a number of well-known Socialists, including Mrs Besant, John Burns, and Keir Hardie. Owing to some bungling in the invitations or credentials, no Germans or Austrians were present; the British were in the majority, with seventy-nine delegates. France sent eighteen, Belgium ten (including Anseele), Denmark two, Italy one. The conference was held in Newman Hall, Oxford Street, London. No decisions of vital import were arrived at. I was responsible for a resolution dealing with unemployment, and was vigorously supported by Mr William Parnell, of the West End branch of the Furniture Trades' Union, one of the best men of the time in the trade-union world. How the voting went I forget, but I have a feeling that the conveners of the congress were doing their best to prevent any success on Socialist lines. The chairman was George Shipton, at that time secretary of the London Trades Council, supported by Henry Broadhurst, MP, who had for long been officially connected with the Stone Masons' Union. Thomas Burt of the Northumberland Miners and Charles Fenwick of the same organization, both MP's, also William Abraham, MP (Mabon) of the South Wales Miners. I knew Keir Hardie pretty well, as I had earlier in the same year put in a couple of weeks at electioneering work with him when he stood as Labour candidate for Mid-Lanark. I had opportunities of getting into close contact with the dour side of a certain type of Scotsman amongst the electorate, also I came to know their fanatical devotion to the Liberal Party. Keir Hardie polled 617 votes. In after years I became a close fellow-worker with Keir Hardie, and our relations were always harmonious. Another man who later became world-famous, and who was one of Hardie's chief workers at that Mid-Lanark election, was Bob Smillie, one of the finest men in the Labour movement. Two years ago, when Mr Smillie was reported to be seriously ill, I wrote of him as follows, in the columns of the *Engineers' Journal*:

> I have known Robert Smillie for over thirty years, since the early days of the attempts to run Labour candidates for Parliamentary elections. When Keir Hardie contested Mid-Lanark more than thirty years ago, Bob Smillie was one of the most energetic and capable fighters, and never a year has passed over his head in all the time since then but Bob has been right in the forefront of the militant working-class movement. Although Bob has spent so much of his life in Scotland, he is really a Belfast man, and a most genial and lovable man at that.
>
> Brother Bob has known every phase of working-class struggle, and early in life realized the necessity for industrial organization. He knew by continuous personal contact with the hardships of mining life that there was no hope for betterment unless the miners could learn to organize and to consolidate with all other miners throughout the country. Never has a man worked more faithfully, more consistently, or successfully. He has lived to see the miners become organized equal to any body of men in any industry, to obtain influence in the community, to compel respectful consideration in the chief councils of the nation, and, what is more pleasing to him, to have obtained substantial reductions of working hours and increases in pay.
>
> Mr Smillie has consistently remained an advocate of nationalization, presumably believing that if the personnel of Parliament could be changed and the machinery of Government democratized that public ownership of the right kind would follow, and in any

case Smillie has stood for public ownership by legislation, and apparently he still has faith in the good results likely to follow nationalization.

It is necessary to make this clear to those who wish to understand Bob Smillie and his policy. The capitalist press has in recent years referred to him as an out-and-out devotee of direct action. This is very far from correct. Bob is not and never has been, a direct actionist in the sense implied, which means that one resorts to trade-union or industrial-union methods to achieve economic changes, having no belief in the necessity for, or the efficacy of, parliamentary action through and by the machinery of State.

Mr Smillie simply recognized that in order to command any attention in Parliament it was necessary to possess industrial power, and to have the intelligence and courage to dare to use it as occasion required to force the position, but Robert was all through a parliamentarian.

It would not be fair to Bob to attribute to him the attitude of mind of the thorough-going direct actionist, and indeed it is preposterous to think that one who had no belief in the parliamentary institutions would be identified with the formation of a programme whose chief item was nationalization.

Elsewhere I propose to discuss this and kindred questions. Here I simply want to pay my full meed of praise to a splendid character, a clean man, a straight man, a reliable man, and a first-rate comrade in humanity's cause.

... He is loved by hundreds of thousands, he lives in the hearts of not only the Scottish miners, but also of a very large percentage of all the workers throughout the British Isles. May he ... live to see increasing thousands of young men he has helped to educate and inspire participate in the great work for the uplift of the workers in all lands.

Good luck and long life to you, Bob; lang may your lum reek.

While attending the International Conference already described, I learned that Sir John Lubbock (afterwards Lord Avebury) had successfully piloted a measure through Parliament stipulating that no person under eighteen years of age might work for more than seventy-four hours a week including meal times; but since no inspectors were appointed to see that the Act was complied with, it remained practically a dead letter. The Act also provided that the regulations embodied in it were to be exhibited in a conspicuous place, where the young persons could see them. A voluntary committee was formed to see that the measure was enforced. This body decided to appoint a voluntary inspector, until such time as an amendment to the Act could be carried putting the responsibility definitely upon a public official. I was asked if I would come to London and serve as inspector, looking up cases, taking out summonses, and conducting the cases in court when there were no complications. A barrister who was friendly to the work of the committee, Mr Thomas Sutherst (went down in the *Lusitania*), would be ready to advise and help when expert assistance was required. I accepted the proposal, which necessitated my returning to London early in 1889. I was given a free hand as to the use of my leisure time.

I soon obtained evidence of violations of the measure, applied for summonses, and secured convictions, thus enforcing compliance with the Act to the limited extent within which I was able to operate. These cases I regularly reported in the columns of the *Labour Elector*, a weekly paper run by Mr Champion.

I had already been closely associated with the paper, which was written very smartly, and delighted in exposing those employers who posed as benefactors, and made fortunes out of the low-paid workers.

One special case to which attention was drawn in this way was that of a large firm of chemical manufacturers. The head of the firm was a Member of Parliament, being reputed to be an advanced Radical and a keen sympathizer with the poor.

Information reached the *Labour Elector* that the conditions of work in many departments at the establishment referred to were, in some cases, exceedingly fatiguing, and in others very dangerous. There was the milk of lime department, known to the men as 'Milky Lime'. The duties involved were that a man should push a heavy iron wheel-barrow to a furnace where it was loaded with red hot lime; thence along planks up to a big tank, into which the barrow-load was tipped; then back to the furnace; and so on for a twelve-hour shift.

In another department the effects of the alkali were such that a strong young man getting work there would soon show signs of the bad effects upon his system. A dark man's hair would turn a deadly dull, lifeless brown, his gums would gradually but surely grow black, his teeth would drop out one by one, until some of the men would not have a tooth left.

In yet another department a 'muzzle' had to be worn. This was in the soda-ash chamber, where no man could freely inhale without being 'gassed', that is, overcome by the powerful fumes, taking time to come round and requiring restoratives. So the method of work, was first to get a length of thick flannel, some four or five feet long, and about five or six inches wide. This was placed one end over the mouth the edge close up against the nostrils, and folded to and fro until the whole length formed a pad covering the mouth with an inch-thick material, and with strong cord tied over the head and under the chin, thus keeping the 'muzzle' tight over the mouth and nostrils, so that no breath could be drawn except through all these folds of flannel. The object was, of course, to filter the poison-laden atmosphere of the soda chamber. This apparatus alone made it difficult to breathe; but in addition, the workman had to grease the parts of the cheeks not covered by the flannel, to wear large goggles to protect the eyes, to don a paper hat, and, in this complicated rig-out, to shovel the soda ash. Two minutes was the limit of time a practised shoveller could work before putting his head out of the chamber to inhale better air; if by any chance the flannel was knocked off, or was loose enough to permit the unfiltered dusty air of the chamber to reach the nostrils or mouth, then the man was 'gassed'.

At this time the company's balance sheets showed that debenture-holders were receiving the usual interest, while the ordinary shareholders – I am writing from memory after this lapse of years, but the details are still firmly impressed on my mind – received forty-nine per cent. The workmen, under the conditions I have described worked twelve-hour shifts.

I should explain that the 'process men' – to use the local term – worked twelve-hour shifts; the mechanics, such as engineers, carpenters, plumbers, etc., worked the customary, nine-hour day also the labourers in the same departments; but the others, all those actually engaged in the manufacture of the chemicals, not only were on twelve-hour shifts, but seven shifts a week at that! The machinery ran day and night, continuously. If a breakage took place, it was so arranged that the part could be disconnected and repaired without a general stoppage. The average hours, therefore, were eighty-four a week – seven times twelve; but in order to change the men to alternate weeks of days and nights, the hours were regulated as follows: The day shift began on Monday morning at six o'clock, and these men continued till five in the evening, without any stop for meals. Then the night shift men took up duty, and continued at work till six the next morning, or thirteen hours continuous work without stoppage for meals; thus making in five shifts from Monday evening till Saturday morning, sixty-five hours work. The same men who left work at six on Saturday morning returned to work at two o'clock on Saturday afternoon, and commenced a shift of seventeen hours consecutive work, till seven o'clock on Sunday morning, thus making a total of eighty-two hours for the week.

The day-shift men who worked eleven hours each day on Monday, Tuesday, Wednesday, Thursday, and Friday, worked only eight hours on Saturday, leaving work at two o'clock, so far having made sixty-three hours, but these men relieved their mates on Sunday morning at seven o'clock, and commenced a twenty-three hour shift, till six o'clock on the Monday morning, thus making a week of eighty-six hours for the week.

Of course, I do not mean that the men did not get any food on these long shifts; I mean that each man was continuously at his work the whole of the time. At intervals one man would be responsible for his own work and that of his mate, while the latter had a snack; but the mill went on unceasingly, grinding away at top speed. Mr Champion, as editor of the *Labour Elector* received a great deal of information respecting these working conditions, and had published much of it, when a writ was served by a firm of solicitors, acting on behalf of the chemical works, demanding an apology, and claiming – I think it was £5,000 damages. The next issue of the *Labour Elector* contained a statement to the effect that no apology would be given, and that it was the intention of the editor to continue the systematic issue of statements concerning the conditions of labour, until the hours were reduced by one-third, giving three shifts of men instead of two, without reduction of wages. Being in touch with trade unionists who could advise me as to the best course to take, in order to get work under conditions that would enable me to substantiate the information, I decided to apply for a job as labourer, and dressed the part. Since caution was necessary, I adopted the name of 'Joe Miller'. I learned the customary time and place of taking on, etc., and applied. The second morning I was started as a general labourer, and put with a gang emptying trucks of slack. I was not on the 'process' but on general works, so I was liable to be moved about to any rough job; also, I had meal hours. I was 'posted' as to what departments to take stock of, etc., and in about ten days I had all the confirmatory detail required. Just at this time a public meeting was advertised a few miles distant chiefly political in character, really to serve the political interests of the head of the firm. I had now left the firm as an employee, and attended the meeting where eulogies of the firm were indulged in largely. When question time came I took part in a manner that caused some consternation; but very few knew me by sight, and not more than two knew me by my own name. Suffice it to say that in a few months all legal proceedings against the *Labour Elector* were suspended, and the eight-hour day was established at the works of Messrs Brunner, Mond & Co., Cheshire.

This was some achievement, and there was a sequel to it. A few weeks after the inauguration of the eight-hour day, 'Tom Man' received an invitation to be present at a meeting to be held by the employees of the firm, in a schoolroom adjacent to the works. The meeting was to celebrate the inauguration of the eight-hour day, which had resulted in starting one-third more men. The letter inviting my attendance referred to various other advantages of the change, now that the men had some lesiure. I accepted gladly, and I duly presented myself at the committee room a little while before the appointed hour. Not more than one on that committee had an inkling that the 'Joe Miller' who had taken part in the public meeting of some weeks earlier, and who had made comments upon the firm, was really Tom Mann. One member of the committee was a trade-union official who, doubtless, knew me by reputation; but he had never seen me before except at the public meeting previously referred to, and he had not appreciated the part I had taken in it. His astonishment when he realized that 'Joe Miller' was none other than Tom Mann, was so pronounced that it took him some time to get over it. But he did get over it, and as may be easily imagined, a very successful celebration meeting was held. Of all those present, no one was likely to be more genuinely interested than myself.

During 1888, the years of propagandist effort on the part of Socialists, urging the people to bestir themselves and try to find a way out of the terrible poverty that existed were beginning to show results. The first considerable movement came from the women and girls employed at Bryant & May's Match Factory at Bow. Kindly-disposed persons had written about the awful conditions under which many of the girls worked, resulting in the terrible disease known as 'phossy jaw', and other serious troubles, it being argued that better methods might be applied that would materially minimize these evils. In addition, the wages were shamefully low. No response to appeals from the workers was made by the firm. Lists of shareholders were published showing that a considerable percentage of these were clergymen; but nothing brought any change for the better until the women and girls went on strike. This immediately attracted public attention, and Mrs Annie Besant – at that time devoting her whole energies to the Socialist movement, and doing splendid work as a member of the now superseded London School Board – at once gave close personal attention to the girls on strike. She was ably assisted by Mr Herbert Burrows, the girls were soon organized in a trade union. Their case was conducted with great skill. A club was formed, which was used as an educational and social centre, and a spirit of hopefulness characterized the proceedings. The girls won. This had a stimulating effect upon other sections of workers, some of whom were also showing signs of intelligent dissatisfaction.

In 1889, a few weeks subsequent to my return to London after a two years' absence, the employees at the Beckton gasworks began to voice their desire for an eight-hour day. I do not remember exactly how I first came in contact with them, but I have a clear recollection of being with Mr John Burns one day when we met Mr Will Thorne, and other workmates of his, telling how they had been to visit Mr Sydney Buxton (now Lord Buxton), the then MP for Poplar, to ask if he could do anything to help them get an Act of Parliament to fix their hours of work at eight a day instead of twelve; and how they had met with but little encouragement, as Mr Buxton had told them there was not the slightest hope of introducing and carrying a measure such as they desired.

As the result of the conversation with John Burns and myself, the group of gasworkers saw the necessity of our contention that they must first organize industrially, and then put in the claim direct to the Gas Companies. Will Thorne said it would mean a very big job, as the men in all the Gas Companies of London desired improved conditions. They had already arrived at a decision as to what they intended trying to get. They had to work thirteen shifts a fortnight, and they wanted one knocked off, so as to work twelve. They had to work twelve-hour shifts, and they wanted eight-hour shifts instead, or three shifts in the twenty-four hours instead of two; and, further they wanted, a shilling a day more in wages than they were getting, on top of a one-third reduction of hours.

John Burns and I promised to help all we could, if they would show they were in real earnest about it. We had not long to wait; they set to work immediately, and arranged for a series of demonstrations on Sundays, this being the only possible day for meeting under the conditions they were working, and the demonstrations were fixed at various places so as to give the men of every district a fair chance of attending. The campaign proved remarkably successful, and in a few weeks ninety per cent of the men were organized. It was in connection with this agitation for the gas workers that I first met Ben Tillett. He also was helping them, and at the same time was missing no opportunity of putting the dockers' case. The negotiations that followed upon the organization of the men very soon yielded results. The Metropolitan Gas Companies, all save one, the South, granted the eight-hour day, the twelve shifts a fortnight, and sixpence per shift increase in wages over and above what the men had previously received for a twelve-hour shift. This was so substantial an improvement that everyone who gave the least thought to the subject could see the advantages of industrial organization.

CHAPTER V

THE DOCK STRIKE OF 1889

THE London Dock Strike of 1889 involved a much wider issue than that of a large number of port workers fighting for better conditions. There had long been no more than a dogged acquiescence in the conditions insisted upon by the employers, more particularly on the part of those classed as unskilled labourers. Skilled and unskilled alike were dominated over by their employers; and at the same time the unskilled, not being yet organized, were in many instances subject to further dictation and domination by the organized skilled men. The industrial system was (as it still is, with some modification), creating an army of surplus workers, who, never having been decently paid for their work, had never been decently fed; every occupation had its proportion of this surplus. Irregularity of work, coupled with liability to arduous and dangerous toil when employed, characterized the dock workers in an exceptional degree; and although dock labour was classed as unskilled, in grim reality it often required a considerable amount of skill; moreover, accidents were frequent. Nevertheless, in the struggle against death by starvation, a larger percentage of worn-out men (cast-offs from other occupations) made their way to compete for casual labour at the docks and wharves of London, than to any other place or to any similar occupation.

This does not mean that all the dock workers were weaklings! Far from it. Some of the finest built men in the country would always be found amongst the dockers; but the above generalization was true. Again, whilst dockers were in a very large number of cases badly paid per hour, and could only get a few hours' work per week, in the work of a large port there is always a number who get regular work, and some, of course, who get relatively good wages.

Many circumstances seem to have conspired to make the upheaval of 1889 the assertion of the rights of a large class in the community – the rights of those who had never before been recognized as possessing the rights and the title to respect of civilized humans. It was nothing less than a challenge to all hostile forces, and an assertion of the claim for proper treatment. The challenge was successful; the claim was enforced.

I was at the office of the *Labour Elector* in Paternoster Row, on 14th August in that year, when, about midday, I received a wire from Ben Tillett asking me to make my way to the South West India Dock. I went at once. There was no difficulty in finding the men, for Ben was with them, and they were about to hold a meeting. I was soon put in possession of the main facts. The men had been discharging a sailing ship named the *Lady Armstrong*. They were working for fivepence an hour and 'plus', this meaning that in a vague fashion, very ill defined, there was a recognized time for discharging certain goods, and if the men did the work in less time they received a surplus of a halfpenny or penny per hour. The men argued they had kept correct tally, but the dock superintendent refused to admit the claim. The dockers were told that their demand for more pay would have to be dealt with by the chief authority. The London and India Docks Joint Committee. The men refused to return to work.

Serious discussion must have taken place prior to the *Lady Armstrong* difficulty, because almost immediately it was proposed that now they were out, they should insist in the future upon an established minimum of sixpence per hour for ordinary time, and eightpence per hour for overtime. When I arrived they had already decided to claim at least as much as this, and to call upon their fellow dockers to help them. No need here to go into detail beyond that of giving a correct idea of the definiteness of aim, and the effect of the achievement. For myself, I kept at that strike until it was over; and for long after I remained in touch with the dockers, and with the movement of which they were a part.

Burns, as all know, was, like Tillett, in the thick of the struggle, being active in every phase of it, except when absolutely compelled to take rest. The Strike Committee at the start made its headquarters at Wroots' Coffee House, Poplar, and the first day that relief tickets were given out I had a very difficult duty. There was a crowd of several thousand men to deal with, and each had to be given one ticket, and only one. As yet there had been no time to organize the distribution systematically. The men were in urgent need; they had been told a few hours before that tickets would be issued that day. Now they had assembled, and the committee had just received the tickets from the printer. Wroots' Coffee House door opened out on to a main thoroughfare. If only we could admit the men at a quiet walking pace they could go out at a side door; but naturally they were eager; they were fearful there might not be enough tickets to go round; they would hardly listen to instructions that order must be preserved. I, therefore, stood on the doorstep and briefly addressed the crowd, telling them that every one would get a ticket, but that we must keep control of the position, and I asked them to pass me quietly. To their great credit, they entirely agreed. Almost immediately a thousand men were right close to me, but endeavouring to be perfectly orderly. I put my back against one of the doorposts, and stretched out my leg with my foot on the opposite post, jamming myself in. I talked pleasantly to the men, and passed each man in under my leg, by this means steadying the rush. The fact that they did not make it impossible for me to remain at the task was exceedingly creditable, for, to prevent a stampede, many had to keep their mates back, and it was all done in good humour. At the close I was so stiff and bruised, I could scarcely walk for a while. I pulled my shirt off and wrung it out. It was soaked with perspiration, and my back had a good deal of skin off; but the job was completed satisfactorily.

The stevedores, the men who load the long-distance boats, and therefore stow the cargo, had organized in 1872, and had established a rate of eightpence an hour ordinary time and one shilling an hour overtime, thus giving evidence of the disciplinary effects of organization. Their meeting place was at the Wades' Arms, Jeremiah Street, Poplar; and as the accommodation was more suitable there than at Wroots', the Strike Committee moved to the stevedores' headquarters. Tom McCarthy (dead now this twenty-two years) was a prominent and active member. Another stevedore, James Twomey, was chairman of the Strike Committee – for these and all other waterside workers were out in sympathy, if not directly affected.

The Strike Committee sat every day and evening, usually till midnight. The questions to be dealt with were multitudinous;

occasionally there would be warmth of temper shown, but generally speaking the proceedings were conducted in a most orderly fashion. I was told off to give special attention to picketing, and to the organization of forces on the south side of the river. This left others available for public speaking, attempts at negotiations, etc. I usually turned up at committee about 11 p.m., unless special questions demanded consideration.

What stress and strain and responsibility! What opportunities for demonstrating capacity, a knowledge of what was necessary, a readiness to do it! And, speaking generally, wonderfully good work was done. Apart from public speaking, picketing, and negotiating, a thousand things every day required attention, and as a rule they were well attended to. Besides the thirty thousand dock and wharf workers, there were sailors and firemen, carmen, lightermen, and dry-dock workers, making another thirty thousand. These, with their dependants, all had to be provided for. Four hundred and forty thousand food tickets were distributed during the five weeks the dispute lasted, and many thousands of meals were organized and provided by friendly agencies. Public sympathy was entirely with the men, and practically the whole press was kindly disposed. Large sums were collected, but in spite of this help the time came when finances were at a very low ebb and the prospects of a settlement seemed remote. Next day, however, came a cable from Australia sending two thousand pounds, with promise of more; a few days later, the Australians cabled fifteen hundred pounds more. All told they sent no less than thirty thousand pounds. What a godsend! How it delighted the men: how it encouraged the leaders; and how it must have told the other way on the dock directors!

The dockers' fight in London fired the imagination of all classes in Australia; and employers, as readily and as heartily as workers, contributed to the London Dockers' Fund. I have had opportunities of thanking the people of Australia by addressing them in person at public meetings in nearly every city and township. What of it, that many Australians who subscribed to the London Dockers' Fund in 1889, fought determinedly against the transport workers in Australasia in 1890? There are the vagaries of human nature. As Yorkshire people say: 'Ther's nowt so queer as folk.'

John Burns and Ben Tillett were two very different men in

temperament and style, but each of them possessed exactly the right qualities to fire audiences and keep up the struggle to a successful finish. John Burns – with his assertiveness, his businesslike readiness to deal with emergencies, his power and disposition to keep at arm's length those who would have foisted themselves on the movement to its disadvantage, his cheery jocularity and homely remarks to the men on the march or on Tower Hill, his scathing criticism of hostile comments in the press or on the part of the dock directors – vitally contributed to the continuous encouragement of the mass of the strikers.

Ben Tillett, who had a close relationship to the men as general secretary of the Tea Operatives' and General Labourers' Union, would pour forth invectives upon all opponents, would reach the heart's core of the dockers by his description of the way in which they had to beg for work and the paltry pittance they received, and by his homely illustrations of their life as it was and as it ought to be. He was short in stature, but tough; pallid, but dauntless; affected with a stammer at this time, but the real orator of the group. Ben was a force to be reckoned with all through the fight.

H. H. Champion, cooler than a cucumber, would make statements of a revolutionary character, would deal with the weak points in the men's position, and would encourage them to rectify the same. Occasionally R. B. Cunninghame Graham would appear, as neat as a West End dude, with an eye keener than a hawk's, and a voice and manner that riveted attention as he drove home his satirical points, but always leaving a nice impression.

Tom McCarthy was a keen-witted, eloquent, versatile Irishman, full of personal knowledge of the actual life and work of a waterside man. Harry Orbell was a simple-spoken, frank, honest fellow, familiar with all the difficulties of the unskilled labourer, but was himself a highly-skilled man in the furnishing business. He had been squeezed out of this employment by the exigencies of trade depression. On the south side, Harry Quelch took a keen interest in the organization of the men, and built up the Labour Protection League.

When at length the dock directors agreed to the demands with, certain reservations as to the date when they should become operative, the position became critical. At the Mansion House many conferences had been held. The Lord Mayor, the dock directors, the men's representatives, and with general acquiescence a few prominent persons not identified directly with the business side of life, including the Bishop of London and Cardinal Manning, participated.

I had never seen the Cardinal before, and it was a matter of no small interest to me to find myself closely identified with such a man for a colleague.

A large percentage of the men at the docks were (and are) Roman Catholics. Now that a stage had been reached when the men's representatives were of opinion that the offers of the company merited serious consideration, the Cardinal, on the suggestion of the Strike Committee chairman, agreed to go to Poplar and put the case to the men, who held him in the greatest respect and reverence.

The meeting was held in the Kirby Street Catholic School at Poplar. The Cardinal was a very slender man; his face was most arresting, so thin, so refined, so kindly. In the whole of my life I have never seen another like unto it. He spoke to the dockers in such a quiet, firm, and advising fatherly manner, that minute by minute as he was speaking one could feel the mental atmosphere changing. The result was an agreement that the conditions should be accepted, to become operative in November.

The chief gains were: a minimum of sixpence an hour instead of fivepence (only fourpence formerly at Tilbury); eightpence an hour for overtime; none to be paid off with less than two shillings, or four hours' work. This seems a trifling gain now, but it was an important matter then, to have regular taking-on times instead of taking-on at any hour of the day, and to have gangs properly made up. The last point was not included in the original settlement, but it became a current practice at the docks and wharves, to the great advantage of the men. The change for the better was very real; and although subsequently difficulties arose, when many of the men became careless, and when petty bosses sought to score over the dockers, still, all who knew and know the facts will admit that the struggle of 1889 was a real landmark.

Ben Tillett, who had been general secretary all the time, writing of what happened in 1889 and its effects, when reviewing the position twenty-one years later, in *A Brief History of the Dockers' Union*, wrote:

We had established a new spirit: the bully and the thief, for a time at least, were squelched; no more would the old man be driven and cursed to death by the younger man, threatened and egged on to murder by an overmastering bully. The whole tone and conduct of work, of management of the men, was altered, and for the best.

The goad of the sack was not so fearful; the filthiness and foulness of language was altered for an attempt at courtesy, which, if not refined, was at least a recognition of the manhood of our brothers.

From a condition of the foulest blackguardism in directing the work, the men found a greater respect shown them; they, too, grew in self-respect, and the men we saw after the strike were comparable to the most self-respecting of the other grades of labour.

The 'calls' worked out satisfactorily; organization took the place of the haphazard; the bosses who lazed and loafed on their subordinates were perforce obliged to earn instead of thieving their money; the work was better done; the men's lives were more regular as their work was – the docker had, in fact, become a man!

The man became greater in the happiness of a better supplied larder and home; and the women-folk, with the children, shared the sense of security and peace the victory at the docks had wrought.

I must give myself the satisfaction here of putting on record the great kindness and forbearance shown to the Strike Committee, and to the stream of deputations they had to deal with, by Mrs Hickey of the Wades' Arms, The hostess, her son, and her daughters had, indeed, a heavy task. We practically took possession of the house, not for an hour or two, but for all day and every day during the five weeks the strike lasted. But Mrs Hickey treated these fellows – ourselves of the Committee included – as though she had been mother to the lot. She literally kept a shillelah handy, with which she frequently in, a half-serious way, would threaten any young fellow who was too noisy; but it was fine that these rough chaps respected her so thoroughly, and that she had the splendid tact to make it easy for them to keep good order all through the trying time.

I was generally one of the last members of the committee to get away. Often enough I left the premises nearer one o'clock than midnight – not to go home, for there was little chance of doing that, but to get to the house of Brother Jem Twomey, the chairman of the Strike Committee, with whom I used to stay.

I can honestly say, for my own part, that I cared nothing at all for the public meetings, whether on Tower Hill or elsewhere, or for what was thought of the fight by the public. I concentrated on the work of organization, and was indifferent to outside opinion. I had been at it about three weeks, and was now dealing specially with the South Side of the Thames. One day I realized that my boots had become so worn out, and that I must get others, or go barefoot (we always had long marches, and I invariably marched with the crowd). I slipped away from the marching column as soon as I noticed a boot shop. Hastily buying a pair of boots, I put them on and hurried to catch up with the crowd. When we reached Sayes Court, Deptford, I spoke as usual upon the general situation. A few days later, we were marching again along the thoroughfare where I had bought the boots. My eye lighted on the shop window, and to my amazement I noticed my name on a card. I approached the window, and to my still greater astonishment I saw that the card bearing my name was on the pair of old boots I had shed a few days before. The writing on the card ran: 'The boots worn by Tom Mann during the long marches in the Dock Strike.' I was positively flabbergasted, to think that importance of any kind could attach to such an articles, or to me.

I had become so inextricably involved in the dispute, and felt so completely a part of everything that was taking place, that I had left work, home, and all else, and paid no regard to anything other than the fight I was in. I scarcely noticed the papers, and had it not been for the subscriptions from Australia, I doubt if I should have known that the activities in which I was swallowed up had arrested attention outside this country. But, as events proved, the dock strike started a wave which spread over a great part of the world, and the working conditions of many millions were affected by it.

Offers of clerical help were numerous during the strike. One of these volunteers who rendered valuable service was Eleanor Marx Aveling, the daughter of Karl Marx, a most capable woman. Possessing a complete mastery of economics, she was able alike in conversation and on a public platform, to hold her own with the best. Furthermore, she was ever ready, as in this case, to give close attention to detailed work, when by so doing she could help the movement. I am the proud possessor of a very fine photograph of her father, given me by Eleanor.

Those who desire a consecutive history of the dockers' strike, will find the best account in *The Story of the Dockers' Strike*, by H. Llewellyn Smith (now Sir Hubert Llewellyn Smith) and Vaughan Nash, published by T. Fisher Unwin in 1889.

The revolutionary song, 'The Red Flag', was written at the end of 1889 by Jim Connell.

He was a Socialist then, and remains a Socialist yet. He is still very vigorous, and carries on a 'Legal Aid' business in Chancery Lane. I have known Jim for five-and-thirty years, and he has ever been the proud revolutionary Irishman, proud of his nationality, and proud of his Socialism, but terribly disappointed with the tune to which all Socialist societies, audiences, and individuals, sing his song, 'The Red Flag'.

Jim has explained how he wrote the song, as follows:

> I was 'inspired' to write 'The Red Flag' by the Paris Commune, the heroism of the Russian Nihilists, the firmness and self-sacrifice of the Irish Land Leaguers, the devotion unto death of the Chicago Anarchists, and other similar events. I felt my mind exalted by all these. On the night I wrote the song I was returning home from hearing a lecture by Herbert Burrows.
>
> He spoke in a semi-devout manner, as if he wished to convey that Socialism was his religion. This inspired me to write something in the train. The only tune that ever has or ever will suit 'The Red Flag' is the one I hummed as I wrote it. I mean 'The White Cockade' (Irish version). This was given as the tune when the song first appeared, in the Christmas number of *Justice*, 1889. A. S. Headingly took on himself to change the tune. May God forgive him, for I never shall! He linked the words to 'Maryland' the correct name of which is 'Tannenbaum', an old German Roman Catholic hymn. I never intended that 'The Red Flag' should be sung to church music to remind people of their sins!

The song has been subjected to considerable criticism, words and music both, but no other song is half so popular in the

Socialist movement in this country. During recent years 'The International' is increasingly used, and will, perhaps, ultimately take the first place; but the 'Red Flag' has had a magnificent popularity, and at the present time, of those Socialist bodies who close their meetings with singing, in the majority of cases it is the first and last stanzas of 'The Red Flag' that are used:

> *The people's flag is deepest red,*
> *It shrouded oft our martyred dead,*
> *And ere their limbs grew stiff and cold,*
> *Their heart's blood dyed its every fold.*
>
> * * * *
>
> *With heads uncovered swear we all,*
> *To bear it onward till we fall,*
> *Come dungeon dark or gallows grim,*
> *This song shall be our parting hymn.*
>
> *Then raise the scarlet standard high!*
> *Within its shade we'll live and die.*
> *Though cowards flinch and traitors sneer,*
> *We'll keep the Red Flag flying here.*

CHAPTER VI

AFTER THE DOCKERS' STRIKE
1890

THE stimulus that the dock strike gave to trade unionism was very great, and far-reaching; it led to a real revival. In order to enable those readers who are giving attention to consecutive developments, to the relationship which the activities of this particular period bear to other periods of activity, I here quote some paragraphs from the Webb's *History of Trade Unionism*, written in 1894, five years after the strike. There is a natural risk that one who closely participated in the work of this period, as I did, might attach an unjustifiable importance thereto. But Sidney and Beatrice Webb (p. 391, first edition) write:

> The immediate result of the dockers' success was the formation of a large number of Trade Unions among the unskilled labourers. Branches of the Dock, Wharf and Riverside Labourers' Union were established at all the principal ports. A rival Society of Dockers, established at Liverpool, enrolled thousands of members at Glasgow and Belfast. The unskilled labourers in Newcastle joined the Tyneside and National Labour Union, which soon extended to all the neighbouring towns. The Gas Workers' Union enrolled tens of thousands of labourers of all kinds in the provincial cities. The General Railway Workers' Union, originally established in 1889 as a rival to the Amalgamated Society of Railway Servants, took in great numbers of general labourers. The National Amalgamated Sailors' and Firemen's Union, established in 1887, expanded during 1889 to a membership of 65,000. Within a year after the dockers' victory, probably over 200,000 workers had been added to the Trade Union ranks, recruited from sections of the labour world formerly abandoned as incapable of organization....
>
> A wave of Trade Unionism, comparable in extent with those of 1833–4 and 1873–4, was now spreading into every corner of British

industry. Already in 1888 the revival of trade had led to a marked increase in Trade-Union membership. This normal growth now received a great impulse from the sensational events of the Dock Strike. Even the oldest and most aristocratic Unions were affected by the revivalist fervour of the new leaders. The eleven principal societies in the Shipbuilding and Metal Trades, which had been, since 1885, on the decline, increased from 115,000 at the end of 1888 to 130,000 in 1889, 145,000 in 1890 and 155,000 in 1891. The ten largest Unions in the building trades, which between 1885 and 1888 had likewise declined in numbers, rose from 57,000 in 1888 to 63,000 in 1889, 80,000 in 1890, and 94,000 in 1891. In certain individual societies the increase in membership during these years was unparalleled in their history. The Operative Society of Bricklayers grew from a fairly stationary 7,000 in 1888 to over 17,000 in 1891. The Boot and Shoe Operatives went from 11,000 in 1888 to 30,000 in 1891. . . .

The victory of the London Dockers and the impetus it gave to Trade Unionism throughout the country at last opened the eyes of the Trade-Union world to the significance of the new movement. . . .

In many instances the older members now supported the new faith. In other cases they found themselves submerged by the large accessions to their membership, which resulted from the general expansion.

It is, however, necessary to say that there was a great deal of criticism levelled at those who were termed the 'New Unionists.' Mr Broadhurst, MP, Mr George Howell, MP, Mr Robert Knight, Mr C. J. Drummond, and Mr George Shipton expressed themselves in unfriendly terms, and at times severely censured those of us who were specially active. Mr Shipton in particular wrote an article which appeared in the June issue, 1890, of *Murray's Magazine*, on 'Trades Unionism: The Old and the New'. A more detailed criticism was contained in a volume penned by George Howell, and published in 1891, *Trade Unionism New and Old*. the 'New Unionists' were alleged to be too ready to achieve their ends by strikes. They were blamed for insisting upon all in a department or works being members of a union, aiming as they did at one hundred per cent organized. It was accounted a fault that they made use of demonstrations, of bands and banners, thereby making needless public display.

At this period I was president of the Dockers' Union, having accepted that position after the strike to help in solidifying and extending the organization. Ben Tillett was secretary, and he and I decided that the best way in which to reply to Mr Shipton was to issue a penny pamphlet. We did so, under the title of *The 'New' Trades Unionism – a Reply to Mr George Shipton*. The following extracts therefrom will serve to show that the differences were in spirit and outlook rather than in form and method.

> Many of those who are identified with the 'new' trades unionism have been connected with their own trade societies for many years past, and it was a continual source of bitter grief to them that so much poverty should exist amongst workers of all sections, but especially among the unskilled and unorganized, and that the old Societies should be so utterly callous to this poverty as not to make any special exertion to alter matters for the better....
>
> The methods adopted by us of determining a change in our present industrial system, are on a strictly trade-union basis. All our public utterances, all our talks to our members, have been directed towards cultivating a sturdy spirit of independence, and instilling a deep sense of responsibility. In fact we have been at pains to discredit appeals to the legislature, contending that the political machine will fall into our hands as a matter of course, so soon as the educational work has been done in our labour organizations. We are convinced that not until Parliament is an integral part of the workers, representing and responsible to industrial toilers, shall we be able to effect any reform by its means ...
>
> The statement that the 'new' trade unionists look to Governments and legislation, is bunkum; the keynote is to *organize* first, and take action in the most effective way, so soon as organization warrants action, instead of specially looking to Government. The lesson is being thoroughly well taught and learned that we must look to ourselves alone, though this, of course, does not preclude us from exercising our rights of citizenship.
>
> It is quite true that most of the newly-formed unions pay contributions for trade purposes only, leaving sick and funeral benefits to be dealt with by sick and insurance Societies. The work of the trade unionist is primarily to obtain such a re-adjustment of conditions between employers and employed as shall secure to the latter a better

share of the wealth they produce, in the form of reduced working hours and higher wages, and our experience has taught us that many of the older unions are very reluctant to engage in a labour struggle, no matter how great the necessity, because they are hemmed in by sick and funeral claims, so that to a large extent they have lost their true characteristic of being fighting organizations, and the sooner they revert to their original programme the better for the well-being of the working masses. We, therefore, advocate strongly the necessity for labour organizations dealing with trade matters only.

At every opportunity that presented itself we have paid our willing tribute to our old leaders, the *real fighters*. We attribute the apathy of many of the wealthy unions to the lack of new vitality, many of them up till within recent years not being in advance of the stage where they have been left by the men who suffered imprisonment and starvation for their convictions.

Our ideal is a *Co-operative Commonwealth*. This we believe will be reached by honest effort in various directions, chief among which will be the efforts of the trade unionists; and while striving for the ideal, we are glad to know that we need not wait for years before further advantages can be obtained, but that by discreet conduct on our part, we can be continually gaining some advantage for one or other section of the workers.

The Trade-Union Congress was held at Liverpool in 1890, and the 'old' and 'new' schools were necessarily striving for ascendancy. The 'old' school were more in agreement with the 'new' than they had ever been before, most of them being instructed by their members how to vote on matters considered vital. The big fight was on the eight-hours' question. The 'new' school favoured our eight-hours' bill, and this was carried. John Burns and I were two of the five delegates sent to the congress by the Amalgamated Engineers.

About this time I received a letter from a firm of lawyers, saying that a client of theirs who preferred to remain anonymous authorized them to offer me two pounds (or two guineas) a week on condition that I should become the candidate for a parliamentary constituency. This sum would be paid me until the election should take place. I replied, thanking the unknown would-be patron, but saying I was of the opinion that I could render better service by remaining identified with the industrial movement. I heard no more of the matter.

The wave that started round the world in 1889 did not abate throughout 1890. The maritime strike of Australasia had its rise in Sydney in 1890 and spread until it covered Australia and New Zealand. Originating with the ships' officers, it was a prolonged and fierce struggle, whose result was not satisfactory to the men. This failure on the industrial field was one of the chief reasons why the Australian movement subsequently took on so markedly political a complexion.

During the same year, hundreds of disputes took place in Great Britain, some of them affecting very large numbers of workers. Among these disputes was the Scottish railway strike, which was fought very tenaciously. The Government now announced its intention to appoint a Royal Commission on Labour. I received intimation that I was likely to be nominated as one of the members. The matter having been discussed, it was held desirable that the interests of the workers should be watched and defended, and time to attend the sittings was granted me. The appointment duly came, the Commission Warrant being dated 21 April, 1891.

The total membership of the commission was twenty-seven; the representatives of the Labour interest numbered seven. The full list was as follows:

The Marquis of Hartington (subsequently Duke of Devonshire);
Lord Derby;
Sir Michael Hicks-Beach;
A. J. Mundella;
H. H. Fowler;
Leonard H. Courtney (subsequently Lord Courtney);
Sir John E. Gorst;
Sir Frederick Pollock;
Sir Edward J. Harland;
Sir W. T. Lewis;
Professor Marshall;
William Abraham (Mabon);
Michael Austin;
Gerald W. Balfour;
J. C. Bolton;

Thomas Burt;
Jesse Collings;
David Dale (subsequently Sir David Dale);
Alfred Hewlett (subsequently Sir Alfred Hewlett);
T. H. Ismay;
George Livesey;
Tom Mann;
James Maudsley;
Samuel Plimsoll;
Henry Tait;
Edward Trow;
William Tunstall.

The reference was:

A Royal Commission to inquire into the questions affecting the relations between employer and employed; the combinations of employers and employed, and the conditions of labour which have been raised during the recent trade disputes in the United Kingdom; and to report whether legislation can with advantage be directed to the remedy of any evils that may be disclosed, and, if so, in what manner.

I gave a large part of three years to the work of the commission, and I found it most interesting. There were days when a humdrum, stolid type of witness gave evidence that had little or no value to anyone; and occasionally it seemed farcical to spend time listening to such drivel. Often enough, however, the witnesses were genuine experts, who had well prepared their case, who exhibited ability, and who gave much useful information.

I was especially interested in studying the personal characteristics of the commissioners, in noticing their behaviour when witnesses were giving evidence that conflicted with the views they themselves held. Particularly significant was their manner when examining witnesses.

To expedite business, the commission split up into three sub-committees to deal with special groups of trades; but the members of each sub-committee were free to attend and to participate in the work of the other sub-committees. When the evidence of any witness was accounted of national importance, the commission sat as a whole. At such meetings, the Duke of Devonshire presided, and conducted the examination-in-chief of each witness, individual commissioners having the right to ask supplementary questions.

The Duke made an excellent chairman. He never tried to browbeat a witness, or to take advantage of any clumsiness of expression. Sometimes, of course, a commissioner or a witness would show irascibility. On such occasions the Duke would interpose with a question that invariably damped the ardour of one or other of the disputants; but his action was so tactful that no awkwardness was left behind.

The other three chairmen, one for each sub-committee, were Lord Derby, Sir David Dale, and Mr Mundella. Sir David Dale was particularly suave and deferential to witnesses. Mundella was assertive and disposed to be argumentative. When the evidence elicited by his questions failed to square with his own views, it was his custom to ask further questions, hoping to get his opinion endorsed if possible. Such a practice might be tolerated in individual commissioners, but was unsuitable in a chairman.

Two capitalist members of the commission specially interested me when conducting an examination. One was the prominent shipowner Sir T. H. Ismay, then chairman of the White Star Line. The other was Sir Edward Harland, of Harland & Wolffs, Belfast. Sir Thomas Ismay invariably questioned witnesses in a kindly tone, even when dealing with matters in which he was keenly concerned as a business man. Sir Edward Harland, on the contrary, always put his questions in a markedly hostile fashion, his tone of voice and facial expression combining to create the impression that his main object was to score points, and to secure admissions damaging to any witness who appeared on behalf of the workers.

Professor Marshall of Cambridge, was a very diligent commissioner, and gave close attention to all the evidence. It was obvious that his questions were carefully elaborated beforehand. The professor had an academic and somewhat pedantic style. I remember that when Sidney Webb was being examined by Marshall, the witness showed unmistakable signs of annoyance, and frequently replied in curt and satirical terms.

When the problem of the State Regulation of Labour came up for consideration, I was myself a witness. In addition, I submitted a statement on the Eight-Hour Work Day by trade and local option. In this connection I was under examination for three whole days, fifteen hundred questions being addressed to me, and the replies to some of these were pretty lengthy. I could not judge how far individual members of the commission were endeavouring to make use of the evidence elicited in order to aid them in their parliamentary work: but Gerald Balfour always impressed me as being really keen to understand the trend of opinion with a view to arriving at conclusions that might be helpful legislatively.

The Labour members were:

Thos. Burt of the Northumberland Miners;
William Abraham of the South Wales Miners;
Michael Austin of Ireland – Typographical;
Henry Tait of Scotland – Railwaymen's Union;
Edward Trow of Darlington – Iron Workers' Association;
James Maudsley of Lancashire – Cotton Spinners; and Tom Mann.

When the recommendations came to be made in the final report, four of us were unable to agree, and so a minority report was also presented. It is frequently asserted that the main object of a Government in appointing a commission or select committee, is to shelve a troublesome question. I regard the criticism as substantially sound. Still, I am sure that much genuine effort was put forth to make proposals of a remedial character in the Labour Commission reports; but I am unable to point to any legislative measure as a direct result of recommendations made by the Labour Commission.

Among the various proposals I submitted was one to dockise the river Thames, and to unify the authority that should control the Port of London.

The docks at that time were not under one authority; there were four competing dock companies, and over one hundred-and-fifty wharves and granaries, all in the Port of London. The dock companies were: the London and St Katherine's Company; the East and West India Company; the Surrey and Commercial Docks Company; and the Millwall Docks Company. For business purposes, however, the London and St Katherine's and the East and West India Companies were controlled by a joint committee, known as The London and India Docks Joint Committee. This committee managed the St Katherine's Docks, the London Docks, the West India Docks, the East India Docks, the Victoria Dock, the Albert Dock, and the Tilbury Docks. The Millwall Docks Company controlled the Millwall Docks at the Isle of Dogs, Poplar. The Surrey Commercial Company controlled the Surrey Commercial group at Rotherhithe on the south side; but in addition to these was a small dock at Limehouse controlled by the Regent's Canal and Dock Company, and there was another at Blackwall, known as the Poplar Dock, controlled by the North London Railway Company, and yet another small one, but with considerable warehouses, controlled by the Midland Railway Company. In addition, there were between Blackfriars Bridge and Greenwich Ferry, 141 wharves and 44 granaries; 110 of the wharves were classed as shipping wharves. At 34 of these, ships could be run along the side of the wharf; 21 of them were on the north side of the river, and 13 on the south. The dock companies sent experts to give evidence before the commission, their aim being to saddle upon the dockers and other waterside workers the blame for the comparative costliness of receiving, discharging, and loading a ship in the Port of London. Knowing the location of the various groups of docks and wharves, and the peculiar formation of the river, I made it my task to demonstrate to the commission: first, that the numerous vested interests conflicting with each other in the port prevented anything approaching real efficiency; and, secondly, that the docks were far apart from each other, and so many miles in some instances from the warehouses, that several handlings of the freight were necessary, resulting in unwarrantable expenditure.

I, therefore, submitted a plan for dockising the three-and-a-half-mile loop from Limehouse to Blackwall, where the neck of the Isle of Dogs narrows to one and one-eighth of a mile. I submitted that a cut should be made across this neck. Along the existing course of the river (the loop as I have termed it), the foreshore should be built up; and the same thing thould be done on the foreshore of the cutting. This would give three and a half miles on each side of the bend, and a mile and an eighth on each side of the proposed cutting, or a total of nearly nine and a half miles for scientifically arranged warehouses, to which any vessel could get right up. There should be a big basin built at North Woolwich, opposite Blackwall, so that vessels could enter the basin as they came up the river and have no occasion to trouble about suitable tides to enter the docks. I elaborated lengthily upon this, showing in detail the character of the tonnage that entered the port every month, and the nature of the work that had to be done in connection with it. I also contended that dock labour, at present disastrously casual, might be so systematized that the dockers would be enabled to work just as regularly as railway employees. Vested interests have, however, been too strong for such plans to be adopted. Time and money are still wasted, and the public is badly served owing to the hotch-potch character of the dock accommodation. Nevertheless, some years later, when I was in Australia, I was interested to learn that steps were being taken to unify a good deal of the responsibility for controlling the port. I had advocated that the County Council should be the fully recognized authority for this purpose, but this I suppose was too drastic, so the Port of London Authority was brought into existence, and its new home, near the Tower Bridge, has just been completed.

The discussion as to the relative merits of the 'new' and the 'old' unionism continued. As always happens, attempts to change established conditions brought condemnation from those who did not desire any change, while approving those who, though undoubtedly identified with working-class organizations, did not attempt to use these organizations for changing the industrial and social conditions.

At Toynbee Hall and other settlements in the metropolitan area, frequent discussions took place on one or other phase of trade unionism. Quite a number of the young men residing there, or in one way or another identified with Toynbee Hall, had rendered considerable help during the dock strike. A few ex-Oxford men who had so helped, remained associated with the dockers when they formed themselves into branches of the union; and in several instances the Toynbee men themselves became branch members, accepted positions as officers, and did much useful detail work. So it came about that the Oxford Committee of the Universities' Settlement Association (Toynbee Hall) organized a conference which was held in the Town Hall, Oxford, on 29 November, 1890. The syllabus set forth the subjects, and mentions the speakers who were considered representative in their respective circles:

FIRST SESSION, 2.30 PM

Mr A. H. D. Acland, MP, in the Chair.
Principles and Methods of newer and older forms of Trade Unionism. The relation of both to the employer. The possibility of conciliation.
Mr Tom Mann (President of the Dockers' Union).
Mr J. H. Tod (Of the Dock House Joint Committee).
Mr H. Slatter (Secretary to the Typographical Association).
The Chairman.

SECOND SESSION, 8 PM

Rt Hon. Leonard H. Courtney, MP, in the Chair.
The adequacy of Unionism, in whatever form, as a solution of economic difficulties; proposed supplements or alternatives in Co-operation and Legislation. Economic aspect of the question.
Mr Benjamin Jones (of the London Co-operative Wholesale).
Mr Graham Wallas (of the Fabian Society).
Mr William Hey (Secretary of the Ironfounders' Union).
Mr George Hawkins (of the Oxford Trades' Council and Co-operative Wholesale Board).
The Chairman.

I will not give a résumé of the discussion. It was considered a useful one, and was published by the Oxford Committee. When I look at the speech I made now, more than thirty-five years ago, I find that many of the sentences correspond almost word for word with what I have used recently from the platform. The following paragraph is a specimen:

> We have abundance of raw material from Mother Earth, and the capacity of our workers is increasing each year, so that from the raw material we can with a less expenditure of energy create a greater number of commodities for the energy expended. That being so, we argue that there is no divinely ordained reason, no natural reason, why any man, woman, or child need be short of food or clothing, or the necessities of human existence; and therefore we contend that,

as soon as the present chaos gives place to industrial order, there will be a chance for all to live proper lives: and that is the work of us trade unionists at the present time – so to organize ourselves, and to get the workers generally so effectively organized, that we can insist on the necessary changes taking place.

It is interesting to see the dock directors' estimate of old and new unionism. Said Mr Tod: 'The old unions protect and assert the demands of particular trades, and even of special branches in those trades, and on the whole they do not trouble themselves much with other branches of the same trade. I should say generally – and again I speak as an outsider – that the fault of unionism, either old or new, is that energy and ability are rather levelled down and not up. There is too much uniformity. But when we come to the new unionism it may be protective, but it is eminently aggressive. It deals chiefly with unskilled labour, the supply of which is practically inexhaustible. That is one difficulty. Another thing they do now is to federate branches of the same trade: even though some branches thus federated may have no grievance of their own to cause a strike, they all strike together, or rather they go farther than that, they bring outside trades into the matter. Of course, that is all to bring on greater pressure.'

Dealing with the limitations of unions, Mr Graham Wallas said: 'We believe it is impossible for trades unions or the co-operative system by themselves to absorb what we call the differential advantages – those advantages which are in the nature of rent. We believe it is by a system of progressive taxation that we shall have to extinguish the landlord's right, and the right of the mine-owner, in the natural advantages of the soil, and the acquired advantages of town sites. We believe, in order to do so, it may be necessary to pass various legislative measures, taxing out the landlord and mine-owner, and throwing the compensation for any landlord or mine-owner whom we entirely dispossess, not upon the general body of workers in the community, but upon the holders of what we call idle incomes.'

My duties as president of the Dockers' Union were numerous and interesting. I had responsibilities to discharge in dealing with the pressing requirements of the men. At all times where large numbers of men are under conditions that vary in manner like unto the work at the docks and wharves, it is impossible, even with well-established methods, to avoid stoppages of work through unadjusted grievances. I worked comfortably with my colleagues, and harmoniously with the men: but one set of men were rather trying, perhaps exceptionally so. Their work was very laborious – to discharge grain by hand. There were seven men in each gang, and their duties were – the grain being in bulk – to fill the sacks, which would be hauled up out of the hold, then weighed and put on to the quayside, or 'overside' into a barge. This was piece-work, and, compared with other work at the docks, it was well paid.

I must here explain that it was our rule as officers of the Dockers' Union to organize large meetings, usually on Sunday mornings, for educational purposes; i.e. to get beyond the immediate concerns of the hour, and to deal with the Labour movement nationally and internationally. As was my custom, at one of these meetings I had referred to the estimated wealth production of the nation, and to the distribution of this wealth, quoting statistical authorities. I had stated that 'the workers did not receive more than one-half of the total wealth produced by Labour'. The little story I have now to tell will show that the corn porters of the Victoria Dock district were not only at the meeting, but took note of what was said.

These men were paid a fixed sum per hundred quarters of grain discharged. But frequently the grain, during transit, would 'sweat', and the work then would be exceptionally hot and fatiguing: so an extra claim called 'hot money' would be put in by the men, and often granted by the company. Sometimes the grain would be very dusty also, nearly choking the men at work, and necessitating much drinking: so claims were put in for 'dirty money', and sometimes granted. Further, when a ship was not specially adapted for carrying grain, some of the bunkers were exceptionally awkward to work, which necessitated one of the gang spending time in trimming or shovelling the grain forward, thus hindering the work of the gang and reducing wages: so claims were also put in for 'awkward money', and sometimes were recognized. In time it reached the stage when the Docks Committee said it would be necessary to have a conference with respect to the methods of remuneration and these repeated claims for extras. The conference was held. I was present. As a result, the company agreed to pay a higher overall rate per hundred quarters, and to disallow the claims for extras. Said the men: 'We are prepared to accept this as general principle; but, as all who know how the grain comes over will admit, there are times when the grain is so exceptionally hot or so very dirty, and sometimes both, that recognition for something extra must be made in such cases.' To this the company agreed, provided that there was some qualified person to judge as to the merit of such an extra claim. This, too, was arranged, and for a time matters went smoothly, claims being very rare, and only when conditions were exceptional. Then one morning at the dockers' office I received a message from the Dock House to the effect that work on a certain grain vessel had been stopped, for the men had put in a claim which the umpire disallowed. I was requested to attend to same without delay. I did so, telling them at the office to phone to Victoria Docks and get in touch with the men and meet me in the club room near Tidal Basin station. On my arrival all the men were sitting in the room, quietly awaiting me. I at once took the chair and opened out:

'Good day, lads. Word came from the Dock House about you putting in a claim which their official says is not justified. Since the increased over-all rate was agreed to, this is the first time there has been a stoppage: if the case is a sound one I shall do my best to get the claim recognized, so I've come down to get the facts, and then go and see the cargo if need be. Who'll state the case?'

After a few seconds one of the biggest fellows, well over six foot, came up to me at the table, and said:

'Look here, Mr Tom Mann, the other Sunday morning there was a meeting on the waste ground, wasn't there?'

'Yes, and I was there.'

'Yes, and you told us then the workers didn't get more than one-half the wealth they produced, didn't you?'

'Yes, that's so.'

'Well, we bloody well want some of the other half!' And he returned to his seat.

If the Dock House people could have witnessed and heard this little episode they would, I expect, have laughed well at my being so confronted. The real fact was, the men had worked consecutively for four days under very heavy conditions, and they could not go on without a rest, the work being really exhausting. The claim was not seriously put in; it was chiefly an excuse to get a necessary rest.

CHAPTER VII

THE LABOUR MOVEMENT AND THE CHURCHES
1890 to 1894

DURING the winter of 1890–1, unemployment was rife, and I was battling as best I could for 'maintenance or work' for the sufferers. Cardinal Manning wrote me a very encouraging letter, saying that the claim was a valid one. 'Under the Act of Elizabeth the authorities are responsible for providing one or the other, and this Act has never been repealed.'

As the Cardinal had been so closely identified with the wind-up negotiations of the dock strike, he maintained his interest in the welfare of the dockers, and on a number of occasions he wrote asking me to call on him in order to tell him how matters were developing. I have before commented upon his wonderful features, and upon the ultra-refined manner that always characterized him. He was perfectly natural, and simple, and I was entirely at ease with him. Never once did he broach the question of religion; always his concern was to know how the men were behaving, to inquire whether the improved conditions were being maintained, and to ask if the union was thriving.

I will now relate an incident that caused me to appreciate him in an exceptional degree for the wonderfully kind disposition he showed towards me. I received a letter from him asking me to call, and adding: 'This time I do not wish to talk about the docks or the dockers, but about yourself.' I went. He looked steadily at me, and said: 'The first thing I have to say to you is, that a living dog is better than a dead lion. You need a rest, and must have one.'

I expressed my sincere appreciation of his kindly regard, and said:

'I really do not feel particularly in need of a rest. In any case, I am too full up with work in London and the provinces to consider your proposal.'

'Yes, I know you are busy; but think it over, and decide when you are least busy.'

I had now taken out my diary. Looking at my numerous fixtures, I said:

'Naturally, people always think their own meeting the most important, and I am booked up with meetings several months ahead.'

'Well, try and fix upon a couple of weeks, and let me know. And now, where would you like to go? Do you know Ireland?'

'I have paid short visits to Dublin and Belfast, but I don't know it in a holiday sense.'

'Well, when you have fixed upon the time, if you agree to go to Ireland, I'll give you an introduction where you can have a suitable rest, and come back refreshed for your work.'

I thanked him, and promised I would write and let him know how I succeeded in cancelling some of the engagements; but this proved too difficult, and I wrote and told the Cardinal so, and said possibly I should be able to manage a week-end holiday. Perhaps I would take a run over to the Continent. He replied, regretting I could not spare time for a longer holiday, and enclosing a card of introduction which I might use when I managed a week-end. He advised me to go to the Rhine. I was not able to get off for a week-end or any holiday for a very long time, but I shall never forget the genuine kindheartedness of His Eminence the Cardinal.

About this time I was active in addressing many public meetings in and out of London. I frequently commented upon the Church, and condemned it for not grappling with the social problem. One of the young clergymen who had helped us during the dock strike (the Rev. Thorry Gardiner, I think), was responsible for my receiving a number of invitations to address meetings, and I was ever ready to do so within the limits of physical possibility. One such invitation came from Lady Aberdeen, asking if I would address a meeting at her house, at which would be present a number of people interested in the social problem, who would be glad if I would talk to them about the dockers and their conditions. I went. It was a fashionable gathering indeed – West End with a vengeance, I thought – and, quite a number of clergymen were present. I spoke for an hour, dealt with industrial and social conditions, and denounced the Church for its deadly apathy.

Discussion followed. The whole affair was, if not an opportunity for useful propaganda, at least an opportunity for me to speak in the plainest of terms to members of the exploiting class, and especially to the professors of religion.

A few days afterwards I received a letter from the Archbishop of Canterbury (Benson) stating that he had been much interested in a report given to him by Miss Tait, daughter of the late Archbishop Tait, his predecessor. She had been present at the meeting at Lady Aberdeen's, when I had commented upon the attitude of the Church to social problems, and it would please him much if I would call on him at Lambeth. He had arranged to have tea in a small library, the only other person present besides ourselves being the Suffragan Bishop of Dover. After a few pleasantries, the Archbishop said he had been greatly interested in the comments I had made so far as he had heard. Was it my opinion that the Church should endeavour to solve the social problem? I said that such had certainly been my contention, and that I held the Church to be negligent of what seemed to me the most sacred work in which she could engage, and so on. The Archbishop did not combat anything I said; on the contrary, he expressed his general agreement with me, adding, however, that perhaps I hardly realized the nature of the difficulties that confronted the Church. Then, reaching down a book from a shelf, he went on:

'I should like to read a passage and get your opinion on it.'

He read as follows:

> The problems on which Christ has been consulted, and has given no uncertain answer, are the greatest problems of the past. The present has a problem of its own which may be not much less difficult or less extensive than any past questions. ... The problem now before us, or rather upon us, is what is called in a special way the social problem ... the social problem presented by the conditions of lifelong wretchedness under which a vast part of our town populations lives its life, works its works, etc., etc. But all these social difficulties and solutions, what have they to do with the Church's work? Are these not secular and economic questions?
>
> Yes, and therefore Church questions of deepest moment. These are the phenomena of the world in which Christ is now living. These form the times of Christ.

He asked me:

'Does that touch the same idea that you had?'

'Yes,' I replied, 'it does. What I say is that the Church fails to grapple with the social problem.'

'Yes,' he rejoined, 'I understand, and am largely in agreement with you, but you will see that this is a book of my own. I shall ask you to accept it.'

He signed it and handed it to me. I inferred that he wished me to understand that, in his official capacity as Archbishop, he had brought the subject of the social problem before the clergy and Church workers, and had urged them to study the matter carefully. He did not maintain that the Church was giving due attention to this vast subject; but he obviously wanted me to realize that, theoretically at all events, the social problem had not been entirely overlooked. I considered this a clever method of enlightening me. Whenever, subsequently, I had occasion to criticize Churchgoers, I did not forget to mention what I had learned from Archbishop Benson.

Amid a variety of interests and duties, I did not neglect the Amalgamated Society of Engineers, and was amongst those who considered there was ample room for greater activity on its part. At this time I was a member of the Bow branch of the union. The general secretary, Mr Robert Austin, having died in September 1891, the branch decided to nominate me for the position, in the hope that, if elected, I should be able to put life into the organization. I agreed to accept nomination. A large election committee for the London area was formed, with Mr George N. Barnes (now The Rt Hon. G. N. Barnes, MP) as secretary – and a very capable one he proved. The duties were considerable. The membership of the society extended to Australasia, America, and South Africa, all of which had to be dealt with. Since it had been decided to seize the opportunity of the election in order to make a propagandist and educational campaign for broadening the basis of the organization, and if need be changing the constitution, committees were formed throughout the country, and numerous meetings were held. The ASE had a real good shaking up. The only other candidate in the running was Mr John Anderson, who had been at the head office of the union for some years as assistant general secretary. There was a third candidate, William Glennie (now assistant general secretary), but the contest was really between Mr Anderson and myself. The result of the election was:

Anderson	18,102
Mann	17,152
Glennie	738

Mr Anderson took up office in April 1892. About the same time Mr G. N. Barnes became assistant secretary, taking the place of Mr John Wilson, who had died soon after Mr Robert Austin. Mr John Burns, being a member of the ASE frequently addressed meetings on behalf of the society, and in other ways rendered efficient help. In 1896, Mr Barnes, a Scotsman, born at Lochee in 1859, was elected general secretary.

The following year witnessed one of the biggest industrial struggles the ASE or any other Union had ever engaged in. It may not be uninteresting to give some of the facts. I refresh my own memory by turning to the *Jubilee Souvenir* of the ASE, published in 1901, for whose compilation Mr Barnes was responsible.

The year 1897 opened with 87,450 members, and but 2,000 unemployed, and its first month brought the adoption of the fifty-hours standard week's time at Liverpool, and further advances of wages on the Clyde, at Barrow, Rochdale, Newton-le-Willows, and Cleckheaton. Many places soon followed. Messrs. Platt of Oldham had also agreed to overtime conditions which the society recommended should be taken as a model for other districts, namely, time-and-a-quarter for the first two hours, time-and-a-half for the second, double-time afterwards; and for piece-workers an addition equal to the difference between overtime and ordinary rates.

Difficulties existed, however, at Armstrong's of Elswick in regard to outworking conditions, and at the Pallion Forge, Sunderland, there was trouble. The society demanded the standard rate of wages for the manipulation of horizontal boring machines. The then newly formed Employers' Federation issued lock-out notices; and, although attempts to negotiate were made, they were unsuccessful. In London the men were demanding the eight-hour day. Several of the unions, including the boilermakers, agreed to make common cause with the ASE to obtain this. It transpired later that the boilermakers' executive had refused to endorse this, so solidarity did not prevail. However, the joint committee of the three Societies that did take common action, viz.: the Steam Engine Makers, the Machine Workers, and the ASE, struck work in three London firms on 3rd July. The Engineering Employers' Federation, hitherto confined to the north, now extended operations to London, and informed the union executives that they (the employers) would respond to the men's action by a general lock-out in batches of 25 per cent weekly of all the members of the societies involved. This was wired to the men's committees in the federated area, and evoked unanimous decisions in favour of a retaliatory notice being tendered to withdraw the remaining 75 per cent. These notices took effect on 10th July, and for the following six months and a half a trial of strength ensued. In the end the longer purse of the employers secured them the victory.

It must here be said that the semi-skilled and the unskilled labourers were not organized, and that only three societies out of fifty took action, so that the real cause of the failure to win was the absence of solidarity. Since then something has been done to rectify this, but even yet there are quite sixty separate unions in the metal industry when only one should fill the bill. But this I shall deal with later.

Following upon these numerous activities, I devoted an increasing amount of attention to advocating the municipalization of the docks of the Port of London. I addressed meetings on this subject, and with the aid of a lantern showed pictures of the proposed dockside area, detailing the advantages that would accrue. As a result, members of the London County Council and London Members of Parliament became interested, and expressed hearty approval in the main of the proposals I made. Seeing that legislative powers would be required to take such work in hand, and that this would necessitate parliamentary support from members who as yet had no knowledge of the subject, it was suggested that a reform programme be drafted to suit the requirements of Londoners generally, for this would secure larger support for the dockers' proposition than would otherwise be possible. The outcome was the formation of the London Reform Union, of which I became secretary.

I was thus brought into close contact with persons primarily concerned about matters of municipal reform, and I found good scope for effective work. A stimulus was given to a constructive and advanced policy for the London County Council and for the Local Borough Councils. Among those who rendered substantial help as speakers and general propagandists, were two clergymen, the Rev. Percy Dearmer (now Dr Dearmer) and the Rev. Thorry Gardiner. The latter was unmarried, and rector of St George's in the Borough, near London Bridge. He frequently remained with me for a short talk after the meeting, and occasionally we took coffee together. As a result of considerable conversation he knew of my identification with schools and the Church in earlier days, and also of my frequent criticism of the Church. The speeches he made were very much like unto my own, and his views on economics were not materially different. On one occasion he asked me whether I did not look upon the work we were engaged in as religious work. I said I certainly thought it was, and, further, that if the Church did its duty it would be engaged as we were, honestly striving, not only to clear out the slum areas, to provide opportunities for recreation and education, to insist upon adequate housing accommodation, etc., but also to engage definitely in establishing sound economic conditions for the effectual cure of these evils. Mr Gardiner said he heartily agreed with all this, and then surprised me by adding:

'Why not join me in Church work, and do this in Church as well as out?'

'Tell me exactly what you mean?' said I.

'Well,' he replied, 'as you know, I'm in charge of that large church; there is nothing we are saying and advocating at the meetings of the Reform Union that I am not prepared to advocate regularly in church as a matter of religious duty. I have no curate. If you were ordained we could work jointly and do it more effectively.'

I replied with astonishment that although I admired the Church organization, reaching into every village in the country, it was entirely out of the question that I should be so intimately identified with it. Even if I had an inclination that way, there was the stumbling block of the thirty-nine articles. My friend Gardiner here scored against me in the following way. Often, in conversation with him, I had expressed my great admiration for Dean Stanley, whom I frequently heard preach at Westminster Abbey, and who was the nearest approach in the Anglican Church to Cardinal Manning in the Roman Catholic Church, alike in appearance and in manner. But Dean Stanley, more than any other Church dignitary I had knowledge of, put an interpretation upon troublesome and complex doctrines that removed the cloudiness and opened up vistas of true knowledge concordant with the most genuinely scientific development. Mr Gardiner, knowing my appreciation of the Dean, quietly said:

'Well, the Church that is broad enough and tolerant enough for a Dean Stanley might possibly be the same for a Tom Mann!'

I have lost touch with Gardiner for many years, but I know that he became chaplain to the Archbishop of Canterbury in 1903, and has been Canon Resident of Canterbury since 1917. It is possible that during two decades in a cathedral close there has been time for the waning of the keen interest in social questions that characterized him when I first knew him.

The force which impelled me to the before-mentioned efforts on behalf of municipal reform was my desire that something effective should be done for the unification of control in the Port of London, the necessity for which was urgent. It seemed that scarcely anyone was interested in the matter, and the only way in which I could gain support for my proposals was by merging them into a general policy of London municipal reform. Once embarked on such a venture I became involved in a mass of details. At this time the old vestries still retained some power – chiefly the power of preventing anything of value being accomplished for the community. The London Reform Union united the progressive forces on municipal affairs. The administrative bodies in the metropolitan area are still complex in their variety, but three decades back their multiplicity was positively bewildering to the ordinary man who tried to get a grip of the situation.

A number of prominent members of the Fabian Society were closely identified with the London Reform Union, and its policy was characteristically Fabian and Reformist. I omit further details concerning its activities for these have little bearing on the revolutionary problems of today.

My close friendship at this period with various ministers of religion, led to the circulation of a report that I was about to enter the Church. One morning a pressman called upon me to ask what truth there was in the statement that appeared in *The Times* of that date regarding myself and the Church. The brief statement was as follows, under the heading of 'Ecclesiastical Intelligence':

> We are informed that Mr Tom Mann, the well-known Labour leader, is an accepted candidate for Deacon's Orders in the Church of England. Mr Mann has received a title to the curacy of a large and important parish inhabited by the industrial classes, and it is expected that his ordination will take place at Christmas.

This was on 5 October, 1893. I contradicted the statement that matters were arranged, but did not deny that the subject had been under serious consideration.

To my further astonishment I found the afternoon editions of the London papers had on the placards: 'Tom Mann enters the Church', and I was the recipient of numerous messages and some congratulations. One was from the Church Congress, then in session, signed by several well-known clergymen, ardent advocates of the Labour cause, welcoming me among the minority as a coworker, etc.

One of my Nonconformist friends was the Rev. Mr Belcher, minister of St Thomas' Square Congregational Church, Hackney. He invited me to occupy the pulpit, and I did so. There was a great congregation, and when in the heart of my address I denounced the hypocrisy of the churches, there were hisses. As I proceeded there were cheers, and for the space of thirty or forty minutes there was frequent alternations of cheering and hissing.

Another good friend, also a Congregational minister, but whose church in Southgate Road N, was already known as The Brotherhood Church, was the Rev. Bruce Wallace. I preached in his church on much the same lines as I had done at St Thomas' Square, Hackney. The *Christian World Pulpit* reported my sermon in full.

On leaving for Australia at a later date, I entrusted my correspondence and newspaper cuttings to a friend, and these were nearly all lost. My letters included a number that I set special store upon from Cardinal Manning, and a batch that I received at this particular period *re* the Church. One cutting book only was saved; it contains items respecting this period. The following two letters, which appeared in the *Westminster Gazette*, are fair specimens of many others.

'Rev.' Tom Mann!

To The Editor of the *Westminster Gazette*.
SIR,

It won't do. Has our robust brother no true friend to warn him of his fate? The whole trend of clericalism is towards sacerdotalism, and sacerdotalism is the death of manhood. To take Church pay is to wear Church yoke, and for a modern democrat to do this would be to stultify himself for evermore. Fancy the 'Rev.' John Burns! But if this is simply unthinkable, where and what would be the future of Rev. Tom Mann? More than twenty years ago a brave young spirit of my acquaintance who had been educated at New College was lured into the Church of England by the vision of glorious possibilities therein. Alack! I met him the other day at a mutual friend's dinner table. Never was completer wreck! Every hope had been blasted, and he was eking out existence either as a workhouse chaplain or the chaplain of a cemetery. As a Labour leader an exceptionally glorious future seemed to lie before Mr Mann. But an essential condition of service is absolute release from Official trammels. I pity even Nonconformist ministers their fatal handicapping; but a Radical Church parson! 'If any man will serve me, let him follow me,' was the imperative condition 1,800 years ago, and that following was not exactly into a snug church living.

No. There are plenty of small folk for church curacies, but we have none too many Tom Manns!

Yours, etc.,
A.C.

To The Editor of the *Westminster Gazette*.
DEAR SIR,

Mr Tom Mann will hardly be as 'alone' in his capacity of Socialist parson as the 'Star' man imagines. Apart from the seven-and-seventy priests of the Guild of St Matthew, who are all determined Socialists, the Christian Social Union is a large nursery, filled full of Socialists, who are victoriously cutting their teeth; and the still greater fact remains that the Church herself is a Socialist body. Even the Toriest of parsons is forced and bound to read prayers, lessons, and gospels, every line of which is stuffed with the associative ideas and formulas which deny with emphatic anathema the whole gospel of Individualism. As one who has tried it, I can assure Mr Mann that the more thoroughly one knows the ideas set forth by the Prayer-Book the more utterly one feels that they are Socialist to the core. It naturally follows that those who are communists in the imperishable things should be so in the perishable also, as was felt even in the Apostolic times. (See the Epistle to St Barnabas, xix, 8.)

I am, Sir,
Yours,
CHARLES L. MARSON

St Mary's Clergy House,
 Charing Cross Road.
 5 October, 1893.

The one by that sturdy Socialist parson, the Rev. C. L. Marson, I specially appreciated, and very many others similar in spirit, and some as emphatically opposed thereto. However, I concluded, I hope not immodestly, to use the world as my parish, and acted accordingly.

About this period, Mr Andrew Reid, a social reformer, brought together a number of persons similarly interested, each contributing to a volume entitled *Vox Clamantium*. To this volume the Rev. Charles L. Marson contributed a chapter on the 'Social Teaching of the Early Fathers', in which he referred once more to the Epistle of Barnabas. This document cannot date from later than Tatian's time. The most educated among the early Churches, that of Alexandria, accepted it as genuine. It conveys the whole pith of Christian Socialism:

> Thou shalt have all things in common with thy neighbour, and not call them thy private property; for if ye hold the imperishable things in common, how much more the perishable?

Is not this exactly like the words of the Rev. Stewart Headlam:

> Those who come to the Holy Communion are bound to be Holy Communists.

Other contributors included the Rev. Professor Shuttleworth, the

Rev. The Hon. James Adderley, the Very Rev. C. W. Stubbs, and the Hon. Roden Noel. In his essay on 'Christianity and Social Advance,' the Rev. Roden Noel says:

> Surely that man or woman is no Christian at all, except in name, in so far as he or she remains indifferent to the awful abyss that yawns between rich and poor; to the insufficiency of the share in our immense wealth which falls to the lot of those who produce it; the unjust, inhuman, and horrible condition of the toilers in monstrous cities, herded together like swine, with no leisure or opportunity for living a human life, perpetually starved, stinted, stunted, maddened by carking care and anxiety for the health, well-being, and very life of themselves, and of those nearest to them: the image of God well-nigh crushed out of them by the cruel machinery that makes us clean, comfortable, and virtuous, with a virtue and happiness that have their root in a misery and moral degradation is a millionfold more terrible than those of the slave in Greece, Rome, or modern America.

Alfred Russell Wallace, the scientist, had a chapter on 'Economic and Social Justice'. Mr A. E. Fletcher, who had been editor of the *Daily Chronicle* in its palmiest days, wrote on 'Christian Ethics and Practical Politics'. For myself, I had an article on 'Preachers and Churches', in which I said:

> We have a glorious and an inspiring work in hand – nothing less than the purifying of the industrial and social life of our country, and the making of true individuality possible. For, let it be clearly understood, we Labour men are thoroughly in favour of the highest possible development of each individual. We seek no dead level of uniformity, and never did. Our ideal is, 'From each according to his capacity, to each according to his needs.' We can't reach that right off, but when we have done so, we shall not be 'far from the Kingdom'.
>
> To engage in this work is to be occupied in the noblest work the earth affords. To do it well, we want not only men and women of good intention – the Churches have these now – we shall want men and women of sound sense who will understand the science of industrial economics, as well as of the highest standard of ethics. To mean well is one thing, to be able to do well is a better thing, and we

cannot do well, except by accident, unless we know something of the laws that underlie and control the forces with which we shall have to deal.

It seemed to me that I could better fulfil the spirit of this contribution outside any Church than by becoming an ordained churchman. My next endeavour to combine 'doing well' with 'meaning well' led me to become secretary of a political organization.

CHAPTER VIII

SECRETARYSHIP OF THE INDEPENDENT LABOUR PARTY
1894 to 1896

AT a conference of the Independent Labour Party, held in February, 1894, I was appointed secretary of the party. For some time I had been in hearty agreement with the ILP, and while lecturing under various auspices I had supported the principles and policy of that organization. Having become its secretary, I was henceforward actively connected with the work of extending its sphere of operations. Keir Hardie was chairman of the National Administrative Council, and he and I worked together harmoniously. The members of the NAC were Pete Curran, Ben Tillett, George S. Christie, Alderman Tattersall, Leonard Hall, Fred Brocklehurst, and John Lister, who was treasurer. I had been for some years closely connected with the co-operative movement as well as with the trade-union movement, and in my propagandist efforts I laboured to extend ILP influence in the trade unions and co-operative societies, these tactics being vigorously supported by my colleagues. Definite attention was given to the running of candidates for municipalities and for Parliament. Complete independence of Liberals and Conservatives was enjoined and insisted upon. The declaration of adherence was not exactly the same in all districts. That which prevailed in London was as follows:

> Membership of this party shall be open to all men and women who shall sign a declaration of belief that the interests of Labour are paramount to, and must take precedence of, all other interests, and that the advancement of these interests of Labour must be sought by political and constitutional action, and that no member of any organization connected with the Liberal, Liberal-Unionist, or Conservative parties be eligible for membership of the party.
> I................hereby pledge myself to the above.

Keir Hardie and I did much platform propaganda, and although we were pledged to constitutional action, this did not prevent the capitalist newspapers from denouncing us in harsh terms. To dare to declare determined opposition to both the recognized political parties, and to act accordingly, brought condemnation and vilification from the ordinary press. I took especial satisfaction in exposing the principles and methods of the Liberals, showing that they were essentially capitalistic, and were pledged to the maintenance of a profit-making system. However reactionary Tories were, none of them were or could be greater exploiters than the Liberals.

I was candidate for the Colne Valley division of Yorkshire, two reasons being urged as to why I should run in that constituency. First of all, it was at that time exceptionally backward, neither Socialists nor Labour men having given attention to it. Secondly, the reason was that the sitting member was a prominent Liberal capitalist, the head of a well-known engineering firm in Leeds, Mr James Kitson, afterwards Sir James. The electorate was a difficult one to tackle. Industrially it was chiefly textile, partly cotton and partly woollen, for it occupied an intermediate position between the area of the Lancashire cotton trade, and that of the Huddersfield woollen trade. There were also about six hundred small farmers and a few engineering workers.

I nursed the constituency systematically for the three years preceding the General Election of 1895. There was never any chance of my winning the seat. At the election I received rather more than twelve hundred votes, whilst the sitting member received about three times that number.

At this date, Victor Grayson was a boy of thirteen years of age. Twelve years later, in 1907, Victor Grayson as a straight-out Socialist candidate was returned for the Colne Valley division, against a majority of 153 over the Liberal and 421 over the Conservative.

At the 1895 General Election, Keir Hardie, who had been the member for South West Ham since 1892, was defeated. Keir stood for West Bradford in 1896 and was defeated there, but was returned for Merthyr in 1900.

All the time I kept industrial organization to the fore, attaching prime importance thereto. In September, 1894, I issued a pamphlet under the title *What the ILP is driving at*, in which the following appears:

> And now to guard against the view that the whole of our social difficulties are attributable to politicians or employers of labour, I am bound to state my conviction that while both those sections are about as wrong-headed as it's possible to be, the bulk of the workers themselves are far from being able to cast stones, for, as yet, only a small minority of the workers have really tried to understand the causes of these difficulties, and taken such action as lies in their power to rectify them.
>
> Take for instance the relatively small proportion of the workers who as yet belong to the trade unions. Thus out of six and a quarter millions of workmen in the United Kingdom eligible to join the unions, only two million are members, and while the good work these have been enabled to do has undoubtedly proved of enormous advantage to the workers generally, their power for good has been checked much more by the indifference and selfishness of thoughtless workmen than by the opposition of employers. No need here to recite the benefits of trade unionism, still less to defend it, but as a collectivist and a member of the ILP, I know for a certainty that the greatest hindrance to the democratic movement at the present time is the lack of effective industrial organization, backed up by equally effective political organization for purposes of industrial change. A member of the ILP who should have the impudence to act the part of 'blackleg' in his or her trade, is almost unthinkable. Let there be no mistake, we must have the trade unions perfectly organized and adequately financed, and I have no atom of sympathy with those who profess regard for political action on advanced lines who shirk their duties and responsibilities as trade unionists.

The Social Democratic Federation was conducting a vigorous agitation all this time, and was preparing to run candidates at the next parliamentary election. I thoroughly believed in the desirability of harmony between the two propagandist bodies, and lost no opportunity of endeavouring to secure joint action. Thus, in the pamphlet just referred to, I wrote:

> What then is the ideal aimed at by the Independent Labour Party? It is the establishment of a state of society where living upon un-

earned income shall be impossible for any but the physically enfeebled; where the total work of the country shall be scientifically regulated and properly apportioned over the total number of able-bodied citizens; where class domination shall be rendered impossible by the full recognition of social, economic, and sex equality.

It may be well to give here the object of the Social Democratic Federation as stated by that body, reminding readers that the object of the two organizations is identical. It is the socialization of the means of production, distribution, and exchange, to be controlled by a democratic State in the interests of the community, and the complete emancipation of Labour from the domination of capitalism and landlordism, with the establishment of social and economic equality between the sexes.

The above fits perfectly with the following comprehensive and important sentence from Karl Marx: 'The economical subjection of the man of labour to the monopoliser of the means of labour (that is, the sources of life), lies at the bottom of servitude in all its forms, of all misery, mental degradation, and political dependence.'

The economical emancipation of the working class is therefore the great end to which every political movement ought to be subservient as a means.

There were hopes at one time of uniting the various Socialist bodies into one organization; but although there was no vital difference of principle, there was a considerable difference in temperament, and the uniting of forces did not come off.

In May 1896, owing to the retirement of Dr Hunter from the constituency of North Aberdeen, and the local organization being desirous that I should stand as the ILP candidate, it came about that I again stood for Parliament. The Liberal candidate was Captain Pirie, of the well-known firm of paper-makers, whose works are situated in the district. The contest was short, sharp, and vigorous. I did not win, but we materially reduced the Liberal majority, which for four successive elections had been over three thousand. The previous election gave the Liberal a majority of 3,548, which was reduced on this occasion to 430. Up to that time it was the nearest approach to a win of any ILP candidate.

I desire here to record my sincere admiration and deep respect for one who helped very materially at that election, the late Miss Carrie Martyn. She had been actively connected with the ILP for some years, coming from Lincolnshire, where, in consequence of having espoused Socialism, she was made to feel that her absence would be more appreciated than her presence if she continued identified with such views. Miss Martyn soon qualified as an efficient platform speaker, and threw herself into the movement with whole-souled abandon.

Many of the election meetings were held in the open air, not a few of them in stonemasons' yards, the speakers often standing on blocks of granite intended for tombstones. Miss Martyn addressed many meetings under such conditions, and was always most effective. Indeed, I really believe that had she been the candidate, she would have won the election. She was suffering from a cold during the contest, and ought to have had a considerable rest afterwards, until she could have thrown it off, but duty called. The Dundee jute operatives invited her to take up work on their behalf – work which involved a good deal of public speaking. Having accepted this invitation she became worse, and died, literally in consequence of not being able to take the necessary rest.

She lies in the cemetery at Dundee. The tombstone bears the inscription:

CAROLINE E. D. MARTYN,

Born, Lincoln, 3rd May, 1867.

Died, Dundee, 23rd July, 1896.

During 1896 I did much propaganda work in London, the provinces, and on the Continent. One series of meetings was held in what was then known as the Holborn Town Hall, now the Holborn Hall, Grays Inn Road. The advertising was properly attended to, and the organizing of the meetings was well done. We had the organ and soloists and a choir. There was an adequate staff of stewards who understood their duties well, and carried them out attentively. Every Sunday evening at 7.30 o'clock precisely we took the platform, the organist already having played a voluntary. The meeting lasted fully two hours, and was well balanced throughout with singing and speaking. It was universally admitted that this series was a complete success. Here are a few of the press notices indicating the character of the meetings:

Mr Tom Mann had a wonderful audience on Sunday night, when he commenced the first of his series of six lectures on 'Socialism and the Labour Question'. The hall was crammed in every part, and hundreds were standing down the aisles.

The New Age

Tom Mann has evidently made a mistake. It was the Albert Hall, or, at any rate the Queen's Hall, he should have taken to accommodate his audiences in. I have never seen the Holborn Town Hall so packed as it was last Sunday evening since Henry George's last visit to England, and people who want to get in next Sunday had better go early. Hundreds couldn't get in last week, and the lecturer had to pause before he was half-way through, to bid the standing crowd at the back come up to the front and not block the doors. The choir surrounded and backed lecturer and chairman like a bevy of angels, and sang like nightingales.

Weekly Times and Echo

Every succeeding meeting at the Holborn Town Hall beats the record of the preceding one. At Tom Mann's third lecture on Sunday last, the greater hall was packed tighter than ever.

Labour Leader

The International Socialist Congress was held in the Queen's Hall, London, commencing on 27 July, 1896. I was on the Organizing Committee, and had much to do in the fixing of the necessary halls to accommodate the respective national groups when they desired to meet separate from the main congress, also in arranging accommodation and many other things essential to the success of so large a gathering. Many of those who were delegated to the congress were already famous, or have since become famous, in international affairs. In 1889, while the London dock strike was in progress, two International Socialist Congresses were held simultaneously in Paris. There were two in consequence of the disagreements between French sections of the delegates. The next International Socialist Congress was held in Brussels in 1891, when it was decided to hold them every three years. At the Zurich Congress it had been laid down that in future:

All trade unions shall be admitted to the congress, also all those

Socialist parties and organizations which recognize the necessity for the organization of the workers and for political action.

By political action is meant that the working-class organizations seek, as far as is possible, to use or conquer political rights and the machinery of legislation for the furthering of the interests of the proletariat and the conquest of political power.

The interpretation of this caused a very heated debate. There were present many anti-parliamentarians, one-half of the French delegates taking up this position; but there were also prominent anarchists, including Peter Kropotkin, Domela Nieuwenhuis and others, and German and British Social Democrats. Many of the ILP delegates were for refusing all such the right to take part in the congress. Keir Hardie and I made a determined stand upon this, insisting that all present should have the same right to participate in discussion. Much excitement prevailed. Singer, a German delegate, and H. M. Hyndman, were successively in the chair during this discussion. In the end no one was excluded from the congress, but steps were taken to make the conditions of admission in future somewhat more precise.

I refer to this incident chiefly because of the action of some of the ILP delegates, who were all intimate friends of mine. They actually got up a round-robin of emphatic protest against myself – I forget whether they included Hardie in this – for defending the right of the anti-parliamentarian delegates to have a voice in the congress. Nothing came of it, except that it caused me to observe even more closely the psychology of the two schools.

Among many Socialists there was very little appreciation of and no admiration for trade unionism. In Germany, the Social Democratic movement was powerful before trade unionism had made much headway, and many Socialists were lukewarm about the advantages of trade unionism. So at this congress of 1896 in London, a special commission was appointed by the congress to sit apart, and discuss and decide upon what the attitude of the International Socialist movement should be towards industrial organization. The commission consisted of two delegates from each nation: H. M. Hyndman and I were the two for Britain; Legien and Molkenbuhr represented Germany.

We sat the greater part of two days debating the subject, and

Secretaryship of the Independent Labour Party

succeeded in drafting a report for the congress. Its purport was that not only was it desirable that Socialists should be identified with the trade-union movement, but that an instruction should go out from the congress that it was the duty of all Socialists to resort to systematic industrial organization and use the same for the advancement of the economic emancipation of the workers.

One of the delegates to the congress was Rosa Luxemburg, then as ever until her untimely death at the hands of the reactionaries in Berlin, alert and keen, following all important phases of international development, and tactfully exercising great influence in the congress, apart from any speeches she delivered. Millerand was there as a French delegate; also Jaurès; altogether one hundred and one from France, fifty of whom favoured political action, and fifty-one did not, or it may have been the other way about, but there was a majority of one only whichever side had it.

CHAPTER IX

INTERNATIONAL LABOUR ORGANIZATION
1896 to 1898

I HAD maintained my relationship with the various sections of transport workers all this while, and the necessity for a more definite organization on international lines was fully appreciated, so in June, 1896, there was established the International Federation of Ship, Dock, and River Workers. I became the president of this organization. The objects aimed at by the federation were 'the complete organization of all the men engaged in the occupations named in order to raise wages, reduce working hours, get gangs properly constituted, check overtime, insist upon adequate inspection of gear, and secure for sailors and firemen proper rations, ample accommodation, and a satisfactory manning scale. Further, the federation, recognizing the considerable differences in wages paid in different ports for the same work at home and abroad, seeks to establish, as far as may be possible, a uniform rate of pay for the same class of work in all ports, and to establish a recognized working day and other regulations in the ports of the world.'

The shipowners and other firms connected with port work had repeatedly complained that the men in British ports were enforcing claims altogether in excess of what was paid for similar work in continental ports. There was some truth in this, and the dockers and seamen had endeavoured by means of extending organization to level matters; and anyhow we believed fervently in international organization. From past experience we knew that the continental shipowners and others were not likely to give our efforts a kindly welcome; but whatever the risks might be, we knew that visits to foreign ports would be essential. What could be done by letter was done with not much result other than to get from our foreign workmates the message: 'We are anxious to organize; can you help us?'

We were chiefly concerned to deal with Hamburg, Antwerp, and Rotterdam, and we laid our plans to deal with these.

Havelock Wilson and I were sent by our federation, first to Rotterdam, and thence to Antwerp. We accomplished the mission successfully, held meetings in both ports, got groups organized, and in touch with the British unions. It was not long, however, before the Belgian authorities endeavoured to stop our activities. In many cases our delegates were arrested on landing at Antwerp, and if not then, as soon as they became active in the work of organization. In this manner Ben Tillett was arrested and imprisoned under very uncomfortable conditions. The matter was taken up by the Foreign Office and negotiations resulted in his release. Others were arrested in turn, but not all, and in the long run a considerable stimulus was given to organization, with consequent improvement in conditions.

We were genuinely anxious to avoid stoppages of work, and to bring about agreements by negotiation; had the employers been agreeable, this would have taken place.

I was requested by the Hamburg workers to visit that port, as they were anxious to line up as part of the federation. Knowing that no meetings could be held by Germans, and still less foreigners, without police permission, I obtained the regulation form, filled it up, and sent it to the authorities at Hamburg, stating I wished to hold meetings on trade unionism, and giving all details. I received a duly signed authorization to hold such meetings; this was in November 1896. I set out from London and reached Hamburg all right, but early the same day I was arrested. On being brought before the officials I produced the authorization, the validity of which was admitted, but since it had been issued other developments had taken place. The authorization was withdrawn, and an order of expulsion was issued instead. I claimed my right to confer with the British Consul, and was taken to the Consulate. After consultation, the Vice-Consul accompanied me to the Stadthaus to talk over the matter. As the Vice-Consul was stating in some detail who I was, etc., the official, Herr Ravolovski, who was seated at his desk, said:

'Yes, yes; we know, we know.'

Opening a drawer in his desk, he pulled out a number of

newspaper cuttings, giving details of meetings I had addressed. It was plain to me that the German officials knew considerably more about my doings than did the British. I had to depart by the first boat available. This was a small craft of a thousand tons or less, that regularly traded to the Thames. Under favourable conditions she could only travel at nine knots an hour, but under the unfavourable winds that we encountered she could not make more than six knots. However, I reached London safely, and the Germans held the meetings that I should have been present at. The expulsion served our purpose quite as well as if I had been allowed to address the meetings, probably better. The port workers of Hamburg enrolled rapidly, and in December the corn porters attempted negotiations to obtain increased wages. Negotiations failed, so they struck work and soon succeeded. Other sections followed, and the shipowners decided to resist. In a few days the port of Hamburg was practically at a standstill, and again they sent to us in London for someone from the federation to proceed there. Notwithstanding my recent expulsion, I went there again, in my presidential capacity, being authorized by the executive to act on its behalf. I escaped troublesome attention from the police, and reached my destination. It was my duty to get in touch with the Labour forces, particularly the Trades' Council of Altona, to ascertain what were the chances of success, and to decide in what way help could be rendered by the federation.

I watched developments for three days. The last of these was very exciting. I had been with others visiting each vessel that was working; when the crew could understand English I addressed the men, urging them to desist and to make common cause. We were half a dozen in a steam launch, and the weather was bitterly cold. Having done my utmost, I made my way with Herr von Elm, Socialist member of the Reichstag for Schleswig-Holstein, to his home for a meal. Afterwards I went out for a stroll. An officer of police approached me: result – I was taken to the Stadthaus, charged, and put into a cell until the chief official should arrive. I had returned to Hamburg contrary to the terms of the expulsion order of six weeks earlier. Net result – I was again expelled on the only boat going to England, sailing for Hull. So to Hull I was sent; but again it served our purpose. These interferences with our work aroused increasing interest on the part of some other sections, and made for improved international organization. When I reached London I was surprised to find that the *Daily Graphic* artist had been allowed to sketch Cell No 28 in the Stadthaus, the cell I had occupied. An excellent picture of it was published on 23 December, 1896.

Our efforts at international organization were attended with considerable success, and quite a number of our active men had to serve brief spells in prison; but nothing worse happened.

The year 1897 found us very busy, and this work in the industrial field took up the greater part of my time. I wrote a pamphlet called 'The Dockers and Sailors in 1897'. In this I dealt with the number of workers seeking employment in the various ports, not of Britain only but of Europe, and the fluctuating character of the work; the great trouble was the irregularity of employment.

In the early part of 1897 we had an International Transport Workers' Conference in London, attended by delegates from France, Germany, Holland, Belgium, Spain, and Britain. It gave a healthy stimulus to international organization. Here is a list of the officers and the members of the council of the new body:

President:
Tom Mann (London).

Vice-Presidents:

J. H. Wilson, MP (London);   J. Ratheir (Havre).

Central Council:

H. W. Kay	Dock, Wharf, Riverside, and General Labourers' Union
James Sexton	National Union of Dock Labourers
Edward Catheray	National Sailors' and Firemen's Union
Harry Brill	National Amalgamated Coal Porters' Union
J. N. Bell	National Amalgamated Union of Labour
Arthur Harris	Labour Protection League
D. Donovan	Thames Steamship Workers
C. Fisher	Amalgamated Association of Coal Porters (Winchmen)
L. C. Janssens	Port Workers of Antwerp
John de Vries	Port Workers of Rotterdam
L. Neble	Port Workers of Marseilles

Head Office:
181, Queen Victoria Street, London, EC

Later in the year 1897, our French friends were anxious to have organization effort carried on in their ports. A delegate from London, now filling a prominent position on a London newspaper, was sent to confer with the French and to co-operate in the arrangements. I was to go to continue the campaign subsequently. The pioneer delegate referred to was invited to address the trade-union delegates at the Bourse du Travail, and did so. Apparently he spoke effectively, for he was deported in consequence.

It now devolved upon me to carry on the work. I reached Paris all right, and spent the better part of a week addressing what were technically termed private meetings organized by the Allemanists, i.e. by the Socialists grouped round Jean Allemane, an old Communard. This organization insisted that all who joined the party must be members of a trade union. The French for 'trade union' is 'syndicat', and those who were distinctively trade unionist by policy were named Syndicalists, although the term had not yet become famous.

After this series of private meetings, it was announced that I was to address a public meeting. The comrades knew it was the intention of the authorities to prevent my doing so. I was, therefore, advised to write out my speech. It was translated into French, and a copy of it given to the then secretary of the French Railway Workers' Union. He was to take my place if I was prevented from speaking. I was also advised, if arrested, to agree not to attempt to hold any meeting, or I should probably be forcibly detained and expelled. If I followed their advice they would see that I should address a meeting all right.

On the morning of the day that the public meeting was to be held in the evening, as I was leaving the hotel, a well-dressed man approached me, politely raising his hat. He informed me that he was connected with the police, and said I must accompany him to the Chief Commissioner. We drove there: I was put through the usual inordinately long list of questions, as to place of birth, parentage, etc., etc., exactly as if it had been in Berlin. Then an order of expulsion was read to me in English. I was told to sign it. If I were willing to give an assurance that I not only would not speak at the meeting, but would not attend it, I should be granted twenty-four hours longer in Paris; then I must leave. If I refused, I was to be deported forthwith. In any case, I should be kept under police supervision to ensure my not going to the meeting. Having given the required assurance, I was allowed to rejoin my friends, who were awaiting me. I told them that I was under police supervision, and they at once pointed out two individuals in plain clothes, some forty or fifty yards distant. These dogged our steps. I was not in the least perturbed by what was happening, for I was confident that the comrades would turn it all to good account.

At length we reached the house of Jean Allemane, and had a meal. By this time it was six in the evening, and the meeting was fixed for seven o'clock. All, save one, prepared to go to the meeting, but I was to remain in the house till they called for me. It was nearly eight o'clock when Allemane and others came in hurriedly and bustled me into a cab, telling me the meeting was going on splendidly, that G— the railwayman, had delivered every word of my speech, that the meeting would soon be over, and we were now going to take coffee. In a short time the cab pulled up at a large café, with every table occupied, except some that were reserved at one side of the huge room. To these my friends led me. Much cheering took place. I was told we were now under a private roof, that I could say what I liked, and need not worry about the time. I then addressed this considerable gathering, and a most successful meeting was held. I noticed near to me a striking-looking lady, who had apparently been reporting my speech. I was told that the lady was known and trusted, and I was introduced to her. It was Madame Sorgue, and her report appeared in the 'Matin' next morning. I was wondering if the police authorities would not take this as a violation of the arrangement, but there were many influential friends, especially municipal councillors, watching events, and they kept with me until at four in the afternoon the train steamed out of the station and I in it.

I have said that members of the Paris Municipal Council were co-operating in this propagandist effort. At the meeting of the council, following upon my expulsion from France, a Socialist councillor raised the question, charging the Prefect of Police with having exceeded his duty. He quoted the whole of the address I had prepared, the one which had been read at the public meeting by G— of the Railwaymen's Union. The councillor's object was to get the greatest possible amount of propaganda out of it. A full report of the council's proceedings was posted upon the door of every Mairie throughout Paris, and, therefore, my speech was made available for passers-by to read. The interpolation was so successful that the Paris Municipal Council carried a vote of censure upon Monsieur Lepin, the Chief of Police, for having expelled me. It was thought well to carry the matter still further, so the question was raised in the Chamber of Deputies; but here the vote went in the opposite direction.

Following upon this effort it became necessary to give attention to Scandinavia, and arrangements were made for me to visit Sweden, Norway, and Denmark. Mr Charles Lindley, at one time connected with English shipping (now a member of the Upper House in Stockholm), kindly undertook to interpret for me in the Swedish cities and ports. The inaugural meeting was at Gothenburg. I endeavoured to arrange with Mr Lindley that I should speak for ten minutes, and then he should interpret; and so on throughout the meeting. But he was entirely opposed to this; he said that I must not speak for more than two minutes at the outside, so that he could give an exact interpretation, or the critics would censure him strongly; I had to conform to this. It was a crowded gathering. In spite of all the difficulties, it was entirely successful, and was most enthusiastic. Next morning, Charles Lindley brought me the newspapers, smiling brightly as he read out the descriptive accounts. One of the comments was upon the interpreter, saying: 'He interpreted well, and performed an arduous task with much credit, but of course, it was not a literal interpretation; anyone to follow Mr Mann and give a literal interpretation would require a head as long as a horse.' Lindley considered this was a full justification of his insistence upon very short spells. The same plan was, therefore, adhered to at Helsingborg and elsewhere.

When we reached Malmo, two meetings were arranged at the Folkets Hus (People's House). On the first night, Charles Lindley interpreted, and all went well. Next day, we were talking over affairs with the editor of the local Socialist paper, 'Arbetet' (Work) Mr Axel Danielson, a man standing about six feet three and weighing seventeen stones. Mrs Danielson, the editor's wife, and a few other friends were also present. The question was raised whether it might not be an advantage to have a change of interpreter. I readily agreed, if they had someone competent. It transpired that Mrs Danielson could speak English well, for although she had never been in England, she had lived some ten years in America. Mrs Danielson consented to interpret, provided her husband would promise not to attend the meeting, as she was sure his critical presence would make her nervous. Ultimately the kindly husband agreed to this, and the fair interpreter was willing I should speak for seven or eight minute spells uninterruptedly. All went well for about three-quarters of an hour, when suddenly she failed to rise to interpret, and looked very confused. I soon caught sight of her towering husband who had entered the hall, and was standing up some twenty yards from the platform. Those in the know enjoyed the temporary confusion, including the big husband, who, having given himself satisfaction, smilingly withdrew, and we continued successfully to the end.

Having crossed the Sound from Malmo I was met at Copenhagen in grand style, the Social Democratic members of Parliament having gathered to receive me, although my object was the furtherance of industrial organization. I learned that one of the members of Parliament, Comrade Knudson, was to act as interpreter, and that the meeting was to be in the Folkets Hus, a very fine hall. I asked Mr Knudson if he had any special suggestions as to how long I should speak before he interpreted.

'Ah,' exclaimed he, 'I must beg of you to allow me to give a literal interpretation of your speech, and, therefore, that I shall follow you after every two or three sentences.'

'I don't like this plan,' said I.

'Well, you see, there are many critics. Although I am a member of Parliament, I am also a professor of languages. I teach in the public schools, and my reputation would suffer if I were not to interpret you correctly.'

I therefore fell in with the arrangement. At the meeting, after about forty minutes' easy going, as he rose to follow me he looked at me in a very troubled fashion. The veins on his forehead were swollen, and he said pathetically:

'Shall we not soon conclude? I am very tired.'

I had not got half through my speech, so I simply ignored him and went full-steam ahead for about half an hour. I expect he felt very humiliated for a time, but he evidently decided to make the best of it, for when I sat down, up he jumped and delivered a very eloquent speech, as it appeared to me. The audience obviously took the same view judging by the hearty cheers at the finish.

The most amusing experience I had with an interpreter on this run was at Christiania. The friends responsible for the meeting introduced me to their chosen interpreter. He seemed to be quite at ease, and judging by his conversation fluent enough in English. The meeting commenced – a packed hall – and after about four or five minutes, up jumped a scholarly-looking man who made a few remarks which were heartily endorsed by the audience. From that time, the scholarly-looking man did the interpreting, the original man no longer appearing. I did not know what was wrong until at the close of the meeting I asked:

'Why the change?'

'Ah,' came the answer, 'the first man could talk English all right, but he had forgotten Norwegian!'

After these events, renewed attention to France was requisite. The council of the federation had been informed that one of the chief stumbling blocks to further advance in the French ports was the bad state of organization in Bordeaux. Notwithstanding my expulsion from France a few months before, it was thought advisable I should visit some of the French ports, giving Paris a wide berth. Fortunately, I had a good friend at work in connection with the docks at Havre. He could speak English well, and was in full sympathy with our attempt at international organization. I arranged for him to meet me and help me in my mission. I was wearing a blue serge suit, and all I needed to give me the stamp of a sea-faring man was an official-looking cap. This I obtained, and I went in and out and round about the docks taking note of the methods of work and gathering necessary items of information. After a few days at Havre I went to Nantes, thence to St Nazaire, and on to Bordeaux. I found the official of the Bourse du Travail. Having been forewarned of my coming, he kindly placed himself at my disposal. Since the executive of the bureau was to meet that evening, he suggested that I should put my case before the members. He, himself, would interpret. I learned from the executive that numerous attempts had been made to organize the dockers. Sufficient progress had been achieved to bring pressure to bear on the employers, and more than once substantial improvements in wages had been secured. Invariably, however, this had been followed by an influx of Spanish workers, chiefly from Bilbao, who swamped the port with men willing to work for less than the union rate. This had always frustrated their efforts. Before they could hope to be permanently successful, it would be necessary to stop the influx of cheap labour, and they urged me to meet the whole of the Bureau delegates the following evening, and have the matter more exhaustively dealt with. I agreed.

Only one man knew me. To the rest I was 'J. Miller,' as a matter of tactics; but they all knew the name of 'Tom Mann' and asked when he was likely to be coming over! This of course was suitably replied to.

Next day a municipal councillor requested me to accompany him to the Hotel de Ville, on a visit to the Mayor, who could speak a little English and who would be delighted to meet me. I did so, and had quite a nice conversation with His Worship, who was gracious enough to arrange for my being escorted over the Musée. I duly signed the visitors' book as 'J. Miller, mécanicien de Londres'. The meeting with the delegates was quite a success, and very interesting. It would have been more so if I could have made known who I was, but the expulsion order of an earlier date contained a clause 'not to visit French territory without police permission, under a penalty of six months' imprisonment without trial.'

I decided to proceed to Bilbao, and see if organized action could be encouraged there in the interests of the Spanish workers, no less than that of Bordeaux and of the International Federation. On quitting Bordeaux I left a card for each member of the executive explaining why I had been unable to appear in my own name. I also wrote to the Mayor apologizing for my little deception and thanking him for his courtesy. Ere this could have reached him by post, I was at the frontier town of Irun, and beyond French jurisdiction.

This kind of running around was necessary in the early days to lay the basis of the International Federation; nor will it be wondered at by those who realize how exceedingly slow we have been to take action between one country and another, or north with south, or east with west. One visit is worth many letters, and a meeting, with tactful attention to a few individuals, oftentimes lays the basis for a good understanding.

I did not know more than half a dozen words of Spanish on reaching Bilbao, and had no idea where to address myself. On arrival I saw posters announcing a protest meeting on the following Sunday morning at the Circus, and one of the advertized speakers was Pablo Iglesias, whom I had met at the International Congress. I attended the meeting and easily got in touch with comrades who were able to inform me as to the general situation. I was invited to attend, with Pablo Iglesias and others, a strike meeting of miners, some dozen miles out by train, that same afternoon. I went, and spoke at the meeting. I forget who interpreted, perhaps no one, but that would not be a very serious matter!

I learned that three Socialist members of the Bilbao Municipal Council, on the previous Sunday at a miners' demonstration, had vehemently condemned the authorities for having ordered the military to fire on the crowd, when several had been killed. These three councillors had been arrested and imprisoned. I was invited next day to accompany one of the prominent local Labour men to visit the councillors in the prison, and I agreed to do so. The friend who had me in charge knew little more of English than I knew Spanish, so attempts at conversation were but moderately successful. However, we reached the prison, and several persons were waiting at the entrance, where a comfortable-looking man was leaning back smoking cigarettes, in an armchair in the centre of the porch, giving an occasional nod to new arrivals as he had done to my friend and myself. By and by he lit another cigarette and handed his case to my companion and myself. We each took one. I thought him most genial, but could not understand the chair, and the ease of the burly gentleman. Later, I learned that he was the governor of the prison, and we were only kept waiting because those we wished to see already had a group of friends attending them. My companion explained something to the governor, and he beckoned an official who took us over the more interesting portions of the prison winding up by taking us to the large room (not a cell) occupied by the three Socialist councillors. They were not in prison uniform, but wore their own clothes. Their only punishment was confinement to prison quarters during the period of the strike.

I have been in close contact with prison officials, including governors, on my own account since then; but the only prison governor who ever offered me a smoke was the burly gentleman of Bilbao.

CHAPTER X

ORGANIZATION OF GENERAL WORKERS
1898 to 1901

During all this time I was amongst those, who, recognizing the necessity for enormously extended industrial organization, yet could see little hope that the organizations of skilled workers generally would recognize the necessity for this, and so broaden the basis of their organizations as to cover all sections of skilled and unskilled.

The unions that catered for labourers were very few, and in practice were mainly confined to certain sections. The idea that it is necessary to organize by industry, that is, with the whole of the trades and occupations in an entire industry as the unit, was only just emerging. Scarcely anyone gave serious attention to the matter, as it was felt there was no prospect of success in that direction.

The need for organization by industry was in my mind the most outstanding fact; but the existing skilled workers' organizations not only gave no encouragement, but were obstacles in the path. In the engineering industry, a workman who was on a job for which the recognized union rate was neither paid nor expected was looked upon by the members of the union as an outsider. They made the machine, they would not work the machine, neither would they broaden the basis of their union so that the man who had to work it could be organized in relationship with them. It was the same in every trade, and not more than one-fourth of the adult male population was organized. The proper course, had common-sense prevailed, would have been for the existing unions so to broaden the basis of their organizations as to welcome every worker that came into the industry, and with the variations of occupation to have rules comprehensive and elastic enough for the admission of all. Instead of this, not only was there no provision for an ever-growing number of handy men, which the changing methods made necessary; but between existing unions, each catering for highly-skilled men, there existed an absurd hostility. For myself, I refused to be dominated by such an environment and, resolved to face whatever of approval or disapproval it might bring, I determined to attempt at any rate to draft the rules and to prepare the framework of a union that should be open to any section of workers of either sex for whom no proper union already existed.

The name was important. The idea was to have a short name yet genuinely comprehensive. 'The Workers' Union' was decided upon, and it proved to be exactly the right name. It barred none; it welcomed all. It was wide, yet definite; and it has served exceedingly well. Amongst those who assisted in drafting the rules for the new union was Tom Chambers. We aimed at launching the new organization on May Day, 1898. The rules were out and enrolment begun a month earlier than this, but the actual kick-off was as arranged. Advance was by no means rapid. A few branches were opened in London, and I went to a number of provincial towns wherever there was a chance of starting a branch. It was interesting to observe that some of my warmest friends showed a noticeable coolness in connection with my advocacy of the new union, as though it were an interloper. However, I approached Brother Charles Duncan, then of Middlesboro', whom I had known for some years as a member of the A S E, and one who shared my views in the matter of extended organization. I requested him to come to London and accept responsibility in connection with the new organization, as I wanted to be a freelance and move about anywhere, whilst Brother Tom Chambers, who had at its inception acted as secretary of the new union, was fully occupied with the secretarial work of the International Ship, Dock, and River Workers' Federation. Charles Duncan immediately responded, came to London, and became engrossed in the work of the new union. He had to fight through many vicissitudes, often unable to pay his way, and for a time taking no wage. But the day came when the need for organization was more appreciated, and the steady work put into the union gave confidence of ability to organize, to fight, to negotiate, and to administrate. Many great struggles have been conducted by the Workers' Union, many districts have been entirely changed in outlook, in intelligence, and in relative well-being, as the direct outcome of the organizing ability displayed. A change in the relationships between workers and employers has resulted. The report for 1921 shows that the union is over half a million strong.

The Workers' Union and the General Workers' Union, originally the Gas Workers' and General Labourers' Union, have added enormously to their membership, and have done highly creditable work over the entire country. But their success has made it less easy to organize scientifically on the basis of industry, even if the members of the skilled organizations were ready for this, which they certainly are not. The principle that finds most general acceptance is 'organization as a class'. This is necessary, but still it leaves us with the difficulty of sectional action, and no special arrangements to secure common action on the part of all engaged in one or several industries. Thus, if the AEU were responsible for negotiating for all connected with engineering, using the term in its broadest sense, as the result of all sections of workers being under one set of rules, and one administration, no one can doubt that this would mean greater power, more effective solidarity, than anything which obtains under present conditions. Where sometimes overtures are made between the unions to secure common action, this ensues; but always there is the risk of conflicting policies being pursued, of personalities getting at cross purposes, with consequent weakness. In the trade-union movement, as in many other phases of existence, there is more of muddling through than of scientific guidance. So it is with nations. Many things could be far better managed if Europe as a whole were responsible under one administrative department; but pettifogging nationalism asserts itself, and what might be better done on a large scale, is indifferently done on a sectional scale. But are not these the ways of humans, and, therefore, to be expected, though not encouraged?

About this time a group of comrades joined together to organize a series of meetings on successive Sunday evenings at the Lambeth Baths. These were run on lines similar to those at the Holborn Hall some two years previously. We had a good choir and a good orchestra (conducted by H. W. Lee, secretary of the SDF), also good soloists, and a good choice of chairmen. We ran a series of twelve meetings. I was the lecturer on each occasion, following a well-arranged syllabus that covered the whole field of social economics. The singing by the audience, aided by the choir and orchestra, was inspiring. Altogether, the series proved to be the most successful I had undertaken.

At this period I became the tenant of *The Enterprise*, in Long Acre, and so had control of a good-sized room for lectures, and for trade-union, Socialist, and other meetings. This room soon became a rendezvous for those who were in difficulties for a gathering place.

The Young Ireland Society met there, as did also for a time the Central Branch of the S D F, also the Friends of Russian Freedom, and the Cosmopolitans. Amongst those who regularly attended the Russian meetings were Kropotkin, Tchaikovsky, Felix Volkovski, Goldenburg, and when in London, Louise Michel. The Cosmopolitans, true to their name, had a great variety of speakers, and conducted highly successful meetings. John Morrison Davidson lectured there on his favourite topic of 'Winstanley the Digger'. The Diggers were the Communists of the Oliver Cromwell period. Gerard Winstanley was the chief spokesman on their behalf, sharing the views of John Lilburne, the Leveller. They declared that no advantage came to the common people as the result of the Cromwellian revolution; it was simply a change of persons as to who should exercise kingly power; a change from the king to a group which called itself the State. The change in no wise bettered the condition of the people, or secured them liberty. They, therefore, claimed the right to use such land as they needed, to cultivate the same for their maintenance. In April 1649, General Fairfax sent two troops of horse to have account of certain Levellers at St Margaret's Hill, near Cobham, and St George's Hill, inasmuch as they digged the ground and sowed it with roots and beans; and on 20th April Everard and Winstanley, the chief of those that digged at St George's Hill, in Surrey, came to the General and made a large Declaration to justify their proceeding, stating:

> That all the liberties of the people were lost by the coming of William the Conqueror, and that ever since the people of God had lived under tyranny and oppression worse than that under the Egyptians....
>
> That they intend not to meddle with any man's property nor to break down any enclosures, only to meddle with what was common

and untilled to make it fruitful for the use of man, and that the time will be that all men shall willingly come in and give up their lands and estates and submit to the community....

Shall men of other nations say that notwithstanding all those rare wits in the Parliament and Army of England, yet they could not reform the clergy, lawyer and law, and must needs establish all as the kings left them?

Will not this blast our honour, and make all monarchical members laugh in their sleeves to see the government of our Commonwealth still built upon the kingly laws and principles? I have asked divers soldiers what they fought for; they answered they could not tell, and it is very true indeed they cannot tell, if the monarchical law is established without reformation.

Morrison Davidson specially drove home the point in 'The Three Great Modern Revolutions, the English, the American, and the French'. The rank and file never knew what they fought for. We can add that there has been another revolution since, where the people did know what they fought for. Winstanley put it to Fairfax:

And is not this a slavery, say the people, that though there be land enough in England to maintain ten times as many people as are in it, yet some must beg of their brethren, or work in hard drudgery for day wages for them, or starve, or steal, and so be hanged out of the way, as men not fit to live on the earth? Before they are suffered to plant the waste land for a livelihood, they must pay rent to their brethren for it. Well, this is a burden the Creation groans under; and the subjects (so-called) have not their birthright freedom granted them from their brethren, who hold it from them by club law, but not by righteousness.

But, adds Davidson:

Needless to say, all this invincible logic was wasted on Fairfax, Cromwell, and the piously rapacious gang of Ironside Colonels, whose sole aim it was to put down King and Cavalier, that they themselves might live by kingly principles. 'What,' asked Oliver, with true squirearchical imperviousness, 'is the purport of the levelling principle but to make the tenant as liberal a fortune as the landlord? *I was by birth a gentleman.* You must cut these people in pieces, or they will cut you in pieces'; and the old Puritan savage was as good as his word.

Morrison Davidson himself was a great character: he was terribly proud of being a Scotsman, and believed, or pretended to believe, that a very big share of all that was passable in the British Isles originated in Scotland. He was a whole-hearted advocate of 'Home Rule All Round', but he specially wanted it for Scotland. In this regard he was very emphatic as to the Irish being West Britons, and he put the case thus:

> It is sometimes objected to the term 'Britain' that it does not include Ireland, but that is not so. The geographer Ptolemy, in the early part of the second century, speaks of Hibernia as 'Britannia Parva' (Little Britain), and Albion as 'Britannia Magna' (Big Britain). Pliny was still more comprehensive: 'The island of Britain, so famous in the writings both of the Greeks and the Romans, is particularly called Albion, whereas all the isles which are about it are called the Britains.'

In his book *Scotland for the Scots*, Davidson writes further on the same topic, saying:

> 'Anyhow the name of "Briton" is historically far more ancient, comprehensive, and respectable, than that of "Saxon", "Anglo-Saxon", or even "Englishman". We were all Britons before we were either Englishmen, Scotsmen, or Irishmen. In point of fact, when we magniloquently talk of the Anglo-Saxon Race – and our American brethren also indulge in this cant phraseology to a most reprehensible extent – we are speaking of a race that does not exist, and never did exist. Both the Americans and we are Anglo-British, the Romanist British element having never ceased to predominate ethnically, even during the Heptarchy.'

I believe dear old Davidson was quite right in all this, but what is really puzzling is how these Scotsmen can be so brimful of conceit over a Scotsman's tongue twisting itself about with broken English, with a spice of Gaelic, a pinch o' Doric, another o' Danish, until we get a veritable porridge of a language; and yet, here is the debonair Cunninghame Graham who openly laughs at the puerilities of snobocracy, and in his time has even written articles on the English workman's home, and the wife's china dogs on the mantelpiece corners, slyly digging at the worship of such household gods; yet see how he bows down to the gabbled utterances of a braw Scotty!

In this book of Morrison Davidson's, the preface is written by Cunninghame Graham, and a third of his space is devoted to telling the following story of something which happened to him in South America:

And as I sat and smoked, upon a thin old chestnut horse with a torn English saddle over which a sheepskin had been laid, a man of about fifty years of age appeared. Dressed in a suit of Scottish homespun, such as our farmers wore, but twenty years ago, before the looms of Bradford and of Leeds had clothed them all in shoddy, with a grey flannel shirt without a collar, and the whole man surmounted by a battered, flat straw hat, which might have made an indifferent strawberry pottle, I at once descried a brother Scot. Dismounting, and hobbling his horse, he drew a short clay pipe out of his pocket, capped with the tin cover that workmen in the north used to affect, in the pre-briar-root days, and greeting me in a strange Doric-Spanish, he sat him down to smoke.

Some time he talked, till in compassion I said, 'Friend, you appear to make but middling weather of it in the Spanish tongue.' No sign he gave of the least astonishment, but between two draws, and as he rammed the dottle hard into his pipe, he said, 'I see ye speak the English pretty well.' I though at the time just at the age when a man speaks, rides, and shoots better than any other man in all the world, suppressed a smile, and said, 'Yes, how do you like the view?'

'A bonny view, Sir, aye, ou aye; I'd no say onything against the view: but man, may be ye ken a hill – they ca' it Dumyel – just abune Brig o' Allan?' I did so, having climbed it as a boy, and watched the Forth wind out, a silver ribbon, towards Aberfoyle. 'Weel, weel, if ye ken it, ye'll ken that there's a far brawer view frae the Dumyel than frae the wee boranty that we're sittin' on the noo.'

When he had got upon his horse, and shambled down the hill, I fancied that I could smell the heather and sweet gale, hear the whawps calling on the moor, and in the towns see drunken folk a-stotterin' from the public-house.

It was customary to have debates as well as lectures at the Cosmopolitans' meetings. Just at the period when public opinion was highly strung on Italian affairs, Enrico Malatesta opened a debate on Anarchism which aroused so keen an interest that three evenings had to be devoted to it.

Organization of General Workers

About this time, W. M. Thompson, then editor of *Reynold's Newspaper*, and his friends, were particularly keen upon the wiping out of the anomalies of the electoral system, claiming that a man should have the right to a vote because he was a man, and that it should not depend upon the house he occupied or the rent he paid. Many anomalies existed: these were exposed, and a vigorous campaign was conducted under the auspices of the National Democratic League. I became secretary of the league for a time, and helped to carry on the agitation extensively, as far as other duties would admit; but I continued to give attention to the industrial side of the movement, keeping up my relationship with the Amalgamated Engineers and with the Workers' Union. I also helped in the formation of the Waiters' Union, and quite a number of others.

Southern Skies

CHAPTER XI

NEW ZEALAND
1901 to 1902

I HAD been much interested in a book entitled *Wealth versus Commonwealth*, by Henry Demarest Lloyd, of Chicago. It dealt with the growth of trusts in the United States, giving details of the plants and the capital they controlled. One day I was struck with a review of a book by the same author, the title of which was *Newest England*. According to the reviewer, the book dealt chiefly with New Zealand, and to a less extent with Australia; but New Zealand was the country meant by the title 'Newest England'. It presented the latter country in glowing colours, describing the achievements of Labour legislation. One chapter was entitled 'A Country without Strikes', meaning that the method of arbitration resorted to was successful in avoiding Labour disputes. To my agreeable surprise, a few days after this, Henry Demarest Lloyd, the author, who happened then to be in London, called upon me. I soon commented upon the review I had read in the *Daily Telegraph*. He was naturally interested, and said he would send me a copy of the book. We talked of Australasia, and he was enthusiastic about the prospects there.

At this time the *Clarion*, the Socialist weekly, was flourishing, and exercised considerable influence. I had a great admiration for the editor, Robert Blatchford, and the group of friends that ran the paper. It so happened that the editor's brother, Montague Blatchford (now dead) whose home was then in Halifax, was staying in London for a few weeks, and I saw a good deal of him. The *Clarion* was publishing a weekly article from a former member of its staff who had emigrated to New Zealand in order to give opportunities to the younger members of the family. He wrote in glowing terms of his new homeland, describing the prospects of the country as positively glorious. I admit this had a considerable effect upon me. It gave a stimulus to my natural desire to see the new world. Whenever Monty Blatchford and I met, we were keen on discussing the latest from New Zealand. Demarest Lloyd's book coming along at this time, added fuel to the fire, and I was soon so engrossed in New Zealand affairs that I was alive to the probable consequences – that I should not be satisfied till I went there. I felt increasingly that they surely must have hit upon better methods in New Zealand than we had, or there could never be so many emphatic statements as to the absence of poverty and the relatively high standard of working-class life. Anyway, I concluded, experience of such a place ought to be of some value; and after all, it was desirable in my own interest that I should have actual experience of the newer countries. I felt the truth of: 'What should they know of England, who only England know?'

At this stage, another circumstance befell which added to my interest in New Zealand affairs. Mr Chapman, a Cabinet Minister of New Zealand, paid a business visit to this country, accompanied by Mr E. M. Smith, New Zealand Member of Parliament for New Plymouth, in the Taranaki district. I met him at a lecture on New Zealand, given at the Imperial Institute. At the close of the lecture, after commenting appreciatively as regards the pictures that had been shown, I remarked to Mr Smith that what I wanted to hear about was the industrial development of the country and the conditions of working-class life.

'Certainly, certainly,' said Mr Smith; 'it's a shame to give the time to such stuff as we have had to listen to. I'd have give them something different if I'd had the platform.'

'Hello,' thought I, 'now is my chance.'

So we talked at considerable length, and I gathered that his chief object in coming to England with Minister Chapman was to bring specimens of the finished metal products made from the iron-sand in the Taranaki district of New Zealand, where his home was. He told me they had brought these specimens over. They could be seen at the Agent General's office, and he invited me to go there, when he would be on hand. I visited the office in Victoria Street, met Mr Smith again, and saw the specimens in considerable variety. They were much like the hardware products of a Wolverhampton firm, and included a pair of scissors – all products of the iron-sand, of which there were millions of tons waiting to be shovelled up without any mining or any digging. As a result of the talks that followed, Mr Smith promised to give a lecture on New Zealand to the Cosmopolitans already referred to. I undertook to get the lantern, to act as chairman, and attend to matters generally. Mr Smith's lecture proved most interesting. It was the custom of the Cosmopolitans to have discussion after their lectures, and lively interchanges of opinion generally took place. On this occasion, Mr Smith was on my right hand, and near by, on my left hand, was a tall, vigorous, well-dressed man of a decidedly dark complexion, but very different from a Negro or a mulatto. I leaned over to Smith and asked:

'Is this dark-looking gentleman a friend of yours? Is he a Maori?'

'No,' replied Smith, 'I've been noticing him; I thought at first he might be a Maori, but he's not. I don't know him at all.'

I asked the stranger if he would like to join in the discussion. He thanked me heartily, and smilingly said he would be very glad to, adding:

'Let me take this opportunity of saying how glad I am to meet you. I know your name well, though I have never had the pleasure of meeting you before.'

Thereupon he handed me his card, on which I read: J. Ojijatekha Brant-Sero.

'Ignore the long name and call me Brant-Sero!' said he.

Our stalwart friend was dressed very correctly in frock coat, and had quite a refined appearance. I called upon him to speak. I remember clearly how all eyes were turned upon him, as, with good delivery and a pleasant voice, he said:

'I am very glad of the opportunity to briefly join in this discussion, and I first wish to say how delighted I am to meet our chairman, after being familiar with his name for years. The advertisement in the paper brought me to this meeting. I am very glad I came, for I have been most interested in the address given by Mr Smith, on the industries of New Zealand. But I can see that you are all wondering who I am, so I will tell you. I am a Mohawk Indian.'

We looked at each other and at the speaker, and Mr Smith showed the liveliest concern to know more. Brant-Sero continued:

'I have listened with great interest to the description of New

Zealand, its beauties and its industries. Mr Smith has referred to it as the Gem of the Empire. Well, that's what is said about my country, Canada, and if the chairman will provide a lantern for me as he has done for Mr Smith, I will undertake to bring some slides, and to give you an address, which I think I can make interesting and informative on the Indians of America. I will tell you of their methods of government on their Reserves, etc., if this meets with your approval.'

Of course, his offer to lecture was at once closed with, to come off a fortnight later. Strictly on time, our accomplished Mohawk friend was at hand with his lantern slides. A most enjoyable and instructive evening was passed. The lecturer told many things about the race he belonged to, describing their habits and the education that was provided for them; speaking also of the matriarchate and of the possibilities for a higher education. He showed most interesting pictures, including his own photograph in full dress as a Mohawk Chief – and a very fine and picturesque figure he looked. Brant-Sero afterwards joined a theatrical company, and was on tour for years, spending a good deal of his time in Germany. Ten years later we learned of his death – lung trouble.

Back to Mr Smith and the iron-sand. As by this time I had practically made up my mind to visit New Zealand, I saw more of Mr Smith, and he gave me a small bag of the iron-sand which I actually carried to New Zealand, using it frequently to inform others of the natural advantages of such a place.

I left England for New Zealand on 5 December, 1901, and arrived at Wellington, New Zealand, forty-seven days later, travelling on the SS *Ruapehu*, of the New Zealand Shipping Line. The Boer War being on at the time when we arrived at the Cape, it was under military law, and we were not allowed to land; but some passengers were taken on board there, especially time-expired soldiers returning to Australia. One of these young men was going to his home in Gippsland, Victoria, where his father was running a farm. One day I noticed him diligently studying the chart, so I inquired:

'What are you studying, Jem?'

'This beats me,' he replied. 'Here's this little dot of a country,' pointing to the British Isles, 'takes all our stuff from Australia, it gets all from New Zealand, and they tell me in Africa that it takes all theirs too. They must be a lot of hungry beggars in your country, eh?'

Jem had not given much attention to the difference in population; and he was so much amazed when he compared the sizes of the countries mentioned, that some of his remarks were more forcible than polite. But he was a real good type, and I met many such in the years that followed.

In the usual way many evenings at sea were occupied in giving impromptu concerts, but these were varied by a number of short addresses by various passengers that way disposed, and at one of these the iron-sand was in evidence.

I had no difficulty in getting into touch with the Labour and Socialist forces immediately on arrival at Wellington. In less than forty-eight hours I was addressing the Wellington Trades' Council. Two days later, I addressed the local branch of the Amalgamated Engineers. The following day, Sunday, I spoke to a crowded gathering in the Opera House. I now undertook a systematic study of the social, industrial, and political conditions of the Dominion. I hastened to join the local branch of the ASE. It was simply a matter of what is termed getting my 'clearance' from the branch I had been a member of, and being accepted a member of the branch nearest to my new place of residence.

By repute I knew Mr Edward Tregear, the head of the Labour Department in New Zealand, whose office was in Lambton Quay, Wellington, the same thoroughfare in which the ASE branch held its meetings. I called at the Labour Department and was favoured at once with an interview with Mr Tregear, who was most polite and helpful as I believe he always was to all who called on him. I knew that Mr Tregear had written an interesting article on New Zealand conditions, for the Amalgamated Engineers' Monthly Journal then just in circulation. I was not a little surprised to find that Wellington at that time had a number of unemployed. When attending the branch meeting, I saw and heard a number of unemployed members claiming donation or unemployed benefit. Later, I took occasion to ask if there was any explanation why there were so many unemployed members. The branch chairman promptly replied:

'Yes, there is a simple and full explanation; it is that the engineering firms in Wellington insist upon an unjustifiable percentage of boys and youths in the trade, and take every opportunity to dispense with the services of men in favour of the cheaper labour of the young fellows.'

I commented upon the fact that in the monthly issue of their own *Journal* that had just arrived from London, there was an article by Mr Tregear of the Labour Department, eulogizing the labour conditions of New Zealand, and extolling the Arbitration Act. This article had evidently been arranged for by the editor of the journal, Mr G. N. Barnes, the general secretary of the union. The impression likely to be created in the minds of readers of the journal in various parts of the world was that the one place above others where labour conditions were comparatively good was New Zealand. Was it true that the Wellington branch was hostile to the Arbitration Act? The chairman replied that such was the case; they definitely and emphatically refused to resort to the Act, as they had no confidence in being able to get their grievances as engineers effectively dealt with by persons in other occupations who knew nothing about engineering, and they were intending to organize more perfectly and use the power of the union to better their position.

Shortly after this I was in Christchurch, and I called upon the secretary of the Christchurch branch of the Amalgamated Engineers. He informed me of the local conditions, and invited me to attend the branch meeting that evening. I did so. In due course I was called upon to address the branch. I again dealt with the conditions of labour and the article in the *Journal* eulogizing labour conditions in New Zealand, and I referred to the high praise given by Demarest Lloyd, the American writer, to the happenings in New Zealand. I related my experience with the Wellington members, how they declined to resort to the Arbitration Act. I desired to be informed as to how they fared in this regard in Christchurch.

The chairman requested the secretary to reply to my queries, and to give me such information as would enable me to get a knowledge of the conditions. The secretary then stated that they in Christchurch had had similar experiences to those of their fellow engineers in Wellington with regard to boy labour; instead of having about one boy to three men, it was a common thing in some firms to have two or even three boys to one man. Unlike the Wellington members, they had resorted to the Conciliation and Arbitration Act, and had done their best to obtain improved conditions under the Act. They had met with moderate success, as although they had not been able to obtain an increased wage, they had brought up to a higher standard some of the lowest paid shops in the district. This afforded indirect help by reducing the intensity of the competition by the firms employing underpaid non-union men. With regard to establishing a proper ratio of men to boys in the shops, they had requested the courts to deal with this matter, and submitted proposals on the subject; but the employers strongly objected to any legal interference, on the ground that the union could not speak for the whole of the industry in the district, but only for the local members. The plea influenced the court, so that on this troublesome question they were in the same position as the Wellington members. Yet it was an urgent matter, for so many more boys entered the trade than there was room for as journeymen, that when they were out of their apprenticeship and required a journeyman's pay, a large percentage of them had to leave the trade altogether, whilst others went to England to qualify as sea-going engineers. Thus it was clear that the Christchurch men who made use of the Act, were in the same plight as the Wellington men that did not use the Act, and that the real thing that mattered was one hundred per cent organization in the union. Then, with or without the Act, the trouble would be overcome.

Turning to the clothing trades, I was satisfied that the operation of the Act had resulted in substantially bettering the condition of many of the employees, both with regard to working hours and to rates of wages. No doubt equally good changes could have been brought about by organization, but certainly not in the absence of it. However, I determined not to draw hasty conclusions as to the value of the Arbitration Act, and other labour legislation, and resolved to cover both islands, get in contact with all sections of workers, study the effects of labour legislation, and gauge the strength and character of the trade-union movement. In my travels I reached New Plymouth. Mr E. M. Smith, whom I had met in London, had now returned. We renewed our acquaintance, and in his company I had the opportunity of seeing enormous quantities of the iron-sand of the Taranaki Coast. Also I saw old furnaces, quite derelict, which, Mr Smith told me, had been used many years before to test the qualities of the iron-sand. The experiments had been successful, but no results of commercial value had followed. Nevertheless, he believed that by-and-by European steel workers would come to appreciate its merits, and that the iron-sand would yet be exploited. I never learned what was the final result of his efforts in conjunction with Mr Chapman, who, I believe, visited Sheffield firms with a view to interesting steel-makers in the sand. Some years later I knew of experiments being made with the sand in Melbourne. They seemed on the point of success, but failed in the end, as far as I could learn, to give encouraging results to experts. Now I observe that, in the New Zealand display shops in the Strand, London, one window is devoted to specimens of manufactured articles, said to be made by a Darlington firm, from the iron-sand of New Zealand.

I visited the Coromandel Peninsula, via Auckland, and the famous Waihi gold mining district. Here I had another illustration of the working of the Arbitration Act. I found the Waihi miners on strike against the Act. The men did not want it, but the management did. The union was opposed to the men being brought under the Act, so the management easily got over the requirements of the law which provided that societies consisting of two or more employers, or seven or more workers, might register and come under the jurisdiction of the Act. The employers had no difficulty about their own side of the case; and as the miners proper were not disposed to come under the Act, the owners encouraged men engaged about the mine, other than miners, to form themselves into an organization to meet the legal requirements. By this means a case was cited and an award granted.

I will here record my next experience at Waihi, which was five years later, when I revisited New Zealand from Australia. Again there was a dispute at Waihi. The men had been on day work. They had applied for an award under the court, and a wage of eight shillings and sixpence per day was awarded for all daywork men at mining proper. To evade the payment of so high a wage, the manager gave all the day-men notice to finish their jobs, after which he put up advertisements to the effect that he would let the work out to contract parties. This resulted in competition for the jobs, in the men undercutting each other, and in 'racing, or slogging', so that many were thrown out of work altogether, and in other cases the prices were cut, in some instances as much as twenty-five per cent. Thus the award ceased to operate, and the standard of the men was seriously reduced.

I had opportunities of studying the conditions under which dairy farming was conducted in the Taranaki area. This is one of the best dairy districts in New Zealand. Some farmers are, naturally, very well circumstanced; but in a very large majority of cases the children of school age had to help at milking before leaving for school in the morning, and the same when they returned, the reason being that the children's parents could not do all the milking themselves, and could not afford to pay for labour to do it. The cost of land had been run so high by speculation that only by utilizing child labour was it possible to make ends meet. I met some farmers and others who denied that such duties had any ill effects on the children, and a few who even claimed that it did them good; but the conclusion I came to after careful investigation was, that in thousands of instances it proved a positive hindrance to the child's mental and physical development.

On my return visit to New Zealand, I again visited Taranaki, but found no improvement whatever in the condition of the children on the dairy farms. I saw more clearly than ever that many of the New Zealand farmers were simply running farms for a period, until they were able to sell at an advantage, and that they were more keen on making a deal of this sort and scoring financially than they were upon establishing permanent homesteads. It was not pleasing to learn that the farms had already changed hands so frequently that, good as the land was, and excellent the yield, it took a farmer and his family all their time, and seven days a week at that, to pay interest on capital – for, in addition to paying interest on the purchase value of the land, in many instances they had to get farming implements on the hire system and to pay ten or twelve per cent on the amount.

I had an interesting run to the west coast, visiting Greymouth, Westport, Blackspoint, Denniston, etc. New Zealanders regard this as the chief coal-mining district of the southern hemisphere. They claim that the coal of this region is unequalled in Australasia, and is as good as the best steam coal of Wales. On my first visit, now twenty years ago, I had arranged to meet the miners at Coalbrookdale. To reach the place, one travelled from Westport by train to the foot of an enormous hill. The two mines, Coalbrookdale and Ironbridge, were on the top of the hill, a drift in different directions on reaching the plateau leading to the mines. Proud Salopians must have baptized the mines, judging by the names, but I did not learn that such was the case. However, at that time, the only way to get to the top of the plateau was by bridle track. No main road led there, though one was in course of construction. It was about three miles by the track, and I ventured to do it on horseback. I certainly had a good meeting; practically all the mining township was there. I reckon they would have been there equally if I had been the opposite kind of character, or indeed anything in between. The fact is, the people wanted some diversion from the dull monotony of being stuck on that hill-top without variety of any kind, other than an occasional social or concert amongst themselves. I was told that some of the miners' wives present at the meeting had been brought there twenty years before, and had never been off that hill-top the whole of the time. They had a co-operative store there, and if they walked down the bridle track there was nothing worth seeing, just a railway station – and then there was the trouble of getting back up the track. The result was that their knowledge of the world was confined to a stony plateau leading nowhither. What an outlook! That place seemed to me the most completely shunted off from civilized society and from humanity generally of any I had ever seen.

Many will have heard of the remarkable fish known as Pelorus Jack. There were stories galore told of this fish in New Zealand. Some of them were doubtless exaggerations, but the facts in connection with the creature were sufficiently interesting to require no embellishment. It was commonly reported that a large fish, said to be some sixteen feet long, met every vessel in the Pelorus Sound. Vessels leaving Wellington (which is situated at the south end of the North Island), en route for the west coast of the South Island, cross the Cook Strait to Picton as the first port of call, continue their voyage to Nelson via Pelorus Sound and the French Pass, the latter being a very narrow passage separating the mainland from

D'Urville Island. It was said that when a vessel reached the Sound, it was met by a 'Pilot' fish, which went a little ahead of the ship direct to the French Pass. There the marine pilot suddenly disappeared, and would not be seen till the next vessel came along. To give special point to the story, it must be understood that this was the only fish of the kind ever seen in these seas. It was of the dugong genus and therefore not really a fish but a mammal.

On my first run to the west coast, since the boat went through Pelorus Sound at night, although I had in mind the fish story I made no attempt to see Jack. I knew that on the return journey I should be in the right neighbourhood in full daylight, and I had made up my mind to be on the look-out. Some ten days later we approached the Pass about noon. I was on deck, in conversation with a fellow-passenger, when the dinner gong was sounded. I remarked to my companion that I should not go down then as I was anxious to see the notorious fish. He exclaimed:

'What! Pelorus Jack! Oh, there is plenty of time for food. I have seen him often enough; come along, and I'll come back with you. We shall be in time.'

I was reluctant to go below, but I did. We were only about half-way through the meal when another passenger came from deck, saying:

'He's just gone.'

'What has just gone? The fish?'

'Yes, we had a fine view of him.'

I was much annoyed with myself for having been persuaded to leave the deck, the more especially as I had promised friends I would observe the fish carefully and report. I was to go to Australia in a week or two, and perhaps would never be passing through the Sound again. Besides, I was not too sure that after all it was not a case of leg-pulling, and might be a pure fabrication. However, five years later I was making this trip again. The boat was on the same schedule as five years previously, and would therefore be in Pelorus Sound some time after nine o'clock. But I was taking no chances. I said to the steward quite seriously, watching his eyes as I spoke to him, not yet being satisfied as to whether it was a joke or not (for I found no one in Australia who took any other view of it):

'Steward, can you tell me what time we shall be in the part where that fish is said to appear?'

'Yes, sir, soon after nine, about nine-fifteen as near as I can say.'

'So; well, I am anxious to see it; but in case I might be in conversation and overlook the time, will you please be on hand and let me know?'

'Certainly, sir, leave it to me.'

It was a starlit evening; the day had been a fairly warm day I didn't wait for the steward. I put on my overcoat about nine o'clock, and sat in the cabin for a while. A passenger sitting near asked why I had my overcoat on. I said:

'Oh, I'm going to the bow of the boat shortly to see that fish.'

Scornfully he said:

'What! Pelorus Jack?'

'Yes.'

'Why, there's no such fish!'

'Oh! surely there must be some foundation for the stories that are told about it!'

'Well, I've done this trip seven or eight times in as many years, and I've seen no such fish.'

I was just reflecting:

'Confound it! It is leg-pulling after all,' when the steward looked in, and speaking to me, said:

'We are well in the Sound, very near to where Jack appears! Better be on the look-out.'

I made for the bow immediately. Not another person was there save the look-out man, and he seemed anything but the typical sailor. He was some three yards from the bow, walking sharply from port to starboard. I remarked:

'I hope I'm not too late to see the fish?'

He, very abruptly:

'Oh no, he'll be here directly.'

Not another word, and as I stood right at the bow he went further back, but kept up his quick march, port to starboard, starboard to port. I spent about five minutes before speaking again, when I turned to him:

'I see no signs of anything, I hope I haven't missed him.'

'Oh no, he'll come all right; he ain't been yet.'

I turned right into the bow, both elbows resting steadily on the rail, and just got my gaze settled, when, right suddenly, a few yards ahead, was a great splash and a swirl, and I saw the fish as plainly as possible. I could have clapped my hands with satisfaction. The fish blew like a whale, but not so heavily, and continued this about every half-minute. He allowed the boat to overtake him, got right in the swirl, and may have brushed up against the hull. He seemed immediately under me for a few seconds, then he darted off for a dozen yards in front, and appeared to revel in the water as though the big boat were chasing him, but stood no chance. I watched without moving until he disappeared suddenly, as though he had dropped underneath. I had been watching him disporting himself for seven minutes, when he vanished without even a swirl in the water.

The sight of this fish, with the wonderful effects of the phosphorescence, was most striking; so entirely different from anything I had ever seen, that I felt grateful for having been privileged to see it. At the same time I felt quite indignant that there was not one other person besides myself, the look-out man, and the officer on the bridge, that had seen it, or apparently cared to see it. I was leaving the bow and going down the stairs into the well-deck, on my way back to the saloon, when a passenger coming in the opposite direction said:

'Can we see that fish tonight?'

I really had a difficulty in replying becomingly, I was so affected by the (as it seemed then and still seems to me) literal pig-headedness of humans not to show more interest in such an exceptional natural phenomenon. In any case, I was exceedingly pleased that I had had the good luck to secure such a splendid view of Pelorus Jack.

CHAPTER XII

FIRST YEARS IN AUSTRALIA

1902 to 1905

HAVING had a good run through New Zealand, having covered practically the whole of both islands, and having taken nine months to do it in, I made for Australia, arriving in Melbourne at the end of September 1902. I had been in communication with the Labour organizations there, and had learned that the Victorian State election campaign was in full swing. As usual in such cases, the Labour forces were divided into moderates on the one hand, and persons of advanced views on the other. This was made plain when a deputation in a small boat came several miles out to meet the steamer in which I was travelling to Melbourne. Their mission was to put to me the claims of the particular candidates in whom they were interested, that I should agree to speak on their behalf. I made no promise. I considered their methods somewhat unfair, and said that, since I was a stranger to the country I should leave myself entirely in the hands of the Trades' Hall Council. By noon the same day I was in consultation with the members of this body. I addressed six meetings that afternoon and evening, and six more the next day. On the following day the elections took place.

A few days after this, 6th October, was fixed for the annual Eight-Hour Demonstration in Sydney. I was invited to attend, and in this way secured an introduction to the organized workers of New South Wales. The Eight-Hour Day celebrations had long been looked upon as the chief Labour Day of the year in the capital cities of the respective States; but they were held on different dates. Melbourne gave especial attention to the organizing of a most picturesque procession and sports, the latter being supervised on lines commanding the approval of experts. The speeches on the occasion were usually delivered under cover, most often in the luncheon room. There is nothing notable to record in connection with these experiences. The names and records of the speakers gave an indication of the general outlook; and the character of the speeches might be taken as forecasting Labour's programme for the immediate future.

I visited the chief cities in New South Wales, Victoria, and South Australia on free-lance lines. Then I was asked by the Victorian Labour Party to organize on its behalf. I was given a free hand with regard to procedure, and the emphasis I should lay upon the need for industrial organization was left entirely at my discretion. I was sent to districts where little or no propaganda work had been done, and requested to put my whole time into the work. Help in the planning of the tours was furnished by those who knew the country well, and were familiar with the means of communication.

I enjoyed the undertaking, and often I met with kindly cooperation. This was generally so where a branch of the party already existed, or where a few friendly sympathizers were willing to help in forming a branch. Occasionally it was otherwise. In some electorates, no Socialist, and not even a Labour man, had ever addressed a meeting. In such cases, more often than not, the bulk of the population consisted of small farmers who looked askance at the Labour Party, and were hostile to Socialism, so that I had occasion to learn that all reactionaries are not domiciled in the northern hemisphere.

I vividly recall my visit to Kyabram. This was an irrigated agricultural district in which hostility towards town areas and urban workers prevailed. More especially did there exist an animus against organized Labour, and above all against Socialists. No Labour member could give me the address of even one sympathizer; but it was the more necessary that I should go and endeavour to sow the seed, and if possible establish the nucleus of an organization. I had been able by letter to secure the use of a hall. This overcame one difficulty, but there was not anyone to give help. My name and views were well known. Although I was travelling under the auspices of the Labour Party, always and everywhere I advocated Socialism. I reached the hall in good time, saw a number of persons hanging around who recognized me all right, although they had never seen me before. When the doors were opened many sauntered in, but they all kept aloof. No chairman, no committee man, no helper of any kind. On mounting the platform, I first sat in the chair that ordinarily would have been occupied by the chairman. I semi-jocularly referred to the absence of an associate on the platform likely to take up too much of my time, and launched into my subject.

No hostile behaviour was shown beyond scowls, and a cold and unfriendly attitude; but these did not daunt me. I had the necessary energy and I was in my element. I occupied nearly two hours straight off the reel, and the audience sat it out. When I had finished, there was some applause, and I invited questions. These were forthcoming, more or less pointedly hostile to the policy and declared objective of the Labour Party, but nothing of any note. The ice had been broken; a quiet and entirely successful meeting had been held; and I obtained a few names as the nucleus of a branch. In such districts as these the only pleasure was in achieving in spite of the absence of general goodwill. I had the privilege of tackling virgin soil in this regard in a number of districts.

I recall an open-air meeting at Penshurst, the centre of another farming district; here again, no help of any kind. An intimation had been sent that I should be there on a certain date. Having arrived pretty early, finding no one anxious to assist, and being unable to secure a bellman to cry the meeting, I borrowed a good-sized dinner bell from the hotel, and walked around the town in bellman fashion crying the meeting for 7 p.m. I turned up promptly at meeting time, having borrowed a chair for a platform, and, as I was fixing things just prior to commencing, I heard one man say:

'Why, dong it, that's the same fellow that cried the meeting.' 'Yes,' I responded, 'I'm the one that cried the meeting, and now I'm going to do the speaking,' and so I plunged off at the deep end, and no floundering.

October is the month of sheep shearing in Victoria. The secretary of the Shearers' Union arranged with the Labour Party and myself that I should put in three weeks at the shearing sheds. A horse and buggy were placed at my disposal; the route I was to take, and the shearing stations I was to call at were duly marked. The secretary undertook to notify each of the stations when to expect me, and I started off, through what was to me entirely unfamiliar country, and using, what was also to me, a novel method of locomotion. I managed the horse very well. I was driving alone all the day, generally reaching my rendezvous late in the afternoon or early in the evening. I had no difficulty in getting audiences. The men were usually glad to meet me, and I had ample opportunity of seeing a phase of life that naturally was as interesting as it was new.

On one occasion one of the men arranged to accompany me to the next station, for he knew some of the shearers there, and, like most of them, had a horse at his disposal. He cantered along by the side of the buggy which I was driving, talking all the while. He seemed to ride so easily, that I thought now would be a good opportunity for me to try horseback. I suggested it.

'Certainly,' he said, 'any time you like.'

I asked for an assurance that the horse would be as quiet with me on his back as with him.

'Oh, he's as quiet as a lamb,' said my friend, jumping off.

I mounted, and he took the buggy in hand. I was trotting along in a bumpety sort of way, not too comfortable, when my gee-gee took it into his head to slow down. I tried to appear cool and self-possessed, but the gee-gee was boss. My companion said:

'Let him have the rein; don't hold him in.'

Whether I let him have too much rein, or too little, I never knew; but the beast darted off with me at a terrific rate, and I had the greatest difficulty in keeping on his back, but I couldn't pull him up. He shot under the branches of trees unexpectedly and several very near touches I had of getting my head broken against one. Ultimately he pulled up on his own account, and I was delighted to get on my feet. By this time my mate was a long way behind. When he caught up he was laughing most immoderately at my discomfiture, all the time assuring me that really his horse was the quietest of animals, etc., etc. But I returned to my quiet old mare and the buggy for safety – and comfort.

Later, in Queensland, I was with shearers at some of the large stations. A note I made at the time, which I am sure must have been written with care (though it now seems difficult to realize the fact), says:

> A record shearer at ... station in North Queensland shore 208 sheep in eight hours, and forty shearers shore 6,000 sheep a day, or an average of 150 per man, all through the eight-hour day. The highest on record for one man was 340 sheep in one day of eight hours.

It was not for me to doubt it: I saw some quick work, but nothing approaching such a rate as this.

It will be of service to make known the conditions that prevailed industrially, and the standard of life experienced by the workers in Australia, compared to that which obtained in England. At that time a nine-hour work day was almost universal for mechanics in Britain; in Australia the eight-hour day, though not universal, was general. Food stuffs were quite as cheap as here; meat, considerably cheaper; clothing, and other things generally, dearer. Making allowance for the higher prices, I came to the conclusion that a mechanic in Victoria, was quite seven shillings and sixpence a week better off, for one hour's work per day less, than a mechanic in England; and the unskilled labourer likewise had a higher standard. This was the direct outcome of insistence upon that higher standard quite apart from considerations of output. In this new country, where the capitalists were unable for the mere asking, to secure an ample supply of men willing to accept almost any wage, it was much easier for the workers to resist the ever-repeated attempts of employers to reduce wages. The higher standard does not obtain in consequence of any greater goodwill on the part of capitalists towards workers, nor because there is work for all who want it; nor does there exist any institution or agency, governmental or other, to take general action to prevent starvation. There was not and there is not either in Australia or in New Zealand any basic difference in the system of industry as compared with that which obtains here in Britain. Capitalism is dominant throughout Australasia; it is as ruthless there as here; but even in Britain we find districts where the standard of life of the workers varies by as much as ten or even twenty per cent from the normal.

In my advocacy of Labour interests, I traversed the whole of the State of Victoria, some portions of it many times. During the eight years I spent in the southern hemisphere, though I made Melbourne my chief centre, I visited every industrial district and many of the agricultural districts of every State and Dominion – New South Wales, Victoria, South Australia, Western Australia, Queensland, Tasmania, New Zealand, and South Africa. I was not making a casual visit, but a definitely planned and deliberate

First Years in Australia

survey of the whole of these countries, which are at one and the same time very new and very old.

While organizing for the Victorian Labour Party, I frequently visited Ballarat and Bendigo, these being the two largest cities in the State outside of Melbourne, the capital. Both of them are gold-mining towns, and Ballarat has some claim to consideration as a city where attention has been given to street beautification, at least as regards the main thoroughfare. It was a city of some fifty-five thousand inhabitants, and had always been a gold-mining centre from its origin seventy years earlier. The general rate of pay for miners when I was there was from seven and sixpence to eight shillings per day of eight hours. That was for those who worked on a fixed daily wage. It was the custom, as soon as the mines ceased to yield well, for the owners to refuse to pay any fixed daily wage, but to let the mine workings to 'tributing' parties, usually composed of about four men each. This threw all the expense of working on the men, who were paid only for the metal produced.

I visited Ballarat at intervals during a period of seven years, became most friendly with William Hursfield, a Britisher, who was secretary of the Ballarat Trades' Council, and was also well acquainted with the secretary of the Miners' Association, with most of the committee, and with many of the rank and file. I have thus good warrant for the following statements. It frequently happened that a tributing party of four would start work and not get any metal for two or three months. All that time they had to live at the expense of their families, or run into debt – a very common practice with them. Often when they did get gold, and the owners' half had been deducted plus all cost of explosives, picks, and other tools, there would not be left as much as ten shillings per man per week for the time they had worked; and yet they would proceed again on similar lines. I have dealt with the subject at many public meetings in Ballarat and elsewhere in Australia. There was no alteration up to the time of my leaving in 1909. Fully thirty per cent of the miners, in and around Ballarat, were at work 'tributing', and their average income over the year did not exceed one pound per week.

I took down many statements from the men concerned. Here is a specimen:

Bob Patterson, Ballarat miner.

From January 1904 to December 1906 my weekly wages would not average fifteen shillings working full time at 'tributing' in Ballarat East. There are hundreds doing no better and many doing worse than this at the present time, 1909. . . . I have worked in the famous Birthday Mine, Beringa, for four shillings a day tributing. I've worked as a miner from seventeen years of age and I'm now thirty-nine. I have not averaged more than a pound a week all that time, and I've only been laid up by illness for two months.

There was no machinery existent by which this could be altered, and there was no other work to which these men could turn to get a better livelihood. I knew a young miner in Ballarat who determined he would try and get out of it altogether. He desired to go to Queensland to the sugar-growing districts, and his friends collected sufficient to enable him to pay his fare to Queensland. He arrived there before the sugar season began, in June, when he stood no chance of getting work. There were more than enough who had some experience with sugar work or who had Queensland mates to help them in getting a job and so had a better prospect than a stranger from Victoria.

It is, or at any rate was when I was there, much the same in the copper-mining district of Moonta, South Australia. I visited the district on several occasions, during the time when Mr Tom Price was coming to the front – the man who afterwards became the Labour Premier for South Australia. At that time John Verran, a miner from Cornwall, was working at Moonta, and with his and others' aid I studied the conditions. On the death of Mr Price, Mr Verran became Premier. Many of the Moonta miners did not receive a wage higher than twenty-five shillings a week, and a number did not average more than a pound. My object in giving these details is to enable intending emigrants to form a clear picture of Australian conditions.

I do not discourage anyone from going; on the contrary, I think it well that young people should at least have experience there, and stay there if the life suits them. Too often however, they emigrate and they settle only from economic compulsion. Still, if a young man asks me whether I would advise him to go, I place the facts of the economic situation before him, and then wish him the best of luck in his endeavours to get a broader experience. But everyone should bear in mind that capitalism is established there, that capitalism rules there. The workers find the same need for working-class organization there as here. Australasia, like Europe and America, is under the Iron Heel of Capitalism.

So far I had not visited Western Australia. I arranged to take a rest from my organizing work in Victoria, and in the middle of 1904 I took boat from Melbourne to Fremantle. A lecturing tour from Perth, the capital of Western Australia, to the two distant railway terminuses at Leonora and Laverton was soon arranged. At Coolgardie, Kalgoorlie, and Boulder City, I had many meetings. I visited the mines as well as the miners, going down the mines and into the engine shops, and into most places where work was being carried on. Kalgoorlie I found a go-ahead mining city with the characteristics of youth and vigour; but as my destination was ever somewhere beyond, I had to go farther along the main line, sometimes up branch lines, and occasionally journeying by coach to reach the outlying townships and mining camps. While on this run I saw many more aboriginals than I had hitherto seen, and naturally I was interested. Often enough I had gazed at representations of Australian natives at the Crystal Palace; and the West Australian group, whenever I stayed to look at it, always made me feel indignant. I considered it to be a gross exaggeration, a travesty on what I conceived to be the real thing; and I often said those responsible were playing upon our ignorance. I could not believe that the native women would appear as the artist presented them, but I was to get a lesson. I had a meeting in one of the western towns, Menzies I think it was, and the next day I had to move on to another camp, but there was no train till the afternoon. The hotel proprietor kindly asked whether I would care for a drive. The district was terribly barren and desolate looking. I said I certainly would if there were anywhere worth driving to.

'There is the reservoir, and we can take a sweep round and return by a different road.'

So to the reservoir we went; it was almost empty, and there was little else worth seeing. On the way back to the township by the other road, we suddenly came upon clusters of natives, chiefly women, and in a flash I saw what appeared to me to be the original of the Crystal Palace group. My friend was driving at a foot pace, so that I could see them well. One of the women was leaning on a long stick, pipe in mouth, the exact replica of the Palace group, and her features were startlingly like those I had thought exaggerated. I was all eyes and ears as long as we were amongst them, and on arriving at the hotel I felt bound to tell my host how much I had wronged those who had tried to educate us by means of the groups at the Crystal Palace, and how glad I was to have seen the real thing at first-hand. On many occasions since I have endeavoured to make amends to the artist whose work I had, prior to this visit, been unable to appreciate. Visitors to the Palace, if the groups are still there, may look and learn with more patience and satisfaction than I did.

Returning to Victoria, with Melbourne as my centre, I continued working for the Labour Party. I felt it necessary to make certain proposals with a view to the better organization of the Party, and wanted certain pronouncements to be made with regard to the Socialist objective. These suggestions were taken in good part, but nothing was done; so, early in 1905, I resolved upon an extended tour in Queensland.

Commencing the campaign at Brisbane, I had meetings at Ipswich, where the locomotives are built; at Gympie, a gold-mining town; at Maryborough, where there are large engineering works; at Childers and Bundaberg, among the sugar growers; at Mount Perry, with the copper miners and smelters; at Rockhampton, Mount Morgan, Mackay, Bowen, Townsville, Charters Towers, Cairns, Wolfram Camp, Chiligoe, Nymbol, Ravensworth, and other places on the outward journey; revisiting most of these and calling at others on my way back.

It was of much interest to be brought into direct contact with the actual workers building up this new country. I was eager to understand and to experience for myself their standard of life. It is so easy for even a well-balanced investigator to draw wrong conclusions, if only on the spot for a short time, and particularly so when climatic conditions are markedly unfamiliar. Still more difficult is it to get a real grip of the situation when the traveller can command good hotel accommodation, or entertainment by friends in comfortable circumstances.

I had resolved, on reaching New Zealand, and later, when

visiting Australia and South Africa, to make a long stay, and to live under conditions which would approximate (allowing for the changed environment) to those of folk of my own standing at home. In each State I therefore gave close attention to the conditions of work and of home life, to the way men and women dressed, to the pleasures they indulged in, and to their social habits generally. This included a careful observation of the uses they made of industrial and political organization. In the more sparsely-populated regions, conditions were, of course, very different from those of the homeland – and all these places were thinly peopled in comparison with Britain.

Sydney, with a population of 700,000, and Melbourne, with a population of over 600,000, necessarily have characteristics not unlike those of great cities elsewhere; but when one tries to size up a population like that of Western Australia – 280,000, all told including the urban, farming, and mining inhabitants, distributed over a total area of 975,000 square miles (the area of Great Britain, Ireland excluded, is only 88,000 square miles) – one must expect to find marked differences in habits and in methods of development. This population of less than 300,000, including the 6,000 natives, has its own State Parliament and takes its share in the Federal Government. Queensland has a population of 604,000 and a territory of 670,000 square miles.

The chief gold-mining centre of Queensland is Charters Towers. When I was there, trade unionism was at a low ebb, and the working conditions were nothing to be proud of. At Mount Morgan, producing gold and copper in about equal proportions, and admittedly one of the richest mines in Australia, not one miner belonged to a union.

On my arrival at Mount Morgan, the Mayor (who was also the editor and, I think, the proprietor, of the local paper, *The Mount Morgan Argus*,) met me, and was good enough to show me round.

'Are the men here well-organized industrially?' I asked.

'No,' said he, 'I don't think they are in any union. I have never heard of it if they are; and I think, as Mayor of the town and editor of the paper, I should know of it if they were.'

Later we were with a group of the active men in the town, and the Mayor raised the question in this wise:

'Mr Mann was asking me if the men are organized in a union. I said I'd never heard of it. There are no trade unionists here, are there?'

One of the group, Mr Aitken by name, replied:

'Well, I know of one, Mr Mayor, not a miner, but a carpenter; that's myself. I belong to the Rockhampton branch, as there is no branch here; but I don't know of any other member of any union in Mount Morgan.'

Further inquiry confirmed this. I had already been to Gympie, then (and I suppose still) the second largest gold-mining town in the State. It is represented in the State Parliament by two Labour Members, and it was part of the constituency which had returned the Hon. Andrew Fisher as its Federal Member. A group of friends had met me at the station, including the two State Members. After a talk I found myself walking with a friend who seemed to accept responsibility for the meeting arrangements.

'Have you many organized in the unions here?' I inquired.

'We haven't any!'

Thinking he meant only a few, I added:

'I don't suppose there are many, but there is sure to be a group; if I could see the committee or the secretary, I'd like a talk.'

'I mean just what I said; there are none. I should know. I was secretary of the last committee that existed here and that's been dead about two years.'

Such was the condition of trade unionism amongst the Queensland miners. I may add that I arranged with that same friend to take me the following morning to the pit-head of the principal mine and introduce me to a representative mechanic, on the off chance of finding an engineer who might belong to the ASE. The effort, however, was quite fruitless. Not one member could be found of any union. This will indicate the small importance attached at that time to industrial organization. It was one of those spells when practically all attention had been given to organization for the parliamentary campaign, leaving no energy – because no disposition – to deal with industrial affairs.

Sugar-cutting and sugar-crushing are dependent, to some extent, on the season, like the wheat harvest. Usually the cutting begins in June, and work at the crushing mills continues from then on till November or December. At the time I am writing of [1905], the

Kanakas were being deported. Four years were allowed for repatriation. No more were to be brought in. The Kanakas did not cut the sugar; but they did much of the plantation work and were regularly employed. White men worked in the crushing mills; it was heavy work. I was in the company of the Labour Member for the district, Mr Barber (an Englishman) at Bundaberg, and he arranged for me to go over a large sugar estate and to be present when the Kanakas had their food given them. Outside the estate, on the road side, several six-by-four tents were rigged up and the men belonging to them were sitting around. On inquiring what it meant, I learned that these white men were wanting work, and had made their way to the neighbourhood of the sugar estate, not knowing to a week or so when cane-cutting would commence. They were waiting to get work either at cane-cutting or in the crushing mills. The men in the mills worked twelve-hour shifts, six shifts a week, the mills running night and day; and they did this for twenty-two shillings and sixpence a week and 'tucker', the latter being valued at that time at eight shillings a week. I conversed with the men waiting to get a start on these rates and conditions, expressing my astonishment that they worked so long and received so little. I was told that, during the previous season, meetings had been held to ventilate the need for an eight-hour day and higher pay; but the agitation had led to nothing so far.

I also learned on inquiry that most of the men, when discharged at the end of the season after five or six months' work in the sugar mills, 'hump the bluey', 'carry the swag' over the country, or in our phraseology 'go on tramp', getting casual work where they can. They usually average one week's work in four during the tramp, making their way back to be ready for a start at the mills when the next season begins. It does not require much imagination to picture the domestic life of such men. While at the mills they are housed in rough barracks; when on tramp, any old shed serves them as often as a room.

When I went to Australia in 1902, it was at the close of the terrible drought, which in some parts of Queensland had lasted for seven consecutive years. Millions of sheep and cattle had perished and many people had lost everything they had. Australia in that period lost 30,000,000 sheep and 1,000,000 cattle.

As soon as a good season came along, a cheerful optimism

characterized the community, and they set vigorously to work. The soil yielded wonderfully, and the animals were extraordinarily prolific, Mother Nature joining heartily with the efforts of men to make up for the bad times. In consequence of the prolonged drought more attention had been given to the well-sinking. The various States had already done something substantial in this direction and had demonstrated the practicability of getting great supplies of water. Thus the Government of New South Wales reported while I was there, that they had completed eighty-two borings. Fifty-six of these had been successful, the aggregate flow being thirty-three million gallons a day. There were also one hundred and twenty-eight private borings, two of which discharged four million gallons a day each. In Queensland, in 1910 there were some one thousand three hundred and fifty artesian wells in action, yielding four hundred and eighty million gallons per day. The depth of these borings varies greatly; some of them are four thousand feet deep. The average cost of a boring is twenty-six shillings per foot.

The river waters in the interior of the country run underground to a considerable extent; but the inhabitants are coping with adverse conditions, and are making the wilderness blossom like the rose.

Shortly after this period, there came a great revival in industrial organization. Sometimes by direct action, often through and by means of the Arbitration Courts, hours of labour have been reduced, and wages substantially raised.

I am still amazed when I reflect that so few men in so short a time have cleared so much land, made so many roads, built so many cities, and changed so largely the character of the country, as has been done in barely two generations in Australia.

I am Britisher enough to experience in reasonable measure the pride of race, and am not wholly unmoved when I think of the truly wonderful achievements that have been wrought on the small area called the British Isles. From the standpoint of physical and mental energy, exercising an influence upon the world (the nature of this influence not being for the moment under consideration), it must be clear that, despite a hundred drawbacks, the climatic conditions of Britain have not been altogether unfavourable to the growth and perpetuation of a sturdy race. But who would pretend that our climate is a nice one, except for half the year? When the bloom and warmth of spring and summer are really with us, no place is more delightful; and some autumn days and autumn tints are exquisite. But what a price to pay in the long cold wet days of a greater part of our long winter – November to March. Australia has a great variety of climate, as there needs must be in a country covering three million square miles of the earth's surface; but all over the great island continent there is more sun everywhere than we have at home – too much, perhaps, in some places at certain periods! But there are few in Great Britain who would not be glad to give a good three months of our British cold and foggy dampness for the genial, warm atmosphere our kinsmen in Australia are favoured with. It may be that the natural scenery of Australia is for the most part dull and sombre. The gum trees do not shed their leaves and put on new, young, enlivening greens that catch and reflect the sunlight with dazzling brilliancy; but the character of a large part of the country has already undergone a change. European trees are flourishing there, the varied tints are seen there, and the gums give a grand steady balance and a healthful pleasing aroma. Yet, the whole of this enormous area is peopled by no more than five million men, women, and children – barely two-thirds of the population of greater London! Their achievements are positively marvellous. No man who has had the chance to see even as I have seen these new countries, can ever be despondent of the future of the race. Many difficulties are yet to be overcome. The best proof that these will be mastered is the definite knowledge that a thousand similar ones already have been overcome.

Returning to Melbourne, I began a series of lectures on social problems, in the Bijou Theatre on Sunday evenings. Out of these grew a committee called the Social Questions' Committee, which accepted the responsibility of undertaking many social tasks, and especially of helping in connection with the unemployed problem, which at that time was acute. The general attitude of the Government was to treat the matter lightly, ignoring requests, on the ground that there was no special urgency. As the result of the refusal of the authorities to help or to investigate, our Committee decided to make a house-to-house visitation in the industrial districts of Melbourne. Seventy persons undertook this considerable task, helped by capable organizers. They were able to prove that over five thousand adults, and a similar number of young people, were unemployed, and that much real poverty existed. The chairman of the Committee, Mr J. P. Jones, now the Hon. J. P. Jones, Member of the Legislative Council, spent much time in the endeavour to get responsible statesmen to accompany him to the homes of the destitute. At length, after months of effort on our part, several statesmen paid a few visits and admitted that the evidence of their own eyes could alone have convinced them of the reality of what they saw. Various schemes of relief work were resorted to; but no cure of unemployment was achieved, for the outlook of those in authority was as completely bourgeois as that of the Coalition Government in Britain today.

CHAPTER XIII

SOCIALIST WORKERS, WRITERS AND POETS
1906

THE Social Questions Committee had developed into the Victorian Socialist Party, and this body grew rapidly in numbers and influence. Active men in the trade unions who were already declared Socialists joined. They helped to build up the movement, not in hostility to the Labour Party, but untrammelled by its restrictions. Joyfully declaring themselves in favour of International Socialism, they spurred the Labour Party in the same direction. For myself, I enjoyed the work immensely; it was varied and effective. In April 1906 *The Socialist* was started; it soon became a weekly. I was editor. The paper is still running, and my old comrades always send me a copy. We founded a Sunday School. During the sixteen years of its existence, it has exercised a valuable influence over many scholars, passing them on into a Speakers' Class, training them in elocution, and giving such help as was suitable to their various talents. Some have become prominent as musicians, having had their first training in the band, the orchestra, or the choir of the Party.

I lectured for the Party every Sunday evening in the Bijou Theatre, Bourke Street, over a period of three years. We had large outdoor meetings on Sunday afternoons, on the recognized rendezvous – the Yarra Bank, i.e. the bank of the River Yarra Yarra. From this outdoor meeting it was the custom to adjourn to the Socialist Hall, where tea was provided at a small charge, all work in connection therewith being done voluntarily. The original object in thus arranging teas was to make it possible for the friends who came from the suburbs to the afternoon meeting, to get tea without the trouble of going home, so that they would be near at hand for the chief meeting at the Theatre in the evening. The gatherings for tea were very popular, usually about one hundred and fifty partaking, and these occasions were excellent for consolidating friendships and for introducing new sympathizers into the movement.

The Socialist Party aimed at fulfilling the requirements of its members in every phase of life's activities, and was more successful in this respect than have been any of the other organizations I have belonged to. It interests me to recall some of the personalities with whom I had the pleasure of working, among the thousand or more of the members. Should any of my Melbourne friends happen to read these lines they will, I am sure, share my satisfaction in the memory of our comradeship.

There was our sturdy and efficient secretary, Frank Hyett. He may be regarded as an actual product of the Party to which he rendered such excellent service in so many ways and for so many years. It was ever our aim to be well-balanced, blending a thorough appreciation of the highest ideal with the most genuinely practical behaviour in everyday life; therefore we always advocated the vital necessity of every worker belonging to a trade union, insisting at the same time that all our members must understand and rightly appreciate the objective of revolutionary Socialism. Frank Hyett became general secretary of the Victorian Railways Union, and showing first-class ability, delighting in welding together sectional societies, and striving for true solidarity in all industries. Frank was a fine, healthy, clean-living man, a first-class cricketer, a capable and militant trade unionist, and a loyal comrade. He died after a short illness, but not before he had lived the life of a man, and his family and comrades will ever be proud of him.

Next I think of Jack Curtin – to call him 'John' would seem to me to detract from the real warmth of comradeship. He, like Frank Hyett, had an intelligent outlook on life. Curtin was well grounded as a Socialist before the days of the SP, but he takes pleasure, as Frank did, in bearing testimony to the advantages obtained by association with the Party. He became not only an able exponent of advanced principles and policy, but also a proficient union official. For some years now he has been editor of the *Westralian Worker* a paper exercising a wise influence over a very large area. I still hear from him occasionally. I am proud to be Jack Curtin's friend.

Joe Swebleses was born, I believe, in Whitechapel, but in early childhood was taken to Australia. He was another of the devoted young enthusiasts of the movement whose torch he continues to carry.

Comrade H. Scott Bennett was already a capable platform man before the days of our Party. Since joining it, twenty years ago, he has been a constant source of enlightenment to Australia and New Zealand. He undertook a lengthy lecturing tour in the United States, but returned to Australasia and is carrying on the educational work.

Comrade R. S. Ross, familiarly known as Bob Ross, has been closely identified with the vicissitudes of the Party for some fourteen years. As secretary of the SP and editor of *The Socialist*, he became engrossed in the advocacy of socialism and in the task of building up of the Party as an engine of propagandist effort. A man of strong views, he never hesitated to express his dissent from views or policies he was unable to agree with. He was, and is, a great force with the pen which he has used to spread the gospel in all parts of the Southern Hemisphere, and in recent years particularly in the columns of his magazine, *Ross's Monthly*. Still as active as ever, he wields increasing influence. At present he is touring the Australian States on behalf of Daily Newspapers for the Labour Party.

Tom Tunnecliffe, member of the Legislative Assembly, was also a diligent worker. In spite of the pressure of his parliamentary duties he continued to take an interest in the Party. Then there was Angus MacDonell, the present Mayor of Northcote, Melbourne, an ever-ready advocate of our views. There was Percy Laidler, a shrewd debater, excellent worker, and straight goer; now, and for years past, manager of Andrade's Book Store in Bourke Street. H. H. Champion, my comrade-at-arms in the London dock strike of 1889, has lived in Melbourne for the past thirty years; he, too, was on the executive of the Party and took keen interest in its work.

The Hon. J. P. Jones has from early days shown a lively concern for the Party's welfare, though he does not always see eye to eye with its policy. He is an employer of labour, but advocates and conforms to trade-union conditions. A member of the Upper Chamber in the Victorian Parliament he seizes every chance of using his position on behalf of the workers' cause. Some hold that he attaches too much importance to parliamentary institutions. Nevertheless, he is considerably more advanced in his views than most of the manual workers, whose grievances he honestly ventilates to the best of his ability, being always willing to stand up for the 'bottom dog'.

One of the Federal Labour Members of Parliament is Frank Anstey, a man born in Silvertown, London. He left home early in life and became a sailor. Having settled in Australia, he soon became influential in labour circles. Later, he was elected to Parliament for the State of Victoria, and is now in the Federal Parliament. He often lectures for the Socialist Party. An avowed Socialist, he works well for the cause. During the late war, in defiant opposition to Mr W. M. Hughes, the Premier, Anstey championed the No-Conscription campaign. He came to Europe, visited various countries, returned to Australia, and published an arresting book called *Red Europe*. Frank is a man of moods. Should a real revolutionary movement take place in Australia, and Frank be in cheerful mood, he will stick at nothing, but will go the whole hog.

We were fortunate in the Socialist Party in having several poets, at least two of whom stand high and sing true among the worshippers of the Muses. Bernard Patrick O'Dowd, born in Victoria in 1866, frequently helped us with a topical song or poem to give point to and to strengthen our work.

The other poet was Marie E. J. Pitt, Tasmanian by birth, and one who knew what the struggles of the workers were and are. Keen to resent injustice, and to stimulate others to strive for a worthy life, she was in close touch with the toilers, knew the work of the axeman and of the miner, was familiar with the terrible effects of miners' phthisis, and she helped in the Melbourne investigation of unemployment in 1906.

It will be of interest to my readers to see exactly where I stood at this date with regard to political and industrial organization. I had myself been approached several times to accept nomination as a Labour candidate, and although I had emphatically declined, it will be seen by the article which follows that I urged parliamentary action. It was not till some three years after this that I declared definitely in favour of Industrial Unionism. My article appeared in August 1906.

THE SOCIALIST PARTY AND POLITICAL ACTION

Socialists believing in the necessity for working for the speedy realization of a Socialist regime, must also work definitely to bring about the same. To do this we must unceasingly agitate, as by this means we can arouse some of the lethargic who would otherwise sleep till doomsday; we must educate ourselves and the community by working from the inside of existing organizations, as well as by innumerable propagandist meetings and the spread of literature, and we must miss no opportunity at election times, not only of taking part in the work of elections, but also by bringing to the front and popularizing those measures calculated to lead to the realization of our ideal.

We of the Socialist Party are fully alive to the risks attendant upon political activities. We know that many attach undue importance to parliamentary business, and fuss about over the merest trifles, as though they were matters of vital importance.

But we are not of those who contend it is sufficient to preach Socialist doctrines and await results without taking part in political agitation and directing the attention of those we may to the Socialist goal. And so it is necessary to be clear-minded as to programmes, and the measures to be submitted for the consideration of the electorates.

The object of the Socialist Party is to secure economic freedom for the whole community, i.e. that all women and all men shall have equal opportunities of sharing in wealth production and consumption, untrammelled by any restriction it is possible for the State to remove.

Some of our members are accepted candidates for the Senate and the House of Representatives. It is our duty to back them heartily, to work for them cheerfully, and to do all we can to secure their return.

As Socialists, we cannot support opponents of Socialism, no matter what fine fellows they may be in other directions; and it is no secret that in the ranks of Labour are some who have no knowledge of Socialist principles, and therefore no appreciation thereof. Such persons must never expect to get the backing of Socialists; but we must on the other hand sensibly and generously allow for past environment, and not forget that many are actively engaged in courageously fighting with the proletariat in The Great Class War, who have no clear intellectual grasp of the science of industrial and social economics.

Not to allow for and properly appreciate this fact would mean that we should soon become doctrinaire, exclusive, pedantic, and narrow, and therefore should soon become comparatively useless and perhaps even mischievous. Therefore, while we must ever hold up the ideal of Class-Conscious, International, Revolutionary Socialism, we must rejoice when we see men break away from the support of the orthodox parties, whether called Liberal or Tory, Freetrade or Protectionist, Democratic or Republican, and resolve that henceforth they will unite as Labour men and take their stand against the Capitalist parties.

This is the first stage in the War of the Classes as regards the attitude of the masses, and those who thus sever themselves from the old order are in a fair way to receive and make use of sound economic knowledge.

For Socialists to antagonize this section by denouncing them because they do not yet see clearly what is meant by the economic interpretation of history, or are unable to discern the differences between the Socialism of our French comrades, Jean Allemane and Jean Jaurès, or our German stalwarts, Bebel and Bernstein, would show their unfitness to educate and to organize for great and glorious Socialist victories the mass of the people.

Such considerations are necessary in considering our attitude towards the candidates that will be brought out by the Labour Party. It is necessary we should use all becoming means to secure the selection of class-conscious Socialist candidates; but even when this is not done, if the candidates selected stand for the proletariat in the War of the Classes, it becomes our duty to work for them and do our honest best to secure their return.

It will be remembered that there was a considerable increase in the number of Labour Members returned to the British Parliament in 1906; among the new MP's of that year was Mr G. N. Barnes. *Pearson's Weekly* published interviews with the Labour Members, and the following was reproduced in one of the Melbourne papers. I thought it highly creditable to Mr Barnes to show such modest frankness in the matter; most men would have been so important in their own eyes as to have overlooked some of the earlier essentials to their advance.

PUSHED INTO FAME

I don't know that I have much to say about 'How I Got On', said Mr G. N. Barnes, MP for the Blackfriars Division of Glasgow, in the House of Commons, to a reporter of *Pearson's Weekly*, than that I have been pushed on.

Henry George certainly had a great influence upon my career, awakening me to wider interests in life; but it is to Mr Tom Mann that I owe my entry into public life.

I had joined the Amalgamated Society of Engineers as soon as I came to England from Scotland, and in 1891 my work as an agitator brought me to act as secretary to Mr Mann, who contested the post of general secretary to the ASE.

He did not get it, but his propaganda, supported by voluntary contributions from the members, shook the whole society from end to end.

Mr Mann became the talk of the country, and as his secretary I was brought prominently before the members of the ASE, and to some extent before the public.

Eventually I contested the post of assistant-secretary to the ASE, and won it. I held it for three years, and then returned to the 'shops', until, in 1897, the post of general secretary having fallen vacant, I competed for it, and was successful.

As I told you at the beginning, I have been pushed on. But for my connection with Mr Mann I dare say I should never have come into prominence in Labour circles, and very possibly I should have been content to go on working in the 'shops'.

As evidence of the kind of work carried on in Melbourne, I republish another of my articles dealing with our activities at the time and setting forth principles and policy. If I have any reserves to make today concerning what I wrote in 1906, it is because the events of recent years have compelled me to realize that our internationalism of those days was incompetent to prevent the outbreak of war.

WORK OF THE SOCIALIST PARTY

In reviewing the work of the Socialist Party during the past twelve months, it is necessary to realize how relatively deadly anything in the nature of straight-out Socialist propaganda work had fallen eighteen months ago in Melbourne. Meetings were held at the Queen's Hall on Sunday evenings by the SPD, but they were chiefly in the nature of entertainments.

In June 1905 we commenced Sunday afternoon lectures on Socialism in the Gaiety Theatre; these proved a decided success. Then, when the Queen's Hall was available for us on Sunday evenings, we commenced there too. As the summer weather came on we gave up the Gaiety and commenced outdoor agitation on the Yarra Bank. We definitely formed our present organization on Friday, 1st September, at a meeting convened for the purpose in Furlong's Rooms, Royal Arcade.

At first we were known as the Social Questions Committee, whose objects were declared to be the collection and utilization of information bearing upon social questions, with special reference to the proper feeding of children, the advocacy of the claims of the unemployed, the housing question, etc.; but all the time we avowed ourselves straight-out International Revolutionary Socialists.

We commenced open-air propagandist meetings at street corners in most of the suburban districts. Every Sunday morning, without fail, our speakers have appeared at Port Melbourne Pier to preach Socialism, and every afternoon on the Yarra Bank.

We commenced an Economics Class and a Speakers' Training Class, and fully 60 comrades have been engaged in the voluntary work of Socialist advocacy indoors and out during the year. We have averaged fully ten propagandist meetings a week, or 500 meetings during the last twelve months.

In the holding of these meetings, and the conducting of the campaign generally we have ever had in view the necessity for clearly enunciating Socialism of the scientific school, that is, the recognition that the evolutionary development of Capitalism renders Collectivism or Socialism imperatively necessary. That this Socialism is and must be International in character; further, that while of necessity it is evolutionary, it is equally of necessity revolutionary. This is clearly understood by our 1,500 members, and many others who attend our meetings.

Nothing can be done in opposition to the evolutionary growth of the social and industrial forces, but the change involved in the present social unrest, which is also social growth, is a change so wide and deep as to completely transform the existing regime of capitalist private ownership and control of productive forces, and therefore it is revolutionary, BECAUSE THE SYSTEM ITSELF WILL BE CHANGED.

The Class War

We have also habitually preached the Class War as understood and advocated by Socialists the world over. By this we mean, that we are conscious of the fact that present Society is based on Class domination, i.e. the Capitalistic Class dominates in all countries, and the Parliaments of the world are used as Committees of the Capitalist Class to carry out their desires. Class antagonisms exist in every civilized State, and these antagonisms are being daily accentuated. The immediate interests of the capitalists and *petit bourgeois* are not in the same direction as the workers. The growth of the Trusts and Combines renders organization of the workers increasingly necessary to check the harmful effects of the hostile and antagonistic capitalist factions. Therefore, while believing in the necessity for and possibility of getting rid of classes, we know that the way to do this is by the workers – quite distinct from the capitalistic parties – organizing industrially and politically, and so conquering political power to facilitate the change and get rid of the modern CLASS STATE, and establish a regime of Co-operation when there will be no employing class outside of the employed, and where community of interests will be universally recognized.

The Red Flag

Further, a year ago, we aimed at giving a true interpretation of the Red Flag. We resolved to remove the unwarrantably narrow idea that had been attached to it in Melbourne, which caused practically all to shrink from its presence. Now, however, nothing is more cherished by the vast majority of those who turn up and make the vast audiences that have filled the Bijou Theatre and Zion Hall, as well as at the outdoor meetings, than the Red Flag – symbolizing as our comrades know, the oneness of the interests of our common humanity the world over. As we sing 'The Red Flag' song, at all our meetings – undoubtedly the most popular song of its kind in Victoria – we realize that our movement wipes out all racial hatreds, gets rid of national frontiers, and demands of us that we shall recognize all men as brothers, not in words merely, but in deed and in truth.

Narrow patriotism therefore disappears and a true cosmopolitanism takes its place. The 'Red Flag' is to us the symbol of the most sacred principle we can hold, which enables the Frenchman and German to refuse to organize to fight each other, and impels them to organize co-operatively with each other, and all the world; and so with the Britisher and the American, the Dutchman and the Scandinavian, the Latin and the Slav. All alike, wherever Socialism obtains, drop all antagonisms and accept the Common Faith of a United Humanity.

In matters religious, like the Socialists of all countries, we declare theology to be a purely private concern; but as regards righteous dealings, we declare with Moses and the Prophets, with Christ and the early Christians, that there can be no righteousness where land monopoly (or machine monopoly) obtains, or where the accumulated wealth of private individuals may be used as a means of exploitation. To live by exploitation, which is systematically aimed at by the supporters of capitalism, is a gross violation of right dealing; and for such persons to talk of defending religion is mere pharasaical pretence, the making clean the outside, but inwardly being as dead men's bones. Our Sunday School has done, and is doing, excellent work. The children are taught sound ethics, and encouraged to study economics; and right pleasingly they acquitted themselves on the platform at the Town Hall.

Thus are the forces shaping to usher in a Socialist regime. During the same period the anti-Socialists have been actively engaged, both in encouraging the ignorant to remain ignorant, and in the spreading of the falsehoods they themselves have concocted. We smile at their efforts, and are amused at their squirming. Onward marches the vast and ever-increasing army of the world's workers. We are about to leave the conditions of worse than Egyptian bondage, and are making for the glorious freedom of Collectivism, of Socialism, of Co-operation, wherein will be no place for legalized robbery by rent takers, profit takers, and interest receivers; but where the true and righteous principle will prevail, that 'any who will not work, neither shall he eat'.

In that day there will be no Cry of the Unemployed, no children literally dying of starvation in Melbourne, or elsewhere, as is the case now. No wretched cheeseparing to make ends meet, by existing on insufficient food, improperly clothed, and housed in a fashion that would disgrace Hottentots. These bad conditions exist now, but Socialism will drive them out. We of the Socialist Party have done something to usher in the New Time. It is to be our privilege to do more, much more, during the year we have now entered upon.

Courage, comrades, you have done well! At it again, comrades, and you will do still better, and will help materially in securing the economic salvation of the people.

CHAPTER XIV

FREE-SPEECH FIGHT

THE success attending the propagandist efforts of the Melbourne Socialists, received further stimulus by the attempt of the authorities to interfere. In Prahran, one of the Borough Councils of Melbourne, public meetings were held by various bodies in side streets adjacent to main thoroughfares; for a considerable time the Socialists likewise held meetings under similar conditions. Then a campaign of police persecution began. A Socialist speaker, while addressing a small audience, was ordered by the police to desist. Declining to do so, he was arrested and at the Police Court was fined 40 shillings, with the alternative of fourteen days.

This was the beginning of a series of prosecutions which resulted in many arrests and imprisonments (including that of myself). I recount the affair to show that the same reactionary spirit dominates the municipalities in new countries as in old ones. The magistrates, when convicting, said that those only who had permits from the Council could be allowed to speak in the thoroughfares. The Council refused to give a permit to the Socialists, but the magistrate declined to consider this. He was, in fact, a Councillor, and sided with those who refused to grant the permit.

We were determined to fight the matter out. The Party agreed to give full support; it encouraged all who were arrested to refuse, on principle, to pay fines. During the three months that the struggle lasted, over twenty were fined or imprisoned; half of them, refusing to pay the fine. Four of these latter were women comrades who showed as much courage and ability as the men. When I was prosecuted I took the alternative of imprisonment, and was confined in Melbourne gaol for five weeks.

Seeing that I am recording the campaign for the benefit of Australian readers, quite as much as for that of Britishers, I propose to reprint some of the newspaper reports. It should be mentioned that the police, when forbidding us to hold meetings in the same places and under similar conditions as the Salvation Army and the Temperance Advocates, were kind enough to direct us to a piece of waste ground frequented by no one!

The following account is from the Melbourne *Socialist* of 3 November, 1906, written by myself.

TEN SOCIALISTS ARRESTED AT PRAHRAN
Socialists Toe the Line

Instead of tamely backing down, and getting shunted off to vacant land, away from the people, to talk to hoardings and old bottles or kerosene tins, the Socialist Party advertised that their speakers would, at eight o'clock, be present to continue the struggle for Free Speech; and exactly on the stroke of eight the Socialist contingent arrived at Chatham Street, corner of Chapel Street. The police were already on the spot in considerable numbers, and, naturally, their presence attracted a considerable number of persons, who otherwise might not have been interested. Of course, a number of Socialists were there also, and the responsible group marched some 80 yards down Chatham Street from Chapel Street, to just beyond Cato Street (the short thoroughfare running at right angles to Chatham Street), so that there should be no obstruction to traffic.

Ladies to the Front

As had been definitely arranged beforehand, Miss Ahern was the first to mount the little stand. This was at two minutes past eight. The crowd cheered lustily, and the speaker, in very clear and firm language, proceeded to advocate Socialism, making but brief reference to the cause of the special excitement. The inspectors, detectives, uniformed and plain-clothes police, marched single file from the Chapel Street side of the crowd to the back of the speakers. They conferred for a minute or so, and then a half-dozen of them approached and the sergeant told Miss Ahern she must desist. As she declined, he arrested her, and our comrade was marched to the watch-house.

Immediately, Mrs Anderson (as pre-arranged) stepped on to the stool, and in a firm, strong voice, well under control, began to address the crowd. Up came the sergeant, and bade her desist. Our comrade replied she 'would when she had finished – unless they made her before'. The defiant attitude resulted in arrest, and the second of the group was marched off.

With cheers from the crowd, in accordance with programme, W. J. Baxter mounted the primitive rostrum. Not many sentences had been uttered, when, he too, was assisted to the watch-house.

During the short time Comrade Baxter was on the platform, Senior Constable O'Loghlin paid special attention to myself for my activities in keeping the ring round the platform, and otherwise in helping to maintain order. The constable said if I didn't go away he would arrest me for loitering. I scornfully pooh-poohed the loitering charge, and continued to supervize affairs. By this time Comrade Baxter was seized, and I mounted the pulpit, and began, *à la mode*, continuing for a minute or so, in spite of police remonstrance. I was then hauled down by Sergeant Williams and others, and, with more cheering, was escorted like the rest.

On arrival at the watch-house a fifth was brought in, Comrade Quaine, charged with offensive behaviour. He really didn't know what he had done when charged by O'Loghlin, who told him he had 'shouted and boohed'. Quaine replied, 'I didn't booh at the police; it was at the mention of Councillor Miller's name', but apparently it was sufficient.

Shortly afterwards Councillor Miller came in. He shook hands with each of our little batch, one or two of whom extended the hand reluctantly, considering that this gentleman was the chief cause of the trouble that had arisen, including the gaoling of our members.

Councillor Miller at the Watch-house

In conversation with me on the subject Councillor Miller expressed deep regret at the turn of events, and said, although he was credited with being a prime mover, causing action to be taken against us, 'he certainly had no wish to see such action taken, and had not the remotest intention of calling for it'. Reminded that the press reported that he it was that had raised the question in council, Councillor Miller said that it was quite accidental that he had referred to the Socialist meetings, being prompted thereto by another councillor, whilst he (Counciller Miller) was addressing the council on the subject of street obstruction by hawkers, and frankly owned that he did not wish to attack Socialism, as he did not know sufficient about it, never having studied it.

All this may be quite true, but it does not absolve Councillor Miller from exhibiting hostility towards the Socialists in Prahran Council, and as late as last Monday he exhibited a special vindictiveness towards us at the Council; and when questioned at his South Melbourne meeting he continued to ride the high horse of the superior person, siding deliberately with the anti-Socialists, and accepting the blame for having instigated proceedings, resulting in the imprisonment of Comrade Swebleses.

Had Councillor Miller exhibited the slightest regard for fair play to our people, or had he desired to explain his position if wrong conclusions had been drawn, surely there was ample time for him to do so during the fortnight Joe Swebleses was in gaol; and even if he had hoped it would blow over with the imprisonment of Comrade Swebleses when, the very day he was released from gaol, four others were arrested and each of these sentenced to fourteen days' imprisonment, action might have been taken by Councillor Miller to dissociate himself from these proceedings, but he did not.

Permission Refused

It was on Monday of last week, the 22nd October, that Comrades Marsh, Hyett, Beck, and Summers were sentenced. Mr Witt, the presiding magistrate on the occasion, appeared to be under the impression that no application for permission to speak had been made by the Socialists, although Frank Hyett told him such application had been made, and permission refused.

At the close of the proceedings, I personally made direct to the office, and, in the name of the Socialist Party, wrote again, asking permission from the Council for the Socialist Party to hold meetings in the open air in Prahran, not making reference to any particular place. I took care to post this in time to reach the Town Clerk that afternoon, to be in time for the Prahran City Council, who I knew were to meet that night in committee.

I waited several days, and getting no reply, I went down to Prahran and called at the Town Clerk's Office, and inquired if there was any reply to my letter of Monday. The Town Clerk, very abruptly, and without an atom of courtesy, replied, 'No; there will be no reply till after Monday next!' Comrade Fryer was with me when I called.

This left no alternative to the Socialist Party but to continue the fight without further overtures. It appears to have been thought by the authorities that, if they temporarily withdrew the permit from the Salvation Army, they would thereby remove the grounds of dissatisfaction. Therefore, let all concerned understand that, however many permits may have been granted and withdrawn, and however submissive the bodies so dealt with may be, our demand is the right to hold meetings, under reasonable conditions, in the open air, always having reasonable regard for pedestrian and vehicular traffic, and for the general convenience of the public.

This question has been fought out hundreds of times before in other countries. It has been fought and won by our fathers under British law hundreds of times, in Britain and elsewhere. I myself was arrested in Southwark (London) for addressing meetings in Tooley Street, within seven minutes' walk of London Bridge, on the south side of the Thames. I was marched off to Southwark Police Station, and, when the case came on, I was able to show that, during the meeting, I had reasonable regard for keeping the thoroughfare clear for traffic, and the stipendiary magistrate dismissed the case.

On another occasion, for addressing a meeting in the neighbourhood of Queen's Road, W, I was summoned to Marylebone Police Court, but again the case was dismissed, on the ground that, although a considerable number of persons were listening, there was ample room for pedestrian and vehicular traffic.

And this is the only logical position to take up in connection with the subject. As Socialists, we have proper respect for municipal and other regulations made in the general interest, and administered fairly; but not only will we not submit to exceptional treatment, but, however feeble, half-hearted, and impotent other sections may be, we Socialists, at any rate, will not show cowardly servility.

The authorities have taken up a wrongful position. There is only one way to get over the difficulty thus created, and that is, the authorities – the Prahran City Council and the police – must get back to a sensible attitude, and leave citizens free to interchange opinions, always providing they exhibit reasonable regard for the general welfare.

POLICE COURT PROCEEDINGS

The Prahran Court was crowded on Monday, when Comrades Lizzie Ahern, Mrs Anderson, W. J. Baxter, and Tom Mann were charged with having wilfully obstructed a carriage way in Chatham Street on Saturday night, 27th October. Four other comrades, John Quaine, Thomas Hart, Edwin Knight, and Will Thom were charged with behaving in an offensive manner to the police on the same evening.

The plutocrats were mustered in force on the Bench, in the persons of Messrs. Kent, Capt. Panter, Major Clipperton, Witt (chairman), Young, and Hislop.

D. H. Herald prosecuted on behalf of the Prahran City Council.

Miss Ahern was first called on to plead, and, in a straight-out fashion, said she was prepared at all times to claim the right to give expression to her views and principles.

Sergeant Williams and Senior-Constable O'Loghlin gave evidence on behalf of the police. The defendant was addressing the people. They asked her to desist. She refused and they arrested her.

The Chairman: You are fined 30s., with 10s. 6d. costs, in default ten days' imprisonment.

Mrs Anderson was then called on, and declined to plead. The police evidence was the same as the previous case.

The Chairman: Do you wish to say anything?

The Defendant: Why are others allowed free speech and the Socialists refused?

The Chairman said that had nothing to do with it, and fined Mrs Anderson 30s., with 10s. 6d. costs, or ten days' imprisonment.

Comrade Baxter was next charged, and, at the outset, took exception to the presence on the Bench of W. Maxwell Hislop. He considered it unseemly – owing to the peculiar relations that had existed between them formerly in Westralia.

The Chairman announced that under the circumstances Mr Hislop would not adjudicate.

The police evidence as to the arrest, and the Chairman fined our comrade 40s., with 10s. 6d. costs, or ten days' imprisonment.

Tom Mann was next similarly charged. He admitted the offence.

Sergeant Williams stated that when he asked defendant to leave he declined, and spoke over witness's head.

Defendant: Before I spoke did you notice any special behaviour on my part?

Witness: You were moving about, and called out to the people to keep the footpaths clear.

Did you hear anything offensive or unbecoming on my part? – No.

But you distinctly heard me appeal to the people so that the footpaths should be kept clear? – Yes.

Defendant said that he had pleaded guilty because obstruction did take place, and he was one of the central figures. There was no real guilt on their part, because they never sought obstruction. Nor were they willing to obstruct. The direct cause of the obstruction was the attention and the excitement initiated and developed by the presence of the numerous police.

The Chairman: You know why so many constables were there on Saturday night.

The Defendant: Yes; because of the differential treatment meted out to us as Socialists. You stated last week that others had asked for permission, and obtained it. We have asked for permission, and it has been refused. I ask that you will note that exactly similar by-laws are in operation elsewhere. There is a law which gives to every citizen the right of free speech in thoroughfares under reasonable conditions. That has been decided again and again, and that is the right we have been contending for, and the right I shall continue to fight for under all circumstances.

The Chairman: We have decided to fine you 40s., with 10s. 6d. costs, in default fourteen days' imprisonment.

Defendant: I tell you plainly that I certainly shall not pay the 40s.

A man in the audience: I'll pay the fine.

Defendant (loudly): Do nothing of the kind. I protest against its being paid for me.

The fine was paid, in spite of Mr Mann's protest, and, immediately on being released, he went direct and advertized a meeting for the same evening in Chatham Street, where he had previously been arrested.

RE-ARREST OF TOM MANN

Prahran was far and away the liveliest suburb of Melbourne on Monday last. The proceedings at the police court in the morning, and the excitement attending the re-arrest of Tom Mann in Chatham Street, in the evening, the indignation meeting at the Town Hall, and the several overflow meetings in connection therewith, manifested an amount of life that agreeably surprised the old-time residents of the true sort.

Tom Mann Imprisoned
Tom Mann was actually locked up on Friday night, 9th November, after the authorities had waited for a fortnight in order to muster up sufficient courage to do the dreadful deed!

It happened in this fashion. Tom Mann was wondering whether they had forgotten him, and so he decided to go to Prahran station, and see if they knew anything about the matter, and gave them a gentle hint about the warrant. They told him at the station that the warrant was in the hands of the West Melbourne police.

Our comrade then visited the Chief Secretary, and made a few remarks about prison reform, etc., after which he interviewed the West Melbourne authorities and asked whether they had a warrant for his arrest. They replied that they had two, but that the sergeant had not yet given orders for their execution.

Tom Mann then asked, 'When will they be executed?'

The reply was, 'Some time on Saturday'.

'I'd rather go today', replied Tom.

'Very well. What time would be suitable?'

'Oh, after tea!' replied our comrade.

And after tea it was, he being locked up at seven o'clock on Friday, 9th November, for the awful offence of trying to enlighten the people of Prahran on matters that concern the welfare of everyone!

At the trial I was sentenced to four weeks for causing an obstruction, and one week for resisting the police. These five weeks were spent in Old Melbourne Gaol. Here are some more extracts from the Melbourne *Socialist*:

VISIT TO MR TOM MANN

Last Tuesday, having obtained permission from the Inspector-General, Mrs Mann and Mr J. P. Jones visited Tom Mann in gaol. He said he was in good health, and getting on nicely, and his spirits seemed in no way damped. About twenty minutes were spent in conversation of a general character, no bar being placed upon anything said, and Mr Mann received a fair account of happenings in connection with the Party since his imprisonment. He was exceedingly anxious to know whether the youngsters had a good time at the picnic, and asked Mr Jones to engage Zion Hall for Sunday afternoon, 6th January, when he intends giving a special address to scholars and others.

He is allowed special privileges as regards reading matter, and has been forwarded a Shakespeare and several works of Dickens.

YARRA BANK AND SUCH GATHERINGS THREATENED

We repeat here plainly what we have contended elsewhere, that if the Prahran by-law is valid, the rights of free speech and free assembly, except in hired halls, or other private property, are only exercisable in Prahran (and in every other part of Victoria which has a similar by-law) by the permission of any police constable who happens to be passing. For, if the contention of that council is applicable to orderly meetings in unfrequented public streets, such meetings, whether they actually obstruct anyone or not, are also, by the express words of the by-law, illegal in all public places whatsoever.

OUR OBJECTIVE

As Mr Mann contended on last Thursday at the Prahran Court, as recorded in *Hansard*.

'He had done what he had, not with a view of causing any trouble, but with the object of contesting what he believed was his right, as well as the right of others, to hold meetings in public thoroughfares, providing that there was reasonable regard for the general convenience of pedestrian and vehicular traffic. He did not intend to do anything more than protest against what he considered unwarrantable behaviour in prohibiting meetings in the fashion they had been prohibited. He did not contend that he had any right to obstruct the thoroughfare. He only contended that he had the same rights as others to use the public thoroughfares for such purposes when they had reasonable regard for the convenience of others. He was not defying authorities except when he considered their decisions were not in accordance with good law or usage'.

CHAPTER XV

NEW SOUTH WALES; NEW ZEALAND REVISITED
1907 and 1908

WHILE in Melbourne, I represented my branch of the Amalgamated Engineers on the Trades Hall Council, and on behalf of the branch I submitted a proposal in favour of the six-hour work day. This proposal was fully discussed, and was ultimately carried by a large majority. The secretary of the Council was instructed to communicate with all trade unions in Australia, informing them of the resolution and urging them to take similar action.

When I was sent to Tasmania by the Amalgamated Engineers, I visited the Mount Lyell mining and smelting area, and saw the devastating effects of the sulphurous fumes from the smelters at Queenstown. Every tree on the mountain side was destroyed. Nothing but the stumps were left and even these about once a year would catch fire, and the whole area would flame until it burnt itself out. The process was repeated as soon as new sulphurous deposits had formed.

I visited Hobart, Launceston, Zeehan, Strahan, Devonport, and other places. It was an agreeable surprise to find that the Launceston Council was so go-ahead, particularly in its electrical department and in the facilities afforded to householders for the introduction of electrical appliances into their homes. The orchardists in the apple-growing districts of the Huon have won a deserved reputation for apple culture. The fruit is scientifically packed, so that it reached England in good condition, and we have the privilege of enjoying it. Nevertheless many of the growers find it difficult to make both ends meet. I find the following entry among my notes. 'Apples are grown chiefly on the Huon River. It costs the grower 3*s.* 9*d.* per bushel of forty pounds to place them on the London market; frequently he gets only 3*s.* 9*d.* per bushel; sometimes he loses sixpence per bushel. The growers can make a tolerable living if they get 5s. a bushel, i.e. 1s. 3d. a bushel profit. These apples sell retail in London at fourpence a pound. Apple-growers are in some cases giving up the business on the NW coast. There is no co-operation among the growers.'

Undoubtedly a thriving business might be done in Tasmania, Australia, and elsewhere, in growing fruit for Britain. But what an irony when we think of the conditions that obtain here in the homeland! The English climate is well suited to the successful growing of the finest apples, and is as good as any climate for many other fruits. Yet what are our experiences now? Orchards going derelict. In Gloucestershire, Herefordshire, and other counties, with moderate attention, taking averages, apples could be grown with good results to the producers, and might be sent to co-operative centres and sold (at a profit to the dealers) for threepence per pound retail. Instead, we have the pleasure of paying sixpence to one shilling and even more per pound for fruit grown six to twelve thousand miles away. Britain has been industrialized, but at what a sacrifice?

During the whole of 1907 I was occupied in Victoria, with the exception of a month in New South Wales, when I was working on behalf of the Sydney coal lumpers, who were co-operating with the miners of the Newcastle district of New South Wales in a Labour dispute. At this time my old colleague, Ben Tillett, was paying a visit to Australia, and we were both in Melbourne when the miners of New South Wales having vainly endeavoured to get their grievances rectified by negotiation, decided to strike. The immediate object of the strike was quite out of the ordinary. It was to 'cause the employers to meet the men in open conference'. The miners were confident that if only they could meet the employers in open council where the press and the public were admitted, the justice of their claims would be universally recognized. For many months they tried to persuade the employers to participate in such a conference, but without success. Peter Bowling, a Scotsman, president of the Miners' Union, and his fellow members on the executive recommended a strike. The rank-and-file endorsed this, and took action accordingly.

The bunker coal for most of the vessels trading to New South Wales was sent to Sydney and the ships were loaded there. This meant that there was a considerable number of coal lumpers employed at Sydney, who were affected immediately the miners' strike began. The lumpers' officials wired to Melbourne for Ben Tillett and myself to proceed to Sydney to help them during what they rightly anticipated would be a tough struggle. We needed no pressing to hasten to their aid.

The New South Wales Government had in operation a comparatively new Act known as The Industrial Disputes Act, the provisions of which were much more rigid than any Act I had known. Arbitrary powers of arrest were given to the police if the subject of striking was being merely discussed. I was present at a meeting of the lumpers one morning when they were transacting the ordinary business and when a letter came from the miners' executive at Newcastle, telling them of the position of affairs in the mining area, and expressing the hope that the miners would secure the sympathetic backing of the lumpers. The letter was read by the Secretary, Mr O'Connor, a member of the City Council of Sydney, a quiet, steady-going personality. The chairman, Butler by name, simply said to the members:

'You have heard the letter from the Miners' Union. We have already on our own account decided to support them by refusing to work. I suggest we acknowledge the letter, and tell them we shall have pleasure in complying with their request.'

This was formally moved and seconded without speeches, submitted and carried, and the next business was proceeded with. It was an interesting comment upon the freedom enjoyed by Australians that the two officials, O'Connor and Butler, were not only prosecuted but imprisoned for associating themselves with the carrying of the above-mentioned resolution. The same policy was applied to the miners. The miners' executive was summoned to appear in court for having carried the resolution favourable to resorting to a strike. The court decided to fine each member; the executive refused to pay, and imprisonment followed.

During this visit I addressed many meetings on the Sydney Domain, the 'Hyde Park' of the largest Australian city – a very fine place too, genuinely helpful for physical and mental growth. Sydney's lovely harbour is also something to be proud of. Melbourne is, I think, a finer city than Sydney, but the approach to

Melbourne by water is flat, dull, and uninteresting. In Sydney's case it is positively charming. I had the pleasure of a good talk with Mr Percy F. Rowland, author of *The New Nation*. A patriotic Englishman, writing of Sydney in his book, he says:

> In position, Sydney is conspicuously blessed. The proverbially noble harbour, round whose myriad 'sunlit coves of peace' the city is built, has not, perhaps, that romantic loveliness that extorts immediate enthusiasm ... but the longer one lives in Sydney, the more the harbour unfolds its charms. ... There is an unmatched glory in those endless bays of calm deep water, carrying the monsters of the ocean into the city's heart; there is a splendour in the flashing turquoise, the regal robe of the great city, its background of countless streets, its edging of endless gardens. And when night comes, and the scores of gaily lighted ferries flit like fire-flies across the noiseless waters, when the winds are sleeping with the waves, with quivering stars for sentinel, while the glittering lamps of the city, another starry host, send a thousand broken shafts of gold far into blue-grey depths; when every hue is harmonized, when every sound is lulled, when the fragrant air is soft as the breath of sirens; then who could resist the spell of this harbour of harbours, this snatch of unearthly music fallen from Paradise?

This high praise I consider entirely justified. Sydney, also, is fortunate in having at its very door so fine a sea front as Manley Beach, with surf-bathing galore, and the climatic conditions that make sea bathing delightful. For those who enjoy leisure and reasonable freedom from economic worry, many places in the world are delightful!

Mr Rowland comments forcibly upon the life of the shearer-cum-farmer:

> The unmarried shearer, roaming, 'swag' on back, from station to station, chasing summer down the latitudes, leads an active, pleasant life enough. His arduous work (for it takes a vigorous man to shear his hundred a day) is varied by days or weeks of leisurely tramp along bush-track and road; when he sets out, the scent of the gums in his nostrils, in the cool of early morning, and ceases with sunset glow, to boil his 'billy' of tea by the precious 'creek'. He is known at all the stations. Perhaps he has sheared for them for half a score of years; he

knows his shearing mates; rough but merry is the life he leads with them – a temporary communion with one slave – and master – the cook. And if, when the shearing is done, he betakes him to the next 'shanty', and drinks his whole cheque (or what portion of it seems good to the publican), he harms no one but himself, and, a few days after, is on the road again, lighter of pocket and heavier of head, but otherwise apparently no worse.

But if he decides to marry, select and clear a holding in the 'back-blocks', and keep a small sheep-run or grow such crops as the land will bear, he will have chosen a lot among the most arduous on the face of the earth – one which even Odysseus might have hesitated to change for. He will find his life a long and squalid fight against drought and the rabbit-plague, while his children grow up wild creatures, and his wife fades to a haggard drudge. Ten or twenty miles, perhaps, from the nearest neighbour, fifty or sixty from a doctor, beyond all reach of any church or school; nothing to see, nothing to think of, but sun and sheep and gums, gums and sheep and sun....

It will not be until the State Government listen to the voice of a minority with justice on their side, and extend more consideration to the country districts, assisting schemes of irrigation and affording cheaper and better railway accommodation for passengers and freight, that the life conditions of the average 'out-back' selector can be expected to improve.

I resumed my life-work at Melbourne. The work of the Socialist Party developed encouragingly, and it was deemed advisable I should revisit New Zealand. Nearly six years had elapsed since I left there, and many experiments had been made in what was termed Labour Legislation. I was to ascertain the trend of events, and to study actual conditions in the light of my previous experiences. Early in April 1908, I left Melbourne for a lecturing tour through New Zealand, and for general observation purposes.

I had completely lost confidence in various Arbitration Acts. As a result of the working of these Acts, the unions grew in membership, but lost fighting efficiency. The whole of industrial negotiation was in the hands of the legal fraternity. It was clear that a continuation on such lines would result in the unions becoming virtually a part of the Civil Service. They would be dominated by the plutocratic forces of the State.

On arrival at Wellington, I met Professor Sviatloffski, of St Petersburg. I found him an exceedingly interesting man. I had observed, as carefully as I was able at such a distance, the happenings in Russia after the Russo-Japanese War. Sviatloffski gave me much information concerning Russian affairs during the years 1905-7

I covered again practically the whole of the North and South Islands. Prior to reaching Wellington on this occasion. I read of a widespread butcher's strike in New Zealand. They had not found the machinery of the Arbitration Court to their satisfaction. Heavy fines had been inflicted upon the strikers by the Arbitration Court, but very few would pay. The Government hesitated to send the men to prison. I came across an old friend who had been a fellow-member of the ASE. He was now a factory inspector in New Zealand. Part of his duties at the week-end was to catch the butchers who had been fined but had not paid, and to collect, where possible, instalments of the fines.

During the same trip I was in the coal-mining district of Blackball. The men had a grievance against the manager, and refused to work under the conditions he imposed. The men were subject to a court award; they had no means of redress short of striking. In course of time the Arbitration Court imposed a fine on the union as an organization, but the members declared they had no funds. Next, the court imposed a fine upon the strikers individually. The men unanimously refused to pay. Thereupon, the authorities tried to set the law in operation by sending the Sheriff to levy distraint. I happened to be breakfasting with this gentleman in the hotel when the order came. Later in the day I learned that his task had proved trying, not to say impossible. He went quietly to the houses of the miners, and when he saw a bicycle, a sewing machine, or anything else he counted worth taking, he marched off with it. Later he endeavoured to hold a public sale of these articles, but no one would bid for them. Result, the poor Sheriff had to give up the attempt, and to return to his quarters defeated. A general election was at hand, and the Government could not face the consequences of imprisoning the refractory miners, so a declaration was made that, as soon as the new Parliament should meet, an alteration would be made in the law empowering employers to deduct, by weekly instalments, from the wages of any person, the amount of fines imposed by the Arbitration Court. This was actually done!

Of all the cases I came in contact with, showing the absurdity of referring to New Zealand as 'a country without strikes', that of the Wellington bakers was the most remarkable.

I had long known the secretary of the Wellington Bakers' Union, an Englishman, Andrew Collins. He had the profoundest respect for the Labour Legislation of New Zealand, and particularly for the Conciliation and Arbitration Act. He was himself a member of the Conciliation Board under the Act, and had been so since the Act was passed in 1894. The members of the union had all along desired to get their hours reduced to eight a day, and forty-eight a week. Mr Collins, the secretary, entirely agreed with them as to the necessity for this, and undertook to bring the matter before the Court. This was done but without success. On two other occasions, at three-year intervals, a similar attempt was made, by which time the bakers in many other districts of New Zealand had secured an eight-hour day. But again, on both those occasions, the Wellington men failed to get the reduced hours they were striving for. They came to the conclusion that their failure was directly due to their having put themselves under the jurisdiction of the court.

The union, therefore, decided to cut loose from the operation of the Act, and to resort to direct action. I was with them during the strike. The secretary admitted that the court, as far as the Wellington bakers were concerned, had been an utter failure, and he entirely approved of the resort to drastic action. I was in Mr Collins' office conversing with him on the subject, when another incident took place which sheds an interesting light on the methods of the court. A law officer called on Collins and handed him a document. It was the official intimation that he was held liable to a fine of one hundred pounds for having identified himself with the strike!

I had always looked forward to visiting Roto Rua, the hot-lake district, and to seeing the celebrated Green and Blue Lakes. While in the North Island I was able to devote a few days to this expedition. I saw the Maori women place food in an ordinary box, put the box in a crevice on the rocks from which was issuing the steam as generated by nature, and thus cook their food. This was the regular method of cooking in a unique kind of kitchen. The heat is fairly constant, and rarely becomes unpleasant or dangerous. The strangest thing was that hot and cold springs were gushing forth within a few yards of one another. The arrangements of Mother Nature's below-ground furnaces must be peculiar. Geysers were playing near Lake Rotomahana. Our launch was steered across a place where, with a mug provided for the purpose, one dipped and found the water cool and pleasant, though a few yards farther on the water in the same lake was warm. This was in the immediate neighbourhood of where the famous pink-and-white terraces used to be, but were destroyed by volcanic disturbances a few years before my visit. Driving through the now deserted village of Tarawera, the coach reached a considerable-sized lake, the colour of which was said to be exceptional. At first I felt it was rather a 'sell'; it seemed to me quite ordinary. But, after a few minutes' drive, we reached another lake, with the first one still in sight. Looking from one to the other, it was obvious that one was of a pronounced green, and the other an equally pronounced blue. I did not learn the scientific explanation, but I was glad to have seen the renowned 'Blue and Green' Lakes of New Zealand.

CHAPTER XVI

BROKEN HILL DISPUTE
1908 to 1909

RETURNING to Melbourne, I had resumed my usual duties in connection with the Socialist Party, when, in September 1908, I was asked by the Miners' Association of Broken Hill, New South Wales, to visit them and help them to organize their forces. The chairman of the Broken Hill Proprietary Company had announced at the end of the year wages would be reduced by 12½ per cent. Only a minority of the miners were organized. I had been entertaining the idea of a return to England, but the urgency of the appeal made me change my plans. Arrangements were made for a well-known comrade, then in Broken Hill, to come to Melbourne and to take over my work for the Socialist Party, including the weekly paper. This was R. S. Ross, who had long been an active worker in the movement, and who has continued to labour unceasingly for the cause with pen and tongue.

I arrived at Broken Hill on 30th September. The committee posted me as to the position, the percentage organized, etc. The members of ten unions were involved, viz. the Amalgamated Miners' Association, the Engine Drivers' and Firemen's Association, the Amalgamated Engineers', the Carpenters' and Joiners', the Blacksmiths', the Sailor Gang, the Masons' and Bricklayers', the Iron Moulders', the Boilermakers', and the Plumbers'. For the purposes of the campaign a Combined Trade-Union Committee was formed. It was this committee that had invited me to the Barrier, the district of which Broken Hill is the centre. 1st October was a holiday, for the annual celebration of the eight-hour day, and Members of Parliament and others were present to take part in the public demonstration. Next day I was one of the party with the parliamentary contingent to make a visit of inspection to the Proprietary Mine and elsewhere. This excursion was valuable in helping me to a full understanding of local conditions.

We opened the campaign with special meetings at union branches, to which members of other unions were invited. Stress was laid on the need for solidarity. There were also meetings for women at hours to suit their convenience, and street-corner meetings to get in touch with those sections not likely to turn up at indoor meetings. Three or four times a week mass meetings were held. A few weeks of such efforts brought about so complete a change that it soon became difficult to find any qualified person outside the unions. At this juncture I went to Port Pirie in South Australia. While there I received the following letter which indicates the effect of the campaign.

TRADES HALL, BROKEN HILL,
31 *October*, 1908
BARRIER BRANCH OF THE AMALGAMATED
MINERS' ASSOCIATION

DEAR TOM,

Yours of the 29th to hand. I am pleased to say that things are still going along swimmingly, new members coming in wholesale. I really do not think there can be many working along the Line of Lode who are not members of one union or other represented at the Combined Conference. I sincerely hope you will meet with the success at Pirie that you accomplished here. I feel sure that if they will only take the trouble to attend your meetings you will convince them that their place is inside and not outside the union ranks. Remember me to all the boys down there and also please extend fraternal greetings to all old and new members from comrades here, telling them that we expect them to be united by joining the unions of their calling. We have been exceptionally busy taking contributions today, so I know you will forgive me for making this note brief. Wishing you success, and rest assured that if anything crops up I shall advise you at once.

Yours in the cause,

W. D. BARNETT,

Secretary

There was good reason for my journey to Port Pirie. The mines at Broken Hill are known as silver mines, because there is a larger percentage of silver than of any other metal; but, in addition, the mines yield lead, gold, zinc, antimony, and copper. The chief company, known as the Broken Hill Proprietary Company, does not smelt the metal at Broken Hill, but has its furnaces at Port Pirie in South Australia. It would involve much greater expense to carry the fluxing materials inland to Broken Hill, than it does to take the crushed ore in the form of concentrates from the mines to the port of Pirie, to which place various fluxing materials are brought by sea. After the smelting and refining, the metals are shipped direct.

It is now necessary to explain briefly that while each State has an Act (known by different names) for dealing with industrial affairs, the Federal Government has also passed a measure to deal with disputes affecting workers simultaneously in more than one State. In the case of New South Wales, the State measure was known as The Industrial Disputes Act, but its powers were, of course, confined to the limits of the State. Like considerations applied to the Labour legislation of the other States. To meet the requirements when a dispute should extend beyond the boundaries of any one or more States, as in the case of the shearers, whose members work in every State, the Federal Government passed the Federal Arbitration Act, based upon the experience of all the Australian States as well as upon that of New Zealand. The workmen at Port Pirie had never been properly organized, and as the furnaces were never allowed to cool men were wanted constantly. At Port Pirie I came into contact with the men working at the smelters and refineries. Many of them worked eight-hour shifts, and seven shifts a week. Some of the labourers had exceptionally hard and heavy work; these were the men that fed the furnaces, which were twenty feet in diameter and twenty-five feet deep. The men wheeled the materials to the furnaces in what they euphemistically called 'banana carts'. These were iron carts, very heavy, and when loaded it was a considerable strain to drag such a cart along from the place of supply, either of ore, fuel, kaolin or other flux. This was loaded on the 'top floor', on a level with the tops of the furnace, into the mouth of which the cartload was tipped. This tipping process was worse than the dragging of the load, for, when the furnace was opened, out came the sulphurous fumes. Moreoever, since other men were at the same time drawing off the molten slag at the bottom of the furnace, poisonous fumes rose from this also, causing many to be affected with lead colic.

These men had not one recognized holiday all through the year, not at week-end, or year-end, no Bank Holiday, no Easter or Christmas Holiday. The strongest could not endure the work for more than a year, then becoming utterly incapacitated. All this was borne without protest. Port Pirie was represented in Parliament by a Labour Member, and neither the Labour Party, nor the local Member, nor yet the men themselves, had attempted to bring about any change for the better. The object of my visit was to organize the workers, and to get them to make common cause with the men of Broken Hill. I saw easily enough that the first thing to do was to arouse in them sufficient self-respect so that they would be ashamed of the conditions they were quietly tolerating.

I laid my plans, accordingly even though I should at first encounter hostility, for this is only to be expected from men who have long been supinely acquiescent in a low standard of life. I first called a meeting of the few trade unionists connected with the various departments, chiefly on the establishment, such as the mechanics, fitters, plumbers, carpenters, etc,, whose hours were not controlled by furnace conditions, but by the conditions agreed upon between the unions and the employers. I commented in strong terms on the seven-day week of the furnace-men. I declared I would run an organizing campaign for these men and get them enrolled, and would at the same time encourage them to put in a claim for a six-day week. This secured general approval; but the trade unionists expressed doubts as to how the labourers who were working under these conditions would receive the proposal.

However, a mass meeting of the Port Pirie men was called. I addressed them at length on the situation at Broken Hill, and on the necessity that they should organize for the improvement of their own working conditions. This part of the speech received hearty endorsement; but when I came to deal with the actual conditions under which they worked, and especially when I enlarged upon the seven-day week and the necessity to get it altered to six, enthusiasm was less marked. At the close of the meeting none were so ready to dwell on the difficulties in the way of a change as those who were toiling under these conditions. Still, after two or three weeks' continuous educational effort, as at Broken Hill, we obtained a ninety-eight per cent organization, and unanimity in the demand for a six-day week.

I must now explain that the Broken Hill men had decided to make use of the machinery of the Federal Arbitration Court, and that, therefore, the union, through lawyers, had had a case prepared for the court. It was arranged that the demands of the Port Pirie men, the chief of which was the six-day week, should be included as part of the same case.

The Federal Arbitration Act states definitely, 'This is an Act to prevent industrial disputes.' The court consists of the judge and his assistants. The first judge, who filled the office until quite recently, was one of the most genuinely respected men in Australia, Mr Justice Higgins. The miners of Broken Hill took the view that, if they cited their case early, several weeks before the end of the year (the date when the threatened reduction in wages was to come into operation), the court would find some means of preventing a stoppage of work. When the Christmas Holiday began, notices were posted stating that the pits would recommence on such a date, at the reduced wage. Right up to the actual day it was believed by many that some steps would be taken to postpone the change until (at least) the court had had time to adjudicate. However, nothing whatever was done. The company refused to let the men work unless they agreed to the reduced wage; the men refused to accept any alteration until the court had given an award. The court was overburdened with business; it was ten weeks before an award was given in favour of the men. But this did not terminate the lock-out or finish the dispute.

The union lawyer, in citing the case, had omitted to include the demand of the Port Pirie men for the six-day week. This omission was realized before the end of the year, and the solicitors attended the court, explained the situation, and asked leave to amend the case. Justice Higgins, who technically constituted the court, stated that 'as it was evidently a simple omission the court would note the fact and when the court dealt with the Broken Hill case, that of Port Pirie should be dealt with also'. When the award was given the six-day week was granted; but immediately the Companies' lawyers appealed to the High Court against the decision of the Arbitration Court, on the ground that the case of the Port Pirie men was not included in the original citation. It took another eight weeks for this to be dealt with by the High Court, and all the time the mines were closed. The High Court upheld the appeal, the Port Pirie men's claim was quashed.

This experience of the admittedly most perfect Arbitration Court in existence, with a Labour Government in power, damped any enthusiasm I might have felt for such an institution!

Wigs were on the green long before matters reached the stage just recorded, and in order to show how similar capitalist rule is in new and old countries, I will relate now some of the events of the dispute. Incidentally, I shall prove that groups of organized workers, well-disposed towards the miners, really helped to defeat these because their forces were dispersed in different unions.

To reach Broken Hill by rail from Sydney, it was necessary to travel through Victoria and South Australian territory. The authorities sent large numbers of mounted police from Sydney, a journey of over thirteen hundred miles; the distances roughly being, from Sydney to Melbourne, 500 miles, Melbourne to Adelaide, 500 miles, Adelaide to Broken Hill, 333 miles. Broken Hill was a town of 35,000 inhabitants, with a police force proportionate.

Seeing that the mines were closed from the beginning of the year 1909, except on the employers' terms, work in Broken Hill was at a standstill.

The Combined Committee of the unions, now acting as a Disputes' Committee, did its utmost to ensure that the requirements of the community were met. The Co-operative Stores were efficiently conducted. A considerable bakery business was taken over by the committee, and run co-operatively for the general bread supply. Numerous meetings were held. An elaborate system of picketing was inaugurated. After the mass meetings, which were held on open ground adjacent to the Trades Hall, the entire audience would fall into marching order, and, led by a band and the union officials, would pass through a portion of the town and along a thoroughfare near the 'dumps', or 'pit-heaps', being careful not to trespass on the company's property. No unseemly behaviour was indulged in. The Chief of Police reported that the only notable change was a marked diminution in the number of 'drunk' cases, compared with normal times. On Saturday morning, 9th

January, an additional body of police, foot and mounted, reached Broken Hill from Sydney. The mounted men, like their predecessors, were armed with carbines and revolvers. The new arrivals were on duty the same afternoon, and the miners, having held their usual meeting, which I had addressed, proceeded to march as was their custom. I was at the head, in advance of the band. Everything was orderly, and the line of route was the same we had traversed many times before. As the procession approached the thoroughfare on the far side of which was the company's property, we found the way blocked by a body of police. They made a dash for the union banner, tore it off the poles and used the latter on the heads of the men, including the bandsmen. For ten minutes there was as lively a time as I had ever experienced, and I was in the middle of it. At the end of the fray, I was marched off to the police station, together with twenty of my comrades. We were all bunged into one large cell. These events took place on the Saturday afternoon, and we remained in the lock-up till Monday, when most of us were bailed out. The Mayor, Alderman Ivey, became bondsman for me. During the day we had the biggest demonstration ever known in the district. The unjustifiable attack by the police put the necessary ginger into the movement. Although the weather was very hot, this was not altogether a disadvantage, and meetings, concerts, and sports, were kept going in great style. Police court proceedings commenced on 18th January, and on the 25th I was committed for trial to the Quarter Sessions. Then came the question of bail. The Assizes were not due till April, nearly three months ahead. Bail was refused unless I would give an undertaking not to hold any meetings or take part in the dispute at Broken Hill. Consultation with the committee resulted in a decision to give the undertaking, it being arranged that I should go on a lecturing tour in South Australia and other States.

Film pictures had been secured of scenes in connection with the trouble and I went on tour. In spite of the prohibition it was possible for citizens of New South Wales to attend some of my meetings. The town of Cockburn is the border town of South Australia and New South Wales, being less than forty miles from Broken Hill. The committee arranged for special trains, and contracted with the Silvertown Tramway (really Railway) Company so that four thousand people from the Broken Hill district did the journey. On the front of the engine was fixed a banner bearing the inscription in bold letters: 'Tom Mann Train'. At the boundary there is only a barbed-wire fence. With a few minutes' walk on to the South Australian side, we were beyond the jurisdiction of the New South Wales' authorities and had magnificent demonstrations.

With film equipment, I visited all the bigger towns in South Australia and many of those in Victoria, raising funds for Broken Hill and doing propagandist work. This was a most interesting and successful tour.

In April I was informed that the Attorney-General of New South Wales had decided to change the venue of the Sessions, and, therefore, of my trial. Instead of the Sessions, being held as had originally been intended, at Broken Hill, they were now to take place at Albury, a district of large landowners and farmers, more than one thousand miles away. The hope evidently was to secure an unsympathetic jury. Intense excitement prevailed. I was charged on several counts, including sedition and unlawful assembly. My case lasted eight days and the result was acquittal. Ten minutes afterwards I was on the balcony of a hotel addressing an enormous audience which showed the keenest sympathy and liveliest enthusiasm. So the removal to Albury was, after all, void of effect, as far as I was concerned.

Henry Holland, at that time a Labour journalist, now member of Parliament in New Zealand, was sentenced to two years at the same assizes for a speech delivered at Broken Hill. He was released after serving six months. Considerable uneasiness prevailed at Broken Hill for some weeks after the trial.

At length matters settled down and I resumed my work in Melbourne. But before the year was out, I had turned my eyes towards the Old World once more. At this juncture the miners of Johannesburg, South Africa, who had learned I might be returning to Europe, invited me to visit the Transvaal and help them in the matter of organization. Up to this time I had not decided whether to travel via the Cape or the Suez Canal. The request from the Transvaal settled it. I decided to accept the invitation, and proceeded with arrangements accordingly.

During the latter part of 1909, I devoted special attention to industrial unionism. As a result of the Broken Hill experiences, I realized more clearly the need for perfecting industrial organization. It was plain to me that economic organization was indispensable for the achievement of economic freedom. The policy of the various Labour Parties gave no promise in this direction, nor did the superadding of political activies to the extant type of trade-union organization seem any more hopeful. I therefore wrote a pamphlet called *The Way to Win*, wherein I urged the desirability of more complete industrial organization, contending that reliance upon parliamentary action would never bring freedom. I pointed out that the armed police and other henchmen of the companies were transported from Sydney to Broken Hill by the instrumentality of the organized railwaymen of New South Wales. At Albury, the police, etc., were handed over to the care of the organized railwaymen of the State of Victoria. These latter took them to the boundary of the next State, when again the forces hostile to the working class, were handed over to the organized railwaymen of South Australia. These railwaymen were practically all union men, who nevertheless lent themselves to the fighting of the battles of the master class against the working class! Yet they were in full sympathy with the Broken Hill men, and were actually subscribing funds to help the miners in the fight. In their daily labour, however, they not only frustrated all they had done by friendly letters and subscriptions, but took charge of, fed, and carried the persons, ammunition, horses, etc., etc., to the scene of action, thus enabling the master class to have at its disposal the machinery of the State and the services of the organized workmen to beat the miners.

I kept in close touch with the men of Port Pirie, and a singular coincidence occurred just at this time. I received from James Connolly (later shot by the British Government for his activities in founding the Irish Republic), who was then in the United States, some copies of his pamphlets *Socialism Made Easy* and *The Axe to the Root*. His views were identical with those I had expressed in my own pamphlet. I had met Connolly in Edinburgh and in Dublin, and was greatly interested to find that he presented the industrial side of the position in the unmistakable and clear fashion he did.

It will help to show the strong trend towards industrial action of a different character from that formerly prevailing if I reprint the leaflet I issued in July, 1909, soon after the Broken Hill and Port Pirie dispute. Although this is now some thirteen years old, it will refresh the memory of my Australian readers and help to link up events and policies.

INDUSTRIAL UNIONISM

CONFERENCE IN ADELAIDE

TRADE UNIONISTS – READ THIS!

The industrial struggle at Port Pirie brought together the representatives of the different unions in a Combined Committee, and the requests made by this Combined Committee to other unions throughout the State for co-operation in various ways brought vividly before them the serious limitations of the existing 'trade' or 'craft' unionist movement, and it was demonstrated beyond question that working-class solidarity does not yet exist even amongst the organized workers. As a result the Secretary of the Combined Committee (Mr Frank Price) sent a circular to the various union secretaries in South Australia, in which he said: 'My Committee have come to a definite and unanimous conclusion that craft unionism has outlived its usefulness, and that twentieth-century industrial development demands on the part of the workers a more perfect system of organization. With this end in view we urge, as a preliminary step, the holding of a Trades' Union Congress in Adelaide during the month of July next.' The replies to this circular were very encouraging. About twenty unions responded, nearly all of which have appointed delegates to attend the Conference, which is to take place in the Trades Hall, Adelaide, on Tuesday, 27th July.

Some who responded asked for more specific information as to the object of the proposed conference. Partly to supply such information, I wrote a pamphlet on industrial unionism, *The Way to Win*. This sets forth the principles of industrial unionism, and suggests some steps the forthcoming conference might advantageously take, including the following: This conference declares 'that the present system of sectional trades unionism is incapable of combating effectively the capitalist system under which the civilized world is now suffering, and such modifications and alterations should be made in the existing unions as will admit of a genuine federation of

Broken Hill Dispute

all organizations, with power to act unitedly for industrial purposes'. Many other proposals are made in the pamphlet and the reasons given why such a course is vitally necessary. The pamphlet [one penny] can be had from Mr Frank Price, International Hall, Port Pirie, or wholesale from the publishers, Barrier Truth, Broken Hill.

It is barely two months since the pamphlet was published, and, a week later a larger and better pamphlet on the same subject arrived from America. It is called *Socialism made Easy, the Industrial and Political Unity of Labour*. It is from the pen of James Connolly, editor of *The Harp*, published by Kerr & Co., of Chicago, USA. It is an excellent pamphlet of 60 pages. Price 10 cents.

As showing how general this subject is, still another pamphlet came to hand the following week, this time from England. It is called *Revolutionary Socialism*, by E. J. B. Allen, The Industrial League, 25, Queensdale Road, Notting Hill, London, W. Price 1d. Notwithstanding the title, the subject of the pamphlet is *Industrial Unionism*, on the lines sketched in *The Way to Win*. It is known to all who watch European developments that the French and Italian unionists are strong advocates of direct action, and this is spreading rapidly through the various countries.

Already in Australia considerable activity is being shown in favour of this broader and better unionism than the sectional societies admit of, and it is urgently necessary that the first conference should be clear-minded as to the course to be pursued. To those who are going as delegates, it should be said, that unless a clear pronouncement is made that 'craft' unionism fails to meet the necessity of the times, and that such changes shall be made as will make true solidarity possible, then the conference will be abortive, and this would be lamentable. The time is ripe for launching the movement now, and South Australia has the honour of taking the initiative.

Amongst the unions sending delegates to the Conference at Adelaide are the SA Government General Workers' Association; the Commonwealth Public Service Electric Telegraph and Telephone Construction Branch Union; Federated Iron, Brass, and Steel Moulders' Union of Australia, Port Pirie Branch; Australian Boot Trade Federation, Adelaide Branch; General Division Association of SA, Federal Public Service; Adelaide Hairdressers' Employees; Cast Iron Pipe Makers' and Iron Workers' Assistants; the Typographical

Society; Moonta Mines Trades and Labour Association; the Journeymen Plasterers; Glass Bottle Blowers; Bookbinders and Paper Rulers; Wallaroo Mines Workers' Association; South Australian United Labourers; Brickyard Employees' Association; Tobacco Twisters; Third Class Marine Engineers; Australian Workers' Union; Timber Yard and Wood Workers; the Amalgamated Carpenters and Joiners; Drivers' Association of SA; the AMA Port Pirie, and the Engine Drivers' and Firemen. Thus it will be seen that interest is keen and the outlook very promising

Comrade Will Rosser, late of the Barrier, who worked so well in connection with the recent dispute, is now at Cobar, NSW, busy advocating Industrial Unionism. It may be that when the Conference is held a proper method of collecting and disseminating information relative to the movement will be decided upon. Meanwhile, I shall be pleased to receive and tabulate items of information if helpers in the work will communicate with me as follows.

PARK STREET, TOM MANN
SOUTH YARRA, MELBOURNE.
7 *July*, 1909.

In Melbourne likewise I gave attention to the welding together of the sectional trade unions, and to the need for direct action. I lectured on the development of affairs in France, and enlarged upon the growth of Syndicalism in that country, in Italy, and in Spain. It was clear that in the main essentials the Industrial Workers of the World, launched not long before in the United States, was a movement of the same character. Whether parliamentary action was to be dropped or not, increasing importance would evidently attach to industrial organization. The capitalist State would not in future be able to command the sycophantic backing it had hitherto received.

CHAPTER XVII

SOUTH AFRICA
February to May, 1910

HAVING left Melbourne during Christmas week, 1909, and having spent a few weeks in Adelaide and Perth, we set out for South Africa, and reached Durban on 21 February, 1910. I proceeded to Johannesburg and was well received by the trade unionists of that city. As soon as I got the hang of affairs I commenced an organizing campaign. As far as the white workers were concerned, conditions were analogous to those I had already become familiar with in other places. The miners had about one-third of their number organized. The engine-drivers at the mines were better organized numerically, but were clannish and sectional. Conditions in the deeper mines were very unwholesome, the average life of a white miner being less than seven years. Young men were often carried off by miners' phthisis in less than three years. The then miners' secretary, Tom Mathews, a Cornishman, was an exceptionally well-informed man and an ardent worker on behalf of the members of his union. He was fully primed with information on the subjects that directly affected the miners' welfare. He supplied me with many facts and statistics, particularly in relation to phthisis, and the miners' executive requested me to diffuse a knowledge of these details in the interests of the men. My advocacy attracted the attention of the Government, and the Minister of Mines dealt with the subject in Parliament. Referring to my statement about the white miner's life being less than seven years on the Rand, and that the risks could be minimized if proper attention were paid to ventilation, he said: 'This is a gross exaggeration.'

The charge was, however, pressed home over a period of months, and ultimately a parliamentary commission was appointed to investigate and report upon the subject. The evidence showed that the average duration of life of the white miner on the Witwatersrand was only five years. Improvements in ventilation were made in some of the mines; more attention was given to medical inspection, and to compensation for those declared unfit to remain in the mines. There were large accessions of membership to the miners' and other unions. Before long, an Industrial Federation was formed. Nevertheless, in South Africa as elsewhere, every attempt at an advance of the workers was met by a capitalist counter-offensive.

There was a small group of active Socialists at Johannesburg, carrying on propaganda work by meetings and literature; there was also a parliamentary Labour Party beginning to take shape. My own efforts took the form of urging the need for economic organization, and an amalgamation of the unions on the basis of industrial unionism.

I was amazed to find how unconcernedly natives and even whites were buried. The Bramfontein Cemetery was the principal one then in use in Johannesburg, and the man in charge was a most interesting character, a member of the engineers' union, an ex-Leeds man. Under his guidance I was shown some items of interest. He asked:

'Would you care to see the graves we keep in readiness?'

Not being quite clear as to what he meant I said:

'Certainly I should. But what do you mean by "graves in readiness"?'

By this time we were near several rows of graves numbering some twenty-five or thirty. My friend informed me:

'We have to keep a lot like this always in readiness in case there is need for them. In this hot climate bodies can't be kept for many hours, and often there are accidents, when a dozen, twenty or more graves may be required at a few hours notice.'

'Do you bury the natives with the whites?'

'Not in this part – come and see.'

A few minutes' walk and we reached another lot of graves, as many as we had already seen, but here the graves were much larger. My companion said:

'These are for the natives, but natives are not put in coffins. A black blanket or rug is thrown over each body, and five of them are buried in one grave, hence the difference in size. There is no service or ceremony of any kind; the bodies are dropped in, the graves filled up, and the Kaffir's number is stuck on the grave. There is no name or other means of identification.'

Four years later I revisited Johannesburg, and was taken by one of the Labour Councillors to see the graves of those who had been shot during the Labour troubles in 1914, when the Government deported nine of the most active workers to Britain (Bain, Crawford, Livingstone, McKerrell, Mason, Morgan, Watson, Poutsma, and Waterston). I had been sent to South Africa to try and carry on the work of organization in the absence of the deportees. I visited the Brixton Cemetery, for by this time the Bramfontein Cemetery was full. I found at the new cemetery the same conditions that had obtained at the old. There were rows of graves in readiness for whites according to the faith in which they died, and similar rows in another part of the cemetery for the Kaffirs and other coloured folk. The natives were still being dumped in, five to a grave.

In 1910, the railway workers were poorly organized, though a good start had been made; but they had exceptional difficulties, for, in addition to the usual sectionalism of the trades or occupations, there was the racial difficulty. The whites, the Kaffirs, and other coloured people had divergent standards of life, and this added largely to the difficulties of effective organization.

I visited the diamond mine known as the Premier Mine, at Cullinan, near Pretoria. It has no shafts, being a large open cut, oval in shape, and over a half mile wide. Diamonds are found in almost circular areas, like large natural pipes in the earth. I also visited the Kimberley diamond fields and had some excellent meetings there. At each of these centres I found a group of Socialists who were keeping in touch with Europe, by literature, when not by correspondence. Everywhere my gospel was in favour of a complete change of society, and of a perfected system of industrial organization to make this possible.

My last meetings on this South African visit were at Cape Town, from which port we sailed for London on 13th April. After a very pleasant and uneventful voyage, we reached London on 10 May, 1910, having been away eight and a half years. I lost no time in getting to grips with the industrial and social conditions, and my mind was clear as to the line of policy I intended to pursue.

Home Again

CHAPTER XVIII

INDUSTRIAL SOLIDARITY
1910 and 1911

FOR some years considerable efforts had been made in this country to bring about a closer relationship between the various unions, and the French trade unions with their methods of direct action were arousing sympathetic interest. I declared myself definitely in favour of industrial unionism and direct action, not to the exclusion of other methods, but as the main channel for the outflow of our activities.

More especially did I admire the French movement because I knew it to have been the main stimulus that led the Americans, in 1905, to hold the convention which culiminated in the foundation of the Industrial Workers of the World. At that time, a well-known and active Socialist in London, Guy Bowman, translator of Gustave Hervé's book *My Country, Right or Wrong*, proposed that we should go to Paris and visit the CGT (Confédération Générale du Travail) to study its methods of procedure. My old friend Charles Marck, whom I had long known in connection with the seamen's and dockers' movement, was an executive official of the CGT in Paris, so the way was open. To Paris we went, and examined thoroughly the principles and policy of the CGT, the Syndicalists of France.

The term Syndicalism has often been used in this country to frighten the timid and to scare the simple. A brief explanation of the Syndicalist doctrine, and some account of the movement, will therefore be in place here.

Every person who hears that a syndicate has been formed is apt to conclude that it is a group of persons who unite to run some business or other. They think of a 'syndicate' as equivalent to a 'company', and this is in the main correct. *Syndicat* is the French name for an organization of persons to achieve a specific end. When French workers organize themselves into what we in Britain designate a trade union, the French call it a *syndicat*, and the persons who join a union are known as syndicalists, the exact counterpart of trade unionists. Just as in our trade-union movement we have members of every variety and every shade of opinion – industrial, political, and social – and yet, being trade unionists, they are all called by that term; so in France they have every variety of reactionary, moderate, and revolutionary in the syndicalist membership, and the term 'syndicalist' is applied to all alike, seeing that originally it meant nothing more than 'organized worker'. In course of time, however, the word has acquired an additional signification.

About forty years ago the Municipal Council of Paris decided to erect a large hall for the unemployed, and in connection with it a number of offices for the trade-unions. This was the outcome of a demand from a considerable percentage of the electorate of Paris, which had returned Socialists to the Municipal Council, demanding in their programme a Bourse du Travail, or Office of Labour. The hall was to serve as a rendezvous for the unemployed. An official was appointed and paid by the municipality. The main building served as a Labour Exchange; the offices attached were let, for a comparatively low rental, as trade-union headquarters.

This arrangement worked well until some of the unions were engaged in disputes, when the police invaded the union offices at the Bourse du Travail, claiming the right to inspect the books. The municipal authorities supported this claim, and insisted that the police were entitled, in addition, to investigate, at any time, the financial position of the various unions whose headquarters were at the Bourse du Travail. Several of the union executives refused to let the police see the books, and were thereupon informed that unless they gave up the books to the police they would be expelled from the offices, which were the property of the municipality of Paris. The unions persisted in their refusal, and cleared out of the Bourse, joining forces to secure premises elsewhere, at 33, Rue Grange aux Belles.

All along there had been a considerable number of anarchists in the trade unions who were opposed to any kow-towing to the authorities. They were energetic and effective trade unionists. With further experience of the police claim to investigate, and of the use the police made of the information thus obtained, additional unions left the Bourse and joined the original seceders. They now formed themselves into the CGT (General Confederation of Labour). These unions showed increasing dislike for Government – national and municipal alike. They declared themselves antiparliamentarian, and were confident of their ability to achieve the economic emancipation of the workers through industrial organization independently of the machinery of State.

When occasions came round for popular demonstrations, such as the visit to the cemetery of Père Lachaise, in memory of the massacre of the communards in 1871, the Syndicalists, i.e. the trade unionists, of Grange aux Belles would organize their own demonstration, whilst those still working harmoniously at the Bourse and recognizing the authorities, would take steps to organize a demonstration also. Before the date fixed for the celebration arrived, the Prefect of Police would send an intimation that no demonstrations would be allowed; the law-and-order men of the Bourse du Travail would drop the idea, but the CGT men would ignore the Prefect of Police and his (as they said) attempt at dictatorship. They persisted in holding their demonstration. Before it was over the police would interfere and a forcible dispersion would take place with a few lively incidents on either side. The Paris correspondents of the English papers, alert for copy, would inquire who were in collision with the police. Being told that the demonstrators were 'Syndicalists', these journalists referred to this section alone as Syndicalists, unaware that all trade unionists, whatever their views and whatever their activities, were Syndicalists. The result has been that, in the British press the term has been almost exclusively applied to the revolutionary trade-unionist section of the French workers, and this is how the word has become a bogey to frighten the uninformed.

After our visit to Paris, Guy Bowman and I, with the support of a few representative trade unionists, decided to organize in Britain on lines similar to those which had been adopted by the French comrades. We were far from proposing to ignore, belittle, or supersede the extant trade-union movement. We were convinced that the members of the unions could make these organizations what they desired them to be, for the unions are working-class organizations which can be modified and improved as the workers themselves desire. We published a small monthly called *The Industrial Syndicalist*. The first issue appeared in July 1910. In view of what took place a year later, I will give a few excerpts. In July 1910 I wrote, stating the Syndicalist case on broad general lines, but aiming also at precision:

> What is called for? What will have to be the essential conditions for the success of such a movement?
> *That it should be avowedly and clearly revolutionary in aim and method.*
> Revolutionary in aim because it will be out for the abolition of the wages system, and for securing to the workers the full fruits of their labour, thereby seeking to change the system of society from Capitalist to Socialist.
> Revolutionary in method, because it will refuse to enter into any long agreements with the masters, whether with legal or State backing, or merely voluntarily; and because it will seize every chance of fighting for the general betterment – gaining ground and never losing any.
> Does this mean that we should become anti-political? Certainly not.
> Let the politicians do as much as they can, and the chances are that, once there is an economic fighting force in the country ready to back them up by action, they will actually be able to do what would now be hopeless for them to attempt to do.
> The workers should realize that it is the men who manipulate the tools and machinery who are the possessors of the necessary power to achieve something tangible, and they will succeed just in proportion as they agree to apply concerted action.
> The curse of capitalism consists in this – that a handful of capitalists can compel hundreds of thousands of workers to work in such manner and for such wage as will please the capitalists. But this again is solely because of the inability of the workers to agree upon a common plan of action. The hour the workers agree and act, they become all-powerful. We can settle the capitalists' strike-breaking power once for all. We shall have no need to plead with parliamentarians to be good enough to reduce hours as the workers have been doing for fully twenty years without result. We shall be able to do this ourselves, and there will be no power on earth to stop us so long as we do not fall foul of economic principles.

Having been invited to attend an executive meeting of the Dockers' Union by the general secretary, my old colleague, Ben Tillett, I submitted a proposal urging that invitations be sent to the various Transport Workers' Unions with a view to forming a 'National Transport Workers' Federation'. This was done, and a conference, held in London, achieved the object.

In November 1910 an Industrial Syndicalist Conference was held at Manchester. Albert A. Purcell, of the Furnishing Trades Association, presided. Here, an Industrial Syndicalist Educational League was formed, and under its auspices much propaganda work was done. I was continuously on platform work, covering the whole country. I spoke under the auspices of any union, but always advocated the same industrial policy. This went on till the spring of 1911.

Havelock Wilson, of the National Sailors' and Firemen's Union, whom I had known as a colleague from the time of the London dock strike of 1889, had been in the United States during 1910, in part to organize British seamen on the other side of the Atlantic – for in normal times they are easier to get in touch with there than on this side where their homes are. Wilson, and the union of which he was president, had been subjected to many and severe buffetings by the International Shipping Federation. The membership of the union had fallen off seriously, and the shipowners, over a period of many years, with the aid of clever lawyers, did their utmost to make Havelock Wilson a bankrupt. In the whole history of the trade-union movement of Britain, there is no case of such persistent, systematic, and venomous persecution of a union official as that to which Havelock Wilson was subjected by the shipowners of this country.

In ultimate ideals and objective, Havelock Wilson and I have nothing in common, but I have had occasion to work in close relationship with him in trade-union affairs, and we have been colleagues in many industrial disputes. I have always found him a straightforward, honourable, and loyal comrade. Moreover, he was always at his post early in the day, tackling the most difficult tasks with the utmost readiness. I take the opportunity of saying this because there is considerable feeling against Wilson for certain of his activities. I like to dwell upon other phases, and especially upon what happened in 1911, in the industrial arena of Britain, and particularly in connection with the transport industry. Whereas I always aimed at a fight for the complete economic emancipation of the working class, my friend Wilson was not concerned about complete economic freedom, nor did he appreciate the gospel of internationalism for the overthrow of the capitalist system; but I knew well that he had waited long in the hope of a favourable opportunity to reorganize the union.

The shipowners, through the International Shipping Federation, not only gave their officers instructions to refuse to employ any seaman who was a member of the National Sailors' and Firemen's Union, but they actually made it a condition of employment that the men should become members of the organization that they, the shipowners, brought into existence, that the men must pay for and carry the card of membership of the bosses' organization. The conditions under which the medical examination of the men took place after signing on for a voyage, in many firms (not all), was such as to sicken any decent person, and make a man justifiably indignant at the humiliating and disgusting methods. But, having power, the shipowners and the medical staff, used the power ruthlessly.

I had faith in Wilson's ability to seize the opportune time for vigorous action, knowing that he was in deadly earnest and above all things anxious to make no mistake when the right time came. I was informed of conferences held quietly in the chief ports. Wilson told me he was convinced that the summer of 1911 would be the time for the rebuilding of the union and for the putting forward of the men's claims.

I readily agreed to identify myself with the intended effort, for I shared Wilson's hopes and beliefs, though all the time eager for a broader and bigger outlook to prevail. The great movement among the seamen that took place in Britain during the months of June, July, and August 1911, is a matter of history.

A severe struggle had been waged in South Wales between twelve thousand miners and the Cambrian Combine. General interest had been aroused, and in the ports solidarity with the miners had been earnestly advocated. Some union officials, however, positively refused to participate in the effort which they regarded as untimely. In some cases they went further and tried to stultify the movement. In May it became evident that the time for action was at hand. We decided to approach the shipowners through the Shipping Federation once more requesting them to meet us in conference and endeavour to adjust matters. The reply from the chief official of the federation was of that haughty type characteristic of dominant Capitalism. This left us no alternative but drastic action. The Sailors' and Firemen's Union therefore had another conference, and decided to call a strike for the middle of June.

The SS *Olympic*, the largest ocean liner ever built up to that date, had just reached Southampton from the builders at Belfast. She required coaling for the voyage to New York, whence she was to bring back the American millionaires who were to take part in the coronation celebrations. However, the coalies had decided to commence operations for improved conditions. The big ship was held up, and on 14th June the strike was declared in all the chief ports of Britain. The men responded splendidly. On the morning of the 14th the newspapers were pouring scorn and contempt upon those who were connected with the union movement, but they were soon to learn that that strike was something out of the ordinary. The experience was unique in industrial battles. Shipowners who had absolutely refused to have anything to do with the workmen, now earnestly endeavoured to arrange for a conference. The Shipping Federation proved utterly incapable of helping its clients, and, after having dictated conditions for over twenty years, it had in a single day lost all its power. The workmen simply folded their arms, saying that they were quite willing to return to work when their demands were granted, not before. The shipowners begged of union officials to 'instruct the men to take out the mail boats and others', on the assurance that they would meet in conference without delay, and discuss all points desired. But it was too late for such a proposal; the situation had now reached a stage when discussion was out of the question. Nothing but the granting of the men's demands would end the dispute. These consisted of claims for increased pay, alteration of the conditions under which medical examination was to take place, the right of the men to belong to any union they pleased, and to wear the union badge when and where they liked, the Shipping Federation ticket to entirely disappear, the presence of a union delegate on each vessel at 'paying off' and 'signing on' of crews, etc. To the surprise of everybody, all these demands were complied with in a few days.

The fighting spirit had seized other sections of union and non-union men. After the terrible inaction that had lasted for over twenty years, since the dock strike in 1889, dockers and carmen in all ports demanded improved conditions. A spirit of solidarity was shown by those sections that had already obtained better conditions, the men refusing to return to work until the demands of the others were conceded.

It had not been the intention of any of those having special responsibility to include the railwaymen in the struggle; but before the rest of transport workers had achieved their aims, many of the railwaymen had determined upon action on their own account. This was especially the case in Liverpool, where a number of union and non-union railway carters took the initiative. In a few days, thousands of other railway employees, more particularly the lowest paid, joined hands with them. The men waited on the Strike Committee, and asked that their case be taken up; this was done in spite of the fact that the executives of the railwaymen's unions were opposed to any railway men leaving work and making demands, the officials arguing that they were tied down by the decisions of the Conciliation Boards, which they had accepted under the Lloyd George arrangement. The ASRS officials were confident that there would be no concerted action by railwaymen; they were sure that the companies would be able to crush any attempt made at so inopportune a moment; and so on.

In face of all this, the Strike Committee took upon itself the responsibility, grave as it was, of undertaking the railwaymen's case. The shipowners promptly declared that unless the dockers and others returned to work, terrible consequences would follow. They called a joint meeting of union officials and shipowners. The chairman of the White Star Line, who presided at this meeting, read a prepared statement detailing the situation, sermonizing the union delegates and officials, and warning them of the wrath to come. The worthy gentleman looked more like a parson reading a sermon and addressing a homily to those about to be executed than the 'captain of industry' he believed himself to be. The chairman of the White Star Line was thanked for his inspiring address, and the delegates withdrew.

Now came the results of plucky action. The railwaymen's officials, seeing the determined spirit of the men and the strong backing that these were receiving, immediately called their respective executives to meet in Liverpool and decide upon a policy in view of the exceptional situation.

The executives met and unanimously agreed to back the men. Here, indeed, was a departure; those who had hitherto preached of 'law and order' now unanimously endorsed the rebels' stand, and dispatched their secretaries to London to see whether the way was open for negotiation with the heads of the companies.

The reply being satisfactory, the executives proceeded to London, and for some thirty hours maintained a sturdy attitude, and insisted on negotiating direct with the company officials.

At this stage prominent politicians began to exert an influence, with the result that the Government immediately placed at the disposal of the companies an unlimited number of military, not only to guard property, but actually to 'try' and replace men on strike. Some two hundred and fifty thousand of the railwaymen had responded to the appeal of the executives to come out, and there are good reasons for believing that another two hundred thousand would have been out in a couple of days if the strike had been allowed to take its normal course.

The 'statesmen' and the Labour Party politicians got to work, and the Government sent down to Liverpool two MPs and a Board of Trade official, which combination they termed an 'Inquiry Committee'. This Committee never came into contact with the Strike Committee, but saw persons of their own political bias, and kept up communication with the Board of Trade.

It must be remembered that the Liverpool Committee had obtained improved conditions for some seventy thousand seafaring men, dockers, carters, warehousemen, and others, and that these were making common cause with the railway workers; therefore, the shipowners had again declared war. While negotiations were going on, the Strike Committee had found it necessary to call out the tramwaymen to help in the fight of the railwaymen.

To the credit of the railwaymen's executives, when in Liverpool, they declared they would not accept any terms of settlement that did not include the reinstatement in Liverpool of all the men who had been and were still out on their behalf. This resolution was again carried by the joint executives in London, and Mr Williams, of the ASRS, acting as secretary of the joint executives, wired the decision to the chairman of the Strike Committee at Liverpool, and confirmed the same by type-written letter. Without any further communication from them, the Strike Committee only learned of the settlement on the Sunday morning in the same way as the general public, and this though no change had taken place in the situation at Liverpool, where the hostility between the shipowners and others was more intense than ever.

This gave us special trouble in Liverpool. However, it was overcome, and we were all glad that the railwaymen had shown such splendid solidarity. If only they had attended to their own affairs on industrial lines, instead of bringing in the politicians, there is no doubt that their gains would have been far more substantial.

As it was, the Government, and the plutocracy generally, saw that there was a power in the hands of the workers they had never dreamed of.

Solidarity had truly worked wonders, and many of the capitalists thought that already the Social Revolution was upon them.

When the London transport workers demonstrated their ability to decide for themselves and to control the situation, and this in conjunction with the three hundred thousand transport workers of the country; and when unanimity was shown amongst all in Glasgow and the Scottish ports, Dublin and the Irish ports generally, the Bristol Channel, and the North-East Coast – the eyes of the hitherto-blind were opened as to the possibilities of industrial solidarity.

Never in my experience did so many workers in such varied occupations show such thorough solidarity as on the occasion in Liverpool. I was chairman of the Strike Committee for the seventy-two days that the strike lasted, with the exception of three days when I had a hurried run to Paris, which I will refer to later. Further, the seven thousand carters of Liverpool have very close relationship with the North of Ireland, and the much larger number of dockers in Liverpool are correspondingly identified with the South. The differences that arise between these are frequently of a very emphatic character, but I have pleasure in recalling that when we commenced the strike and began committee work, it was definitely agreed that neither political nor theological opinions were to find advocacy or expression on the committee. We were engaged purely on an industrial subject, and that alone should receive attention.

Not only was this undertaking strictly carried out, but no vote was taken until the very end of the proceedings. When a proposal was made, this was dealt with, modified, enlarged, or rejected, without the usual rigmarole of what is called parliamentary procedure. By this means we avoided all those risks of getting a few more votes for one proposition than for another, with the consequent recriminations that so often ensue. Finally, when all our demands had been conceded, we decided to close the strike. The thirty-three members of the committee were present and the decision was unanimous. This was on 24th August. The strike had begun on 14th June.

We had carried it through with the sailors and firemen, cooks and stewards, dockers and carters, and all other sections, until the railwaymen also came in, much against the advice and instruction and in spite of the threats of the officials of the Amalgamated Society of Railway Servants. As the outcome of the success achieved through joint action, the Amalagamated Society of Railway Servants, the General Railway Workers' Union, and the Signalmen and Pointsmen's Society amalgamated into the one organization very shortly after the Liverpool strike, the new body subsequently adopting the name of National Union of Railwaymen.

CHAPTER XIX

POLICE BRUTALITY
1911

IN opening this chapter I propose to give some account of the disturbance in the minds of the capitalists aroused by the events narrated in the previous chapter. For this we must go back a little.

Before the final stage of the struggle was reached in Liverpool, and when there was no serious reason to expect disorder, soldiers were drafted into the city in large numbers and were encamped in the parks. Furthermore, two gun-boats were sent up the Mersey and anchored in mid-stream opposite Birkenhead, with the guns trained on Liverpool.

This last proceeding was particularly senseless, for, had the guns been fired, great damage would have been done to capitalist property. It seemed to cause much annoyance to the authorities that so effective a struggle was being carried on without anything in the way of rioting or tumult, and they therefore decided to brew trouble themselves.

We had recently started a weekly paper called *The Transport Worker*. In the issue of 8th August, the Strike Committee announced a mass meeting to be held on St George's Plateau the following Sunday, 13th August, at 3 p.m. We also stated that cinematograph pictures would be taken of the procession of the trade-union branches with their banners, etc.

The weather had been charming for weeks on end. On Saturday, 12th August, an order was given by the authorities to a wood-working firm in Birkenhead for some hundreds of stout staves for policemen. These were to be of unusual length. On behalf of the Strike Committee, I myself and a colleague interviewed the Liverpool Superintendent of Police, saying that we were quite able to keep our men in hand and that we should have no difficulty in controlling the demonstration on Sunday. We urged him to leave matters to us, and not parade the police force. He heartily agreed, and said he would issue instructions accordingly.

Sunday, 13th August, was a glorious day, and the Liverpool men turned out to participate in the demonstration. Many thousands marched in the lengthy procession, with bands and banners, and made their way to the Plateau in front of St George's Hall. The following report from *The Transport Worker* gives the details, and there are many thousands in Liverpool and district who will perhaps be interested in having their memories refreshed of the tragic events of that Sunday.

As evidence that a formal request had been made for the use of the Plateau on the occasion, and that the same was granted, the following letter may first be quoted:

9 *August*, 1911

DEAR SIR,

Re PLATEAU, ST GEORGE'S HALL

I beg to inform you that your application for the use of the Plateau in front of the above building on the afternoon of the 13th August, has been granted for the purpose of a meeting in connection with the Liverpool District Council, and the National Transport Workers' Federation, subject to satisfactory arrangements being made with the Head Constable, and to your being responsible for any damages which may be done to the property of the Corporation.

Yours truly,

THOMAS SHELMERDINE,
Corporation Surveyor

The report in *The Transport Worker* runs as follows:

In order to do our best for the success of the meeting, the considerations of a peaceful assembly were uppermost in the minds of us all, and to this end the closing sentence in the official route read as follows: 'The Processionists must walk four deep and keep to the left hand side of the roadway giving way to the other traffic as directed by the police authorities'.

The resolution to be submitted to the meeting from the four platforms was, as follows:

'That this meeting heartily congratulates the transport workers of Liverpool and other ports on the successes achieved by the recent effort for improvement of the conditions, and now urges upon all workers to organize industrially, and all unions to unite for solidarity locally, nationally, and internationally, as to the means whereby industrial and social changes can be made, until all workers shall receive the full reward of their labours'.

As duly announced, the carters and dockers played a very prominent part in the procession.

Starting from the branch office, Derby Road, at 2 p.m., the north-end carters, under Mr W. H. Jones, marched to meet their comrades, the north-end dockers, at Bankhall, in charge of Mr G. Milligan. The procession, then consisting of quite 15,000 men, marched in splendid order to the Carters' Offices, in Scotland Road. There the large and magnificent banner of the Carters' Union, placed lengthways on a lorry drawn by a splendid team of horses, entered the ranks in charge of Messrs J. Clayton and T. Ditchfield, and at least 4,000 more carters and dockers formed in line and proceeded south. Meanwhile, the south-end carters, under Mr Edward Arnold, the carters' delegate, had massed at the branch office in Stanhope Street, and the south-end dockers, No. 5 Branch, started from Toxteth Hall at 1.40 p.m. The south-end dockers and carters, having met in Great George Street, proceeded to Seymour Street to meet the north-end bringing up a further strength of 8,000 men, whilst the Birkenhead carters, under Mr Adams, with a band, met at Birkenhead Ferry, and having proceeded across the river, met the dockers of No. 2 Branch, under Bro. Jack Wood, and proceeded up from the Pier Head, to Seymour Street; thus augmenting the procession to a further 5,000 men.

A large number of sailors, firemen, ships' stewards, cooks, butchers, and bakers, engine men, crane men, tram men, railway workers, mill and warehouse workers, canal men, flatmen, and in fact every conceivable branch and section of the transport industry, fell into the procession and marched orderly down London Road.

Brothers Tom Mann, Billal Quilliam, and Thos. Ditchfield, at the head of the procession, in front of the band and the carters' banner, marched at a slow pace amidst rousing cheers down London Road, the whole of the tramway traffic being suspended at the time in that area.

On arriving at the corner of Lime Street, already it was seen that at least 30,000 people had taken part possession of the Plateau and Lime Street. The enthusiasm was great, and as the procession came through the lions in front of St George's Hall, cheer upon cheer was raised as the triumphant fighters took their stands upon the different waggons serving as the platforms. It was found that the crowd was so immense that the Plateau and steps would not hold them all, and, although platforms had been arranged, two other waggons, bearing banners of the dockers and carters, also served as platforms in order that the speeches of the different speakers might easily reach the audience, while at least 10,000 men surrounded the Wellington Column and listened to various leaders of the trade-union movement.

At the south of the Plateau a huge pantechnicon served as a literature waggon, and a body of 100 stewards sold many thousands of the first edition of the *The Transport Worker*, and had not the further events of the day supervened, there is no doubt that no literature would have been left unsold.

Throughout the meeting, it was plainly to be seen that the well-dressed appearance of those taking part, and the orderliness of the huge crowd, were sufficient indications that the men had come there for peaceful demonstration. The attention that was given to the speakers was in itself sufficient evidence that the men wished only for peace.

The Chairman of the different platforms were Brothers Tom Mann, J. Summersgill, Tom Chambers, and Peters.

At the opening of the address on No. 1 platform, Brother Tom Mann said that the railway workers had been without representatives on the Strike Committee, but, having regard to the conditions of their labour, no one could blame them for striking.

In some branches of work, men were receiving from 20s. to 24s. per week for working excessive hours, and others were getting as low as 17s., 15s., and even 13s. 6d., and upon this they were asked to support their wives and families.

The Strike Committee was compelled to have regard to their conditions, to look upon them as comrades, and to do its best to get their grievances adjusted.

He then announced the decision that the Strike Committee had come to in the morning as communicated to the railway companies. He said: 'We have decided on the Strike Committee, adequately representative of other sections of the transport workers, to adopt a peaceful attitude and to show our wish for a speedy settlement by sending a letter to all the companies. There shall be no excuse for them.

They will know that there is some one willing to receive communications from them, and to help in arriving at a settlement. If that brings forth no reply tomorrow, if they ignore us or refuse to take action with a view to a settlement, the Strike Committee advises a general strike all round'. At this moment cheering continued for at least five minutes. Brother Tom Mann remarked: 'We cannot, in the face of the military and extra police drafted into the City, have effectual picketing, and we cannot but accept the display of force as a challenge. We shall be prepared to declare on Tuesday morning a general strike, that will mean a strike of all transport men of all classes; of railway workers, passengers as well as goods men, drivers, stokers. It will mean all connected with the ferry boats, tug boats, river tender men, dock board men, the Overhead and Underground Railways, flatmen, barge men, dockers, coal heavers, crane men, elevator men, warehouse workers, carters, and in fact every conceivable section and branch of the great transport industry in Liverpool will down tools until this business is settled'. (Raising his voice to a pitch that could be heard on the top of the steps of the Plateau, he shouted): 'If you are in favour of that action, if we get no favourable reply from the railway companies, please hold up your hands'. The response to that request was unanimous. All within hearing held up their hands, and at least 20,000 people in front of Brother Tom Mann's platform held up both hands in the air.

It was apparent that a similar resolution was then being put at the other platforms, for they also continued one after the other to hold up their hands at a given signal, and to cheer vociferously. There was then every indication that the men were determined upon what course to adopt, that they would wait and see what would happen during Monday, but that if no negotiations were entered into on Monday, a general transport workers' strike was to take place – with thorough determination, and with all its disastrous effects to the shipping and transport work of the port on Tuesday morning. But little was it dreamt, or even anticipated, that within a few minutes afterwards persons supposed to be possessed of coolness, courage, and foresight, should so lose their heads and act so foolishly, yes, and so murderously, as to put that vast meeting of quite 100,000 men and women into a state of panic and bloodshed. It was fortunate for the meeting that Brother J. Havelock Wilson (who has fought so many fights, and so endangered his health that the doctor has ordered him to withdraw from the front ranks of the fighting line), that his illness had somewhat subsided and his general health recovered sufficiently for him to take part. Standing on No. 2 Platform, with his old comrades Brothers J. A. Seddon and Tom Chambers, also supported by his old colleague, Brother Ned Cathery, Brother Wilson held the audience with his advice to those present.

Following Brother Tom Mann, Brother Quilliam of the Carters' Union, told the men that the only solution to the difficulties of the railway workers was the course that had been taken. It had not been taken rashly, but with a clear deliberation and foresight into the possibilities of every conceivable course that might have been adopted; and it was only after several hours' conference of the Strike Committee that they determined upon what action to pursue.

He advised the men that, while it would mean at least 80,000 men downing tools until the question was settled, and that during such time excitement would be high and the spirit of some might be a little excessive, for the success of the movement it was essential that all parties should keep cool, and collected, and above all not be guilty of any acts of disorder.

He pointed out that it would be only suiting the ends of the persons they were fighting, for some men to get out of hand, to give an opportunity to the police and military to use barbarous tactics to overawe the men and cow them down, and thus cause a state of wild confusion, with the ultimate object of destroying the splendid solidarity that had been shown on all sides.

While Brothers Ditchfield, Clayton, and William Henry Jones, of the Carters' Union, were speaking, it was noticed that something untoward was taking place opposite the Plateau in Lord Nelson Street. A visitor to the London and North Western Hotel assures us he was looking out from a window above Lord Nelson Street, and saw the bother from start to finish. That some youths were sitting on one of the window sills of the Hotel, when three huge burly policemen, without the slightest display of tact, consideration, or common sense, dragged these three youths off the window-sill, and began pushing them down the street towards Lime Street. This agitated a few of the men who were there, and who were there only because Lime Street was filled with people, and there was no room for anyone else, and remarks were passed to the police not to interfere.

This is most important, because the Head Constable had assured

Brother Tom Mann that there would be no display of police more than was sufficient to be ready in case peace was broken, and certainly that none of the police present would do anything which was likely to provoke the crowd. Therefore these wanton acts on the part of the three constables in Lord Nelson Street are highly reprehensible, utterly contrary to the spirit and letter of the Head Constable's assurance, dangerous to the peace, and such conduct that ultimately set the town aflame, and caused such pain, suffering, and disaster on all sides; and it is these three constables of the Liverpool City Police Force that deserve the utmost censure and instant dismissal from the force if not punishment in the courts of law. Other persons present also corroborated this independent witness's statement.

Although these three policemen were appealed to by the men in the crowd to be quiet, evidently knowing that the military were at hand, and extra police in the vicinity, and appreciating at a time like this the military's support, they displayed more vigour than was wise for the peace of the City, and continued their foolishness – in fact their criminal conduct – by drawing their truncheons and knocking the crowd about with severe blows right and left. The crowd would not stand this, and the three policemen were forced back towards the side gates of the station in Lord Nelson Street, and this was the signal for one hundred of the City police to rush madly into the crowd without rhyme or reason, or without any apparent justification or intention of maintaining peace. Such a scene of brutal butchery was never witnessed in Liverpool before. Defenceless men and women, several of whom were infirm, and many of whom were aged, were deliberately knocked down by heavy blows from the truncheons of powerful men, and even as the crowd fled from this onslaught, the police still continued to batter them about as they were running away.

It was not a question of the police using their batons to protect themselves, but utterly and entirely A SAVAGE AND MONSTROUS ATTACK by well-trained men in such a manner as left its severe effect UPON THE HEADS OF HUNDREDS OF PEOPLE. Covered with blood, the poor wretches were falling down stunned all over the street, many lying on the ground either helpless or unconscious.

The police then returned to the gates of the station, and as the crowd began to drift back, apparently to pick up those whom the police had knocked down and left lying unaided, the police again made a savage attack, driving the people forcibly into Lime Street.

This time the police again drew up a cordon, at the bottom of Lord Nelson Street.

Not satisfied with this, not even calculating the severe effect of the attack upon the people, and upon those who could only learn of it from either seeing from a distance what had taken place or from news brought to them on the Plateau, when the crowd again moved from the Plateau into Lime Street, for no reason except that of walking from one part of the street to the other, the police again attacked, this time with the assistance of the imported police, driving the people helter-skelter to both sides of Lime Street, and leaving apparently lifeless men and women lying about in all directions.

After the police had returned and had formed the second cordon, Brother Quilliam left the platform, and entered Lime Street, for the purpose of asking the crowd to keep cool in spite of the attack, and keep back. He succeeded in getting a number of the people who were still wandering about back to the Plateau, although their comrades were lying bleeding on the ground, without assistance. Some, bolder than the rest, went to help their comrades, but the police again made an attack, knocking them about like ninepins, heedless of their screams. The crowd then, and then only, after they had been infuriated by several attacks from the police, and after their comrades had been battered about and left in a most disgraceful and dying condition, began to retaliate.

To the credit of one man who showed his British pluck, and did not display absolutely disgraceful cowardice as did the police with their batons, this pedestrian threw off his coat, and putting up his fists knocked down two constables to the ground, and took their truncheons off them, but he met his fate by half a dozen constables surrounding him, knocking him to the ground, and kicking him.

This was too much for the crowd, and well it might be.

No man if he had the sense of liberty or the feeling of a Britisher could stand such treatment. If the worst and most ferocious brutes in the world had been on the scene they could not have displayed such brutality as the Liverpool City Police, and their imported men, did in the Sunday attacks. To the credit of the audience, they made a bold stand in trying to defend themselves and their comrades from the onslaughts.

Of course by this time the meeting was in utter disorder; despite the great efforts of the speakers in appealing to the men to keep quiet, human nature prevented them from remaining so any longer.

Brother Tom Mann then closed the meeting and ordered those present to get away from the scene, for he knew very well that the police would only take advantage of their conduct, in the excitement that they had caused, by bringing the military and trying to induce the military to fire upon them.

The audience left the Plateau, and even then the police followed in the wake of the people, who were leaving peaceably, and smashed heads with their truncheons. The mounted men then came on the scene, and rushed about the Plateau as if they were wild, and dashed up the steps, clearing women and old men who had taken refuge on the steps, and driving them to seek refuge wherever they could.

We need not enter into what took place afterwards on the Plateau, as there is no doubt that the men, excited as they were by the harsh treatment they had received, were forced to seek shelter in various houses, and they had become so excited by the way they had been treated, that retaliation of course followed upon the attack of the police, and in the retaliation of the crowd, certain brutal policemen received similar blows to those they had themselves inflicted.

But if the authorities think that by this behaviour they can cow the men, they are mistaken. The blood of the men is up, and they will exhibit greater solidarity than ever was evinced before.

We are indebted to every paper in the city, and country, for the accounts given of the strike. In no one paper are the baton charges justified, but on the contrary utterly condemned.

The *Manchester Guardian* has not failed to express itself in no uncertain terms. In the heading to the news of the day's proceedings, loom large the words:

INCREDIBLE STORIES OF VIOLENCE
MERCILESS USE OF TRUNCHEONS

EVEN WHEN THE CROWD WAS SEPARATED INTO GROUPS, THE POLICE CONTINUED THE ONSLAUGHT. They used their truncheons mercilessly and some could be seen taking deliberate aim at the backs of the men's heads before giving them blows which despite the din could be heard yards away. It was when nearly all the crowds had been dispersed that the worst scene of all occurred, and that brutal unnecessary blows were struck by some policemen, mostly young and probably inexperienced. The steps of the Hall had been crowded with men and a few women interested in the demonstration. The orders given for the steps to be cleared, led to scenes. At the top is a wide stone platform with iron railings to protect the ends where there is a sheer drop of 12 feet. When the police charged up the steps, they had the people congregated there in a trap from which escape could only be effected by dropping from the railings to the flags below. Hundreds realized that this was the only thing to do, but in a few seconds the police had won their way to the railings and men, women, young boys, and girls were pushed past them over the edge as rapidly and continually as water down a steep rock. The officers could be seen using their truncheons like flails. Dozens of heads and arms were broken and many shoulders and arms received blows, the marks of which will remain for many a long day, and of those who escaped the blows, many were hurt by the fall. IT WAS A DISPLAY OF VIOLENCE THAT HORRIFIED THOSE WHO SAW IT.

So much for the *Manchester Guardian* report.
Concluding a brief account penned by myself, I wrote:

The workers' movement in Liverpool, and the country generally, is more solid now as a consequence; rapidly growing, truly solidifying as we were, this has added to our growth and our solidification. And although the military are being drafted in daily, and the clatter of the horses hoofs and the noise of the ammunition waggons, disturbs one's rest at night, there is no one in terror or in the least degree afraid. The presence of military in tens of thousands will not prevent our continuing to organize, the presence of Mounted Police with long bludgeons, and fire-arms, and of Cavalry and Infantry with bayonets fixed, will not prevent the workers engaged in this Industrial struggle from still being in it, and conducting their fight with the utmost vigour.

And more, let Churchill do his utmost, his best or his worst, let him order ten times more Military to Liverpool, and let every street be paraded by them, not all the King's horses with all the King's men, can take the vessels out of the Docks to sea. The workers decide the ships shall not go, what Government can say they shall go and make the carters take the freight and the dockers load same, and the seamen man the steamers? Tell us that, gentlemen? Is there really a stronger power than that of the workers in proper organized relationship? If so, trot it out. Demonstrate your power to prevent the liners being held up, prove your capacity to get them loaded, and out again on time, and safely manned, to destination! The confounded impudence of the petti-fogging butter dealers and flour millers, with their petty authority, strolling about full of an imaginary importance, why the whole crowd of them cannot berth, discharge, load, and take away the *Lusitania*! The White Star combine is a powerful combine, the American capitalists that own this big fleet of merchantmen are an important group, but can they handle the vessels or the cargo, or provide for the passengers, or take charge of the ships? And if they cannot, who can? Only the despised worker, he whom the Parochial and Governmental office-fillers affect to treat as human rubbish. Ah! my fine gentlemen, you are up against something at last. You affect to be so superior to the mere labourer, very well get on without him – if you can – if you can – bring in your Military, still further demonstrate your power – to get nothing done; meanwhile the workers' demands had better receive attention at your hands.

The announcement that a cinematograph picture would be taken of the procession and the demonstration had been acted upon. We had two operators, one at either end of the Plateau, and a complete picture was taken, showing the repeated onslaughts of the police.

We had arranged for a first view of the film at a picture theatre at noon the following day, and punctually at noon the picture was showing, but – to our extreme disappointment – the police had already been busy and had ordered the portions that told against them, to be cut out. All we could do to get at our property was unavailing. The theatre manager was fully aware of what had happened, and he was not prepared to risk losing his licence by opposing the police and putting the full picture on in spite of them.

Briefly reviewing the situation in the *The Transport Worker*, I wrote as follows:

INDUSTRIAL SOLIDARITY

Many had declared that the day for successful strikes was past, that strike methods were barbarous, that workers who resorted to them always hurt themselves more than they did those they struck at, and that therefore strikes must be relegated to the history of bygone days and men must in future resort to parliamentary action for any improvement to be secured in their economic and social conditions. The history of the past few weeks has amply demonstrated the power of industrial solidarity throughout the length and breadth of the British Isles. Only a few weeks ago I travelled from London to Liverpool to be present at and take part in the inauguration of the strike of sailors and firemen and cooks and stewards. This was on Tuesday, 13th June, and in the short interval substantial gains in increased wages, recognition of the union, the abolition of the Shipping Federation ticket, and the insistence upon decency at the medical examination, have been obtained for all sea-going men, not only deck hands, and firemen, trimmers, and greasers, but equally for cooks, stewards, butchers, and bakers. These gains in money wages have ranged from 10s. per man per month, to 25s. per man per month, and realizing that British Shipping represents one half of the total shipping of the world, with a mercantile fleet of over 10,000 vessels, it means that the money gains, obtained solely as the result of the strike, for deck hands, stokehold and catering departments equals £600,000 a year.

This money is being received by men whose average wage has not been more than one pound a week, while at work, but whose actual income over the year has been considerably less than that. Thousands of men did not get more than £3 10s. a month as firemen and trimmers, and thousands did not receive more than £3 a month in the catering department. On the weekly boats, where men find their own food, wages ranged from 26s. to 30s. a week, a few have yet to be settled with, but the wages for the same men now average 32s. 6d. with payment for overtime in thousands of cases where it was never paid for before.

Apart from the gains of sea-going men, many thousands of shore workers, dockers, carters, and others, have also received substantial advances, as at Liverpool, Southampton, Hull, Manchester, etc., etc.

COMPLETE ORGANIZATION WANTED

It has commonly been asked what hope there is of ever effectively organizing the mass of the workers? This depends on the methods pursued and the spirit that animates the organizers, even more than that of the men to be organized. As an indication of what can be done by concerted action, the case of the dockers of Liverpool is significant. There are 25,000 dockers in the port of Liverpool, and hitherto there has never been a larger membership in Liverpool than 8,000. A few weeks ago there were only 7,000, at the present hour there are 25,000. One branch whose membership had never exceeded 450 until three weeks ago, now tops 6,000. Of course, it is within the bounds of possibility that many of these will fall away again, but those who have been instrumental in causing the enrolment in one union of over 17,000 members in one port, will probably know how to keep the members in a healthy state of efficient organization.

WHAT LED TO THE STRIKE?

For years past the conditions of sea-faring men had been deteriorating; in spite of all the efforts of the Sailors' and Firemen's Union, the standard of life at sea was going down. The Shipping Federation had imposed its ticket, for which the seaman had to pay 1s. a year to the Shipping Federation. The Seamen's Union stood little chance by the side of it when its impositions were systematically enforced by instruction of the shipowners, who insisted upon a medical examination infinitely more humiliating and brutalizing than could possibly be applied to cattle. Among the scores of thousands of sea-faring men in the various departments, are many refined natures, studious, clean-living men, cultured and sensitive; by the enforcement of the beastly methods of the federation every time these men signed on for a voyage, they all had to line up like cattle, stark naked saving trousers, these to be dropped down on reaching the doctor. The applicants were examined by him in a dictatorial, bullying and often beastly fashion in presence of such officers as were considered requisite (in addition to their shipmates) to exercise a cowing influence over the men. The coarseness, the callousness, the shamefulness, the downright filthiness of this form of examination, beggars description. I venture to predict that any serious attempt to reinaugurate the foul and filthy methods will result in action of so drastic a kind that some will find themselves on what some speak of as the 'spiritual plane' a little earlier than they bargained for. Repeatedly did the National Sailors' and Firemen's Union seek to obtain redress of these grievances by asking for a conference of shipowners, but the shipowners turned a deaf ear. During the past twelve months Mr J. Havelock Wilson has been constantly active endeavouring to bring about such a conference both by direct effort and by requesting the good offices of the Board of Trade. The reply was ever of the contemptuous order, Mr Laws of the Shipping Federation declaring that should a seamen's strike be attempted, it would not be felt, as scarcely any of the men would respond, and those that did would immediately have their places filled by men ready at the disposal of the Shipping Federation.

WHERE IS THAT FEDERATION NOW?

Where is the unlimited supply of blackleg labour they told the world at large so cavalierly they were able to command? What purpose has been served by the ships chartered by the federation in the various ports and placed in convenient spots to receive and dispatch blacklegs? Why did it not get the blacklegs and supply them to the shipowners who most certainly turned to the Shipping Federation for a redemption of its promises? It did not, simply because it could not. What then helped the men in so marked a manner? Three sets of conditions. First, Good Trade; Secondly, the Concurrent Strike in all Ports; and Thirdly, the Exhibition of Working-Class Solidarity. In spite of good trade, if the strike had not been declared and acted upon in all ports at once the men would have been beaten, and even if the strike had taken place simultaneously in all ports, still the men would have been beaten if class solidarity had not been exhibited; but because this solidarity was realized in fact by carters, dockers, and many railwaymen making common cause, therefore the men won.

NO ROOM FOR SECTIONALISM

To make common action possible the National Transport Workers' Federation was formed some six months ago, and although several of the unions connected therewith were very doubtful of the wisdom of action when it was decided upon, the fact that the federation discussed and conferred and demonstrated on behalf of the transport workers, did no doubt help materially to prepare the workers' minds for the exhibition of solidarity in a manner superior to what had before been experienced.

The Dock, Wharf, Riverside and General Labourers' Union, of which Mr Ben Tillet is general secretary, also carried on a vigorous organizing campaign, particularly in the Bristol Channel, Southampton, Hull, and Salford, all of which contributed materially to the results secured. At the present hour this union is engaged in a big movement in London, with the rest of the federated unions. A demand is being made for a minimum wage of eightpence per hour for day work and one shilling per hour for overtime. A few days later these and a number of other demands were conceded.

LIST OF LIVERPOOL STRIKE COMMITTEE

Tom Mann, President, ASE; Frank Pearce, Secretary, Jos. Cotter, Cooks and Stewards; Geo. Parkin, Edward Lamb, J. Clarke, Amalgamated Engineers; James Sexton, John Wood, G. Milligan, NU Dockers; David Kenny, T. Dixon, J. Connor, G. Ruffler, G. Hesson, Sailors and Firemen; T. Ditchfield, W. Jones, W. B. Quilliam, Mersey Carters; Jos. Summersgill, J. Stephenson, J. Peters, — Murphy, Liverpool Trades Council; Clem George, — Williams, ASRS; Pat Kean, South-End Coal Heavers; — Allen, Dock Board Coopers; — Edwards, Operative Bakers; Frank Kilkelly, Arthur Short, J. Hanratty, and Tom Chambers.

As president of the Strike Committee, I was hard at work in Liverpool throughout the affair, except for two brief intervals. In the first week of August 1911, the CGT of France organized a Labour demonstration with speakers of various nationalities, including two from Germany, Comrades Molkenbuhr and Ledebour. This was the first time since the war of 1870 that German Socialists had been invited by the French comrades to take part in a meeting in Paris. At this time the war clouds were threatening in regard to Morocco, and the demonstration was organized as a protest against drifting into war. It was a great success, speakers were present from Germany and Spain, and I was the spokesman for England. The burden of the speeches was the necessity for international action, to refuse to handle war material. As soon as the meeting was over I took the first train back to Liverpool.

In July, during the strike, I had occasion to visit Dublin and Belfast and take part in the struggle there. Brothers Jim Larkin, in Dublin, and Jim Connolly, in Belfast, were very forceful personalities, and were building up a great industrial movement, in many respects a pattern to others. Later, in November of the same year,

I was again in Ireland. I honestly believe that the formation of the Irish Transport Workers' Union, with all that this foreshadowed, gave more hope for drastic and beneficial economic and social change than anything that had ever been tried before.

CHAPTER XX

THE 'DON'T SHOOT' LEAFLET
1912

THE opening of the year 1912 found the Syndicalists exceptionally active. Our little monthly sheet had given place to a monthly paper called *The Syndicalist*. I was much occupied in platform work advocating militant trade unionism, and constantly urging the workers to cease relying upon parliament and to resort to direct action. Six months before this there had appeared an Open Letter to British Soldiers. This had been printed in *The Irish Worker*. It was not signed, but had been written by a comrade in the building trade in Liverpool. In the January number (the first) of *The Syndicalist* the letter was reprinted without comment. Indeed, no special importance was attached to it, but a railwayman, Fred Crowsley, who read it and was impressed with its educational value, decided to have copies printed as a leaflet at his own expense. Having done so, he visited Aldershot and personally distributed the leaflets among the soldiers. This resulted in his arrest, trial, and sentence to four months' imprisonment. Attention was next turned to the editor of *The Syndicalist*, Guy Bowman. He was arrested, and so were the printers, Messrs B. E. & C. E. Buck, of Walthamstow. The latter were sentenced to six months each, and Guy Bowman to nine months. The condemned men had no closer identification with the Open Letter than I had, as chairman of the Industrial Syndicalist League, which was responsible for the paper in which it appeared. I was addressing a series of meetings on behalf of the Worker's Union, in and around Manchester. At this time, February 1912, the miners' strike was on, and was being conducted in a most orderly manner throughout Britain. The whole of the miners had downed tools. It was the first time in their history when complete solidarity amongst all sections of the industry had been exhibited. In Manchester, where I then was, the authorities were having premises prepared as temporary barracks, and were concentrating military forces a few miles out of the city. At public meetings, I drew attention to this, and asked what the temporary barracks were for. I described what had happened the previous year at Liverpool, when everything was orderly until those responsible for Law and Order caused the disturbances. I also directed attention to the imprisonment of my comrades in connection with the 'Don't Shoot' letter, read the letter to the audiences, and declared I believed in every sentence of it. Thereupon, I was arrested, after my return to London. It is, I think, of sufficient interest to put in some of the press reports of the time, especially remembering that a Liberal Government was in power, and that the prospect of a Home Rule Bill stimulated high officeholders, like Sir Edward Carson and the present Lord Chancellor*, to organize rebellion against the State, supplying their followers with arms, and regularly engaging in systematic drilling and preparation for civil war. The following report is from the *Daily Express* for 21 March, 1912:

MR TOM MANN'S ARREST
CHARGE AGAINST THE SYNDICALIST LEADER
TAKEN TO SALFORD

Mr Tom Mann, the Labour leader, who, as reported in the *Express* yesterday, was arrested in London on a charge of inciting to mutiny, will be brought up at the Salford Town Hall Police Court today.

He will be charged before Mr Spencer Hogg, the Salford stipendiary, Mr Gordon Hewart will prosecute for the police, and Mr Quilliam, a Liverpool solicitor, will appear for the defence.

Mr Tom Mann travelled in the custody of Inspector Hestor, of Scotland Yard, and Sergeant Markland, on the 12.15 p.m. train from St Pancras, which was so crowded that both the Labour leader and his guardians had to stand up during most of the journey.

The party of three arrived at Salford Town Hall last evening, having travelled by taxicab from Withington Station, four miles out of Manchester, where the train from London was stopped at the suggestion of the railway authorities to avoid any scene at the Central Station, Manchester.

A small crowd of Socialists gathered to meet the train and were disappointed at the non-arrival of Mr Mann. A few saw his arrival at the Salford Town Hall, and to them Mr Mann raised his hat and

* *i.e.* Lord Birkenhead (publisher's note)

laughed in answer to their cheers. He was taken into the charge-room and the warrant was read over to him.

Mr Mann made no reply to the charges. Four local Socialists paid him a visit, and were allowed to spend an hour with him before he was removed to the cells.

'MAINLY RESPONSIBLE'
ATTORNEY-GENERAL'S REPLY TO MR MANN'S FRIENDS
By our Parliamentary Representative.
House of Commons. Wednesday Night.

Syndicalism and the coal strike have obsessed men's minds, although the long hours of debate down here have been spent on the Navy Estimates.

The sitting had only just begun when the House became aflame over Mr Tom Mann's arrest. There were Socialists and Liberals who could not bear the idea of arresting him and they fusilladed the Attorney-General.

The discussion was as follows:

Mr Charles Duncan (Lab., Barrow): I desire to ask the Attorney-General if he can inform the House what is the charge which is preferred against Mr Tom Mann, who was arrested yesterday in London.

Sir Rufus Isaacs: Mr Tom Mann is charged with the publication of the appeal to soldiers in *The Syndicalist* and the offence with which he is charged is incitement to mutiny, a common-law misdemeanour. Within the last few days application was made by the police authorities at Salford to prosecute Mr Mann. That was based on certain statements made and acts done by him during the past few days.

THE PERSON RESPONSIBLE

The evidence was not before me at the time when I authorized the prosecution of the three persons now at the Old Bailey. As the result of that, I cannot go into the matter further than to say this – that there is sufficient evidence of publication by him as chairman of the committee – and therefore the person mainly responsible for the publication – (*Unionist cheers*) and upon that application by the police and on the evidence before me I authorized the prosecution.

(*Loud Unionist cheers and some Liberal and Socialist cries of dissent.*)

Mr James O'Grady (*Soc., Leeds*): Why has Mr Mann been taken to Salford, especially in view of the statement now made by the Attorney-General that he has not been arrested for any action at Salford but on the fact that he is president of the Syndicalist Education League?

Sir Rufus Isaacs: That is not quite so. I referred to certain statements made by and acts done by him at Salford which would be evidence of publication.

Mr O'Grady: Am I to understand that the Attorney-General has given the instruction for his arrest, and that he so gave it from the fact that he is president of the Syndicalist Education League?

Sir Rufus Isaacs: No, sir, quite the contrary. I was aware that Mr Mann was president of the league, but that, in my opinion, was not sufficient of itself to make him responsible on a criminal charge for the publication of that particular article, but in consequence of certain evidence which has come before us in the last few days, and certain things which happened at Salford in connection with them – I cannot discuss it as the matter is *sub judice* – I therefore came to the conclusion that I was bound, in the ordinary course of my duty, to allow the chief constable at Salford to institute the prosecution he desired. (*Loud Unionist cheers.*)

OTHER PROSECUTIONS

Mr J. C. Wedgwood (*L., Newcastle-under-Lyme*): Will he withdraw the prosecution against the two Bucks and Bowman in consequence of this prosecution?

Sir Rufus Isaacs: No, sir. They are made responsible because they are the publishers and printers of it, and that is a matter of defence equally open to them when the case comes to trial at the Old Bailey, but what I have been desirous of doing is to prosecute the person mainly responsible, and consequently I have authorized the prosecution of Mr Mann. (*Loud Unionist cheers.*)

Mr George Lansbury (*Soc., Bow and Bromley*): Why is it that no proceedings have been taken against those who conspired to prevent the First Lord of the Admiralty from speaking at Belfast?

This lit up all the contending forces in the Chamber. It was all a-boil with noise. Unionists laughed while Liberals cheered, and a few Irishmen threw in jagged contributions to the medley of sound.

The Speaker told Mr Lansbury to put down on the notice paper any question he had to ask.

POLICE COURT PROCEEDINGS.
IS THERE A SEPARATE LAW FOR PRIVY COUNCILLORS?

Mr Tom Mann, the well-known Labour Leader, was arrested at his home at Southfields, Wimbledon, on Tuesday night, on a warrant issued at Salford. The arrest was made by Scotland Yard officers, on a charge preferred in connection with a speech recently delivered at Salford. He was taken to Cannon-row Police Station for the night. After his arrest Mr Mann was visited by Mr Keir Hardie, who conversed with him for some time.

Mr Mann is president of the Industrial Syndicalist Education League, under whose auspices *The Syndicalist* newspaper was published. Mr Tom Mann addressed a meeting called under the auspices of the Workers' Union, of which he is vice-president, in the Salford Town Hall on Wednesday week, and a second meeting on Thursday evening in the Pendleton Town Hall, which is in the Salford Borough. The meetings were orderly. Notes of Mr Mann's speeches were taken by Salford police officers.

In his speech at Pendleton Mr Mann said the Government were preparing a measure to prevent freedom of speech to men like himself, who dared to talk freely and interchange opinions with some degree of courage. Two men associated, as he was, with *The Syndicalist* had been arrested because the paper urged their brothers in the Army not to murder their brothers in the industrial field. He did not know to what extent there were plain-clothes policemen in the hall. Men had been sent by the police for the express purpose of taking notes of his speeches, but even if he were arrested there were hundreds and thousands to take his place.

Mr Tom Mann was brought up before the Salford Stipendiary Magistrate, Mr Spencer Hogg, on Thursday morning on a charge of inciting to mutiny. Mr Gordon Hewart said he appeared for the Director of Public Prosecutions, who, by reason of the gravity and the public mischief of the offences alleged against the prisoner, had found it to be his duty to act in these proceedings. There was at present one charge against the prisoner, but there would be two others. The charges would be threefold, two of them of felony and the other a common-law misdemeanour. The two charges of felony were laid under Section 1 of the Incitement to Mutiny Act, 1797, which provided as follows:

'Any person who shall maliciously and advisedly endeavour to seduce any person or persons serving in His Majesty's Forces by sea or land from his or their duty and allegiance to His Majesty, or to incite or stir up any such person or persons to commit any act of mutiny, or to make or endeavour to make any mutinous assembly, or to commit any traitorous or mutinous practice whatsoever, shall, on being legally convicted of such offence, be adjudged guilty of felony.'

The gist of the offence, said Mr Hewart, was an endeavour to seduce persons serving in His Majesty's forces from their duty and allegiance, and to incite them to mutiny and disobedience. As to the nature of that duty and allegiance, Mr Hewart went on, there could be now no doubt or question, and it seemed hardly necessary to cite legal authority for the purpose of defining it or explaining it. A soldier had a twofold capacity, and owed duties not less in the one capacity than in the other.

The incitement was conveyed in certain printed matter entitled 'An Open Letter to British Soldiers', published in a periodical called *The Syndicalist* and it amounted, in terms, to an appeal to soldiers to disobey the commands of their officers when in certain public emergencies they were called upon to discharge their duty. Mr Hewart said he would read a portion of that 'Open Letter', and then, after a pause, said it would perhaps be more in consonance with the ends of justice if he did not read the letter but handed up copies for the Magistrates to read. Several copies of *The Syndicalist* were handed to the Magistrates. Mr Hewart went on to say that the paper was edited under the auspices of the Industrial Syndicalist Education League, and that in it a man named Bowman was described as publisher of the paper. I wish to refer, said Mr Hewart, to two speeches which the prisoner delivered, the one in Salford and the other in Pendleton, and which showed his responsibility not only for the original but for the subsequent publication of that matter. There was a meeting at the Salford Town Hall on 13th March, a meeting said to be called in connection with the Workers' Union, and a considerable number of persons were present. The prisoner referred to the strike at Liverpool last summer and to the action of the authorities with reference to the troops. He said, referring to the charge which is about to be investigated against Bowman: 'Guy Bowman was editor and I, Mann, secretary of a paper called *The Syndicalist* and Bowman was arrested for publishing and circulating amongst soldiers this paper, which had an article asking soldiers not to shoot down their fellow working men. After his arrest, the police searched Bowman's rooms, and actually stole copies of the paper, but I have about twenty copies of the paper left, which I will sell at 2*d*. each on personal application on the platform for them.' Then he added: 'I don't see how I shall escape as chairman of that committee. You must not be surprised if I, too, am arrested and find myself in court.' Upon that evidence and on the further evidence that there was on sale at the Meeting of 14th March, the paper called *The Syndicalist*, a copy of which was bought by a witness directly from the prisoner, Mr Hewart said he would submit that the prisoner ought to be committed to take his trial upon these charges.

Mr Spencer Hogg said there would be a remand for a week to enable the prisoner to prepare his defence.

Mr Quilliam said there was no doubt that the prisoner was willing to appear for trial, and as several respectable gentlemen were willing by the deposit of reasonable sums to secure his presence he asked for bail. He understood that the prosecution did not object to bail, so that it was left in the hands of the Court. *Mr Hewart:* I hear what is said and I say nothing. Mr Quilliam said the understanding was with Mr Day, who was instructing counsel for the prosecution. *Mr Spencer Hogg (after a consultation with his fellow Magistrates):* There will be no bail. *Mr Quilliam:* Before you say that definitely—. *Mr Spencer Hogg:* I have said it definitely. The prisoner had turned from the dock with a nod of recognition to several friends, one of whom said, 'Good luck, Tom,' when Mr Hewart mentioned that no evidence as to the arrest had been taken. It was agreed by Mr Quilliam that no evidence should be taken until next Thursday, when the case will be called on at eleven o'clock.

I here reprint the text of the document on which the charges were based:

OPEN LETTER TO BRITISH SOLDIERS

Men! Comrades! Brothers!

The 'Don't Shoot' Leaflet

You are in the army.

So are we. You, in the army of Destruction. We, in the Industrial, or army of Construction.

We work at mine, mill, forge, factory, or dock, etc., producing and transporting all the goods, clothing, stuffs, etc., which makes it possible for people to live.

You are Workingmen's Sons.

When We go on Strike to better Our lot, which is the lot also of Your Fathers, Mothers, Brothers, and Sisters, YOU are called upon by your Officers to MURDER US.

Don't do it.

You know how it happens. Always has happened.

We stand out as long as we can. Then one of our (and your) irresponsible Brothers, goaded by the sight and thought of his and his loved ones' misery and hunger, commits a crime on property. Immediately you are ordered to murder Us, as You did at Mitchelstown, at Featherstone, at Belfast.

Don't You know, that when you are out of the colours, and become a 'Civvy' again, that You, like Us, may be on strike, and You, like Us, be liable to be Murdered by other soldiers.

Boys, Don't Do It.

'Thou shalt not kill,' says the Book.

Don't forget that!

It does not say, 'unless you have a uniform on'.

No! MURDER IS MURDER, whether committed in the heat of anger on one who has wronged a loved one, or by clay-piped Tommies with a rifle.

Boys, Don't do it.

Act the Man! Act the Brother! Act the Human Being.

Property can be replaced! Human life, Never!

The Idle Rich Class, who own and order you about, own and order us about also. They and their friends own the land and means of life of Britain.

You Don't! We Don't!

When We kick they order You to murder Us.

When You kick, You get court-martialled and cells.

Your fight is Our fight. Instead of fighting Against each other, We should be fighting With each other.

Out of Our loins, Our lives, Our homes, You came.

Don't disgrace Your Parents, Your Class, by being the willing tools any longer of the Master Class.

You, like Us, are of the Slave Class. When We rise, You rise; When We fall, even by your bullets, Ye fall also.

England with its fertile valleys and dells, its mineral resources, its sea harvests, is the heritage of ages to us.

You no doubt joined the army out of poverty.

We work long hours for small wages at hard work, because of our poverty. And both Your poverty and Ours arises from the fact that, Britain with its resources, belongs to only a few people. These few, owning Britain, own Our jobs. Owning Our jobs they own Our very lives. Comrades, have We called in vain? Think things out and refuse any longer to Murder Your Kindred. Help US to win back Britain for the British, and the World for the Workers.

On 25th March, Mr Josiah Wedgwood raised the question in Parliament by an amendment to a Treasury Vote. The following report is from *Hansard* of that date:

Mr Wedgwood: I beg to move, as an Amendment, to leave out the word 'now', and at the end of the Question to add the words 'upon this day six months'.

I do so in order to enter a protest against the institution by the Government of prosecutions of the Press outside India and Ireland. I would remind this House it has not been the practice for many years for prosecutions of this nature to be indulged in. Prosecutions by the State are always risky business. Prosecutions of the Press have long been notable by their absence. It is true that in Ireland and India we have seen such prosecutions, but they are unknown in England, and for a very good reason. Before the Government undertake a prosecution of the Press there are many risks to be considered. First, there is the risk of increasing the evil by giving wide publicity to printed matter in an obscure publication. There is the classical case of the prosecution instituted against Paine's 'Age of Reason', and Paine's 'Rights of Man', and Campbell of these said:

> 'Its circulation was infinitely increased by the Attorney-General filing an information against the author.'

Then, secondly, there is the risk of interfering with the open expression of opinion and driving it underground. Besides, there is the risk of giving the writer publicity for his libel. I come to the third risk, that of inflaming the opinion, both of those prosecuted and of their friends. There have been some recent prosecutions and certain unfortunate men have gone to prison. They are not even Socialists; they are men who have no interest in politics; they cannot be decreed to be red-hot revolutionists. Their friends throughout the length and breadth of the country feel the injustice done by the Government to them, then in regard to this risk of publicity and inflaming public opinion. It was said that Grenville issued 200 injunctions against the Press in six months. The learned Attorney-General is beginning to learn the lesson. You have already the cases of *The Syndicalist*, the *Labour Leader, Hull Worker, Forward, Justice*, and *Freedom* on your hands. How many more? We are beginning to foresee that by reason of the arrest of Mr Tom Mann, and possibly that of Mr Victor Grayson, there are others to come. The Government has great powers, but it is not always expedient to exercise them. There must be no feeling that they are pandering to panic. There must be absolute impartiality not only of intention, but it must be conveyed to the public mind. Everyone knows the unlimited power of the State in matters of this nature, but before exercising such powers it is always wise in making use of these weapons to bear in mind a certain amount of proportion in the application of any Act of Parliament. It should be the duty of the Law Officers of the Crown to consult the Crown before instituting prosecutions. Was it done in this case? There is a regular Phoenix of a struggle coming up in every age. There is the question whether prosecutions of the Press have ever been justified. The best men in every age have been against it. Milton, Erskine, and Macaulay were against them. There has always been some provocation, some fear-inspiring prosecution. The clamour of propertied classes has again and again deafened the Government to the still, quiet voice of reason and liberty. What did Erskine say:

'I will not say which party is right, but God forbid that honest opinion should ever become a crime'.

There is a curious similarity between the present position and the propriety of basing prosecutions on the Act of 1797, when there was the real danger of the munity at the Nore. The Bill of 1797 was not merely the outcome of the anti-Jacobin terror: the mutiny was fresh in their memory, and the Bill was introduced to put a stop to inciting to mutiny. In the House, Sheridan got up and opposed the Bill, but when one looks back on the condition of the country under Castlereagh and Pitt one cannot help looking on it as a redeeming feature in an age of tyranny that Fox, Grey, and Sheridan night after night led their little band in the Lobby against the Bill. We are carrying on their trade; hon. Members opposite are carrying on the trades of your ancestors, when you go into the Lobby for coercion and tyranny. Then the prosecution took place. The same State prosecutions that we are enjoying today. Hardy, Horne Tooke, Gilbert Wakefield, and others, were prosecuted, and, of course, not only the principals but the printers as well. The only difference is that some of them got off in those days. Those who did not get off had fourteen years' hard labour at Botany Bay. Those who did get off, got off because in those days they were defended by men with magic voices like that of Erskine's. I want to quote one short passage by Erskine directly affecting the problem before us, and dealing with the subject of the freedom of the Press:

'Tempests occasionally shatter our dwellings and dissipate our commerce; but they scourge before them the lazy elements which without them would stagnate into pestilence. In like manner Liberty herself, God's last and best gift to his creatures, must be taken just as she is. You might pare her down into bashful regularity, and shape her into a perfect model of severe, scrupulous law, but she would then be Liberty no longer; and we must be content to die under the lash of this inexorable law that we had exchanged for the banners of freedom'.

These words are as true today as they were then. They are as practical in their application at the present juncture as they were then. I ask all Liberals who know when they read history that Erskine was right and the Government wrong, to express Liberal views now and say that the Government ought to be regarded as wrong now, as it was then. There was the case of prosecution of Muir, of Edinburgh, who was tried in 1793, and this is what Erskine May says of the trial:

'Every incident of this trial marked the unfairness and cruel spirit of his judges'.

The same might be seen today, as I saw it the other day at the Old Bailey. How do we judge the trial of Muir? If anybody goes to Edinburgh he will see on the Calton Hill the Martyr's Memorial. Are these people who are being prosecuted now more extreme than those who were prosecuted then? Let me quote from Charles James Fox. He said in the House of Commons – I do not think he could have said it outside:

> 'If his opinion were asked by the people as to their obedience he should tell them that it was no longer a question of moral obligation and duty, but of prudence'.

Is not that the position today? I do not wish to go about the country saying that the people who issued that pamphlet were right, but I do not intend to go about the country and say it is wrong. I will tell them that it is dangerous to say it so long as the prosecutions are carried on in this way by the Government. The rage of the Government for prosecuting the Press went on till 1831. It was revived in the famous prosecution of Cobbett, and at that time there was the same solid ground for the prosecution that there is at the present day. There was the same terror among the upper classes. There had been the riots at Merthyr Tydfil, when seventy or eighty men who had struck for higher wages were shot. It must be remembered that Cobbett had already spent two years' hard labour in prison before that time. He thundered against these iniquities in the *Political Register*, and directly a weak Government came into power in 1831 he was prosecuted by the Liberal Attorney-General, just as the Liberal Attorney-General is now the prosecutor in this case. I should like to read the passage from the *Political Register* of 1831, which, I regret to say, is thoroughly applicable to the present circumstances:

> 'I may say for myself that I wrote and published under the party of Peel for twenty-one years and under six Attorneys-General called Tories; that I never heard of a prosecution all the while from any one of them; and that the Whigs had not been in power more than about twenty-one days before a deadly-meant prosecution of me was begun; and now, at the end of only six months, there have been more prosecutions against the Press than during the three years that the Duke of Wellington was in power'.

I may mention that Cobbett was tried, like Bowman, at the Old

Bailey. He was acquitted. It is noticeable that from that date to this – from 1831 to 1912 – prosecutions of the Press of this nature have ceased. Erskine May is emphatic in his History that it was from the trial of Cobbett that the freedom of the Press really dates. This is what Erskine May says about it:

> 'However small a minority, however unpopular, irrational, eccentric, perverse, or unpatriotic in sentiment, however despised or pitied, it may speak out forcibly in the full confidence of toleration. The majority, conscious of right, and assured of its proper influence in the State, neither forces nor resents opposition'.

That was the position until this year. Now we see a change. I can quote John Stuart Mill on the same question. He writes in *On Liberty*:

> 'If all mankind minus one were of one opinion, and only one person were of the contrary opinion, mankind would be no more justified in silencing that one person than he, if he had the power, would be justified in silencing mankind'.

These are the opinions of Liberalism today, just as they were the opinions of Liberalism in the time of John Stuart Mill. I come to the consideration of this 'Open Letter', which has been the cause of these prosecutions. I do not want to read the whole of that letter to the House, but this is the material passage:

> 'When we go on strike to better our lot, which is the lot also of your fathers, mothers, brothers and sisters, you are called upon by your officers to murder us. Don't do it. You know how it happens. Always has happened. We stand out as long as we can. Then one of our (and your) irresponsible brothers, goaded by the sight and thought of his and his loved ones' misery and hunger, commits a crime on property. Immediately you are ordered to murder us, as you did at Mitchelstown, at Featherstone, at Belfast'.

That is the strongest paragraph in the whole of this letter. It is for printing that paragraph that these prosecutions have been undertaken. I do not want to tell the soldiers who have taken an oath that it is their duty under any circumstances to break that oath, but we all know that it is their duty to break that oath under certain circumstances. No man would be justified in shooting his father or his brother at the order of any of us. To show the spirit of the people who are writing these protests, who have been sent to prison, or who are being prosecuted, I am going to read to the House the defence of the man Crowsley. He was a common fireman, employed by the London and North-Western Railway Company, and an absolutely sober, honest, working man. I have met him since, and I know him very well. He is getting about 33s. per week wages. At his own expense he takes this 'Open Letter' and has 3,000 copies of it made, paying 15s. for the privilege. He gets home at three o'clock on Sunday morning, and goes by an early train to Aldershot and distributes these leaflets. This is his defence:

'I am not guilty of any crime. Had I been guilty my conscience would tell me so. The law you say I have broken was made over one hundred years ago, when the middle and working classes had no voice in making the law. It was made by a class who live on the labour of another class. But if passed yesterday, I would still tell you that there is a higher law which says, "Thou shalt not commit murder". I have simply made an earnest appeal to the honour of soldiers not to shoot their brothers who are fighting for the right to live. If that is breaking your law, so much the worse for your unjust law. You say my action was undermining society. If society will not stand the attacks of truth, does not that prove the rottenness of your society, and the sooner a more just state exists the better? Your prison missionary called me a traitor for calling attention to the creed he preaches. You and he are entitled to your opinions, and I to mine. But you are traitors to your creed. You say with your mouth, "Love one another". In your heart you say, "Shoot, and shoot straight!" Why are you prosecuting me for distributing leaflets which preach what Tolstoy preached all his life in Russia, undisturbed. You may send me to prison, I shall not be the first or the last to go there unjustly. But you will have to send many more before you can hope to suppress the truth. And you will stand condemned for ever before the eyes of all truth-and freedom-loving people. I know and believe every word on the leaflets to be true. Why are you so afraid of the truth?'

Is that the sort of man you want to send to prison? Is that the sort of man that is worth the Government's breaking a tradition of sixty years in order to prosecute? God forbid that honest opinion should ever be made a crime.

The Attorney-General (Sir Rufus Isaacs): On a point of Order. Sir, I desire to raise the question, for guidance from you, as to how far we are entitled to discuss the merits or demerits of cases which are *sub judice*. The difficulty I shall be placed in is this, that if my hon. friend refers to cases of this kind, which he knows are actually *sub judice* at present, and others, it places me in the position, if I reply to the case made against me, of having to deal with evidence which has not yet been sifted, and upon which I have had to act merely as *prima facie* evidence. I have been careful always to state that that is the view of the case. I find it difficult to deal with the whole of the evidence relating to these matters while the cases are still pending trial. I thought the rule of the House was that we could not discuss the details of cases which were *sub judice*, and I submit we cannot go into them.

Mr Speaker: I think the House has always set its face against discussing any question which is still *sub judice*. Up to the point the hon. Member has reached I understood those cases were disposed of.

Sir Rufus Isaacs: This case and the case actually quoted are *sub judice*.

Mr Speaker: Is it under appeal?

Sir Rufus Isaacs: No. As my hon. Friend knows, Crowsley is committed for trial.

Mr Speaker: I thought the hon. Member referred to six months' hard labour. I think the hon. Member will see that, in the interests of that particular individual and any others whose cases are coming on, it would be most undesirable to refer to it except just incidentally. Of course, what he says on one side may be contradicted on the other, and it would be very undesirable that observations should be made with reference to a case which is still going on. As to any cases which have been concluded, and which have not been appealed against, of course the hon. Member would be entitled to make any comments which he thinks right.

Mr Wedgwood: I certainly accept that. The case of Crowsley is a little peculiar because he offers no defence except one which is of no value in a Court of Law. It is not really a new thing in this country for people to be urged not to shoot under certain circumstances when they are in the Army. In the American War of 1780 it was quite a common thing for officers to resign their commissions sooner than go out to the United States and shoot their brothers there, and at the present day we have the case of the hon. Member (Mr Hamersley) saying that under no circumstances would he allow his son to go and shoot down Unionists in Ireland – a very proper position to take up. May I say, in the absence of the hon. Member (Mr MacCallum Scott), that he gave me this case to speak about, and gave me the extracts from the speech of the hon. Member (Mr Hamersley). I do not think it is necessary to say more about it than that those of us who are against these prosecutions would be equally against any prosecution of the hon. Member (Mr Hamersley) or anyone else who said anything of a similar nature. I will not refer to the prosecution of Mr Tom Mann except to say that there was no question of the soldiers coming in at all. The soldiers were not at the meeting. There you have a case of interference with simple freedom of speech alone, and no direct incitement to anyone. After the outburst of public opinion all over the country among the working classes over that case, I think hon. Members can begin dimly to imagine what is going to happen if this series of prosecutions goes on. Already the working classes have a very shrewd suspicion of the judiciary of this country. They do not think they are getting fair play. Are all these cases which are coming before us likely to increase the respect of the working class for the judicial bench? We have the extraordinary *ex-parte* statement of the Recorder the other day in the charge to the jury. I was very glad that he made that charge to the grand jury, because it merely expressed in words what we know all the people who have to try cases are feeling. However judicial and impartial they may be, they are all human beings like ourselves, and they all, naturally, take either one view or the other in politics. I consider it quite natural that Sir Forrest Fulton should think in that way and should speak in that way; but I am quite certain that the people who read that speech and who see the extraordinarily severe sentences which were given will put two and two together and recognize that the working classes have no chance under existing circumstances of getting justice if that give expression to Syndicalist views.

I come now to the present state of affairs and the difficulty in which the Attorney-General has put the Government. They have proceeded against the Syndicalists and against Mr Tom Mann, well-known politicians, but people who have no personal friends in this

House. Are they going to proceed against people who have personal friends in this House as well? I asked a question today about the *Labour Leader*. The *Labour Leader* is not indeed the organ of the Labour party, but it is intimately associated with the Labour party, and the chairman of that party, Mr W. C. Anderson, is, I think, chairman of directors of the *Labour Leader*, and Crowsley is also one of the directors. They have no editor at present. The *Labour Leader* came out on 22nd March with this in its leading article on the front page:

> 'Before the present prosecutions were instituted we urged the soldiers to refuse to shoot their kinsmen who are battling against poverty if they were ordered to do so, and we repeat that advice now'.

You know what that means. The *Labour Leader* intends either to share the fate of *The Syndicalist* or to show that the Government is partial in the selection of those people who are to be prosecuted. The *Labour Leader* is not by any means the only paper that is putting in paragraphs like that. Are they all going to be prosecuted? Is every man who sells one of Tolstoy's penny pamphlets, and are the publishers and booksellers to be prosecuted by the Government for making use of paragraphs exactly like that? Really, it was madness that the Government should start on this scheme of prosecution. Almost more unpleasant to deal with than the case of the *Labour Leader* is the case of hon. Members opposite who sit for Irish constituencies. I have neither the time nor the taste to scavenge in the old speeches of hon. Members opposite. I do not know whether they have ever specifically made speeches urging that soldiers should not shoot upon the men of the North of Ireland, but hon. Members opposite may be quite certain that the Incitement to Mutiny Act of 1797 was not the only Act passed in those years of Tory reaction. There were the Treasonable Practices Act, and the Seditious Meetings Act. Is the Government going to confine its attentions to the Syndicalists and the Labour parties, and let off the right hon. Gentleman (Sir E. Carson), Privy Councillor, ex-Law Officer? Let me read an extract from a speech by the hon. and gallant Gentleman (Captain Craig). In September 1911 he said:

> 'You need not be a bit afraid of being prosecuted for sedition or

rebellion. Let the Government try to lay a finger on any man for asserting the principles of freedom in civil and religious matters, and they would light a fire in Protestant Ulster which would never be put out'.

I should be the last man to suggest for a moment that it would be an advantage to the State to prosecute the hon. and gallant Gentleman for making a seditious statement.

Mr Malcolm: In what part of that statement was the sedition?

Mr Wedgwood: 'Let the Government try to lay a finger on any man for asserting the principles of freedom, and they would light a fire in Protestant Ulster which would never be put out. You need not be a bit afraid of being prosecuted for sedition or rebellion'.

Captain Craig: So far as we are concerned we repeat the statement in this House and take all responsibility.

Mr Wedgwood: I was quite certain the hon. and gallant Gentleman would. He would repeat it outside too, with perfect safety, I believe; but whether it would be perfectly safe a month or two hence, when we have had a few more of these prosecutions, and when public opinion is beginning to be a little afraid of hon. Members opposite, as they are really afraid of the Syndicalists now, I am not quite so certain.

Captain Craig: We are quite prepared to take all risks. We are not going to funk it in any way.

Mr Wedgwood: We know the hon. and gallant Gentleman. Let me now give a quotation from the Rev. Wm. Wright – I do not know who he is, but it seems to me that he likewise incurs risks for the free expression of his opinion. He said at Newtownards, county Down, on 10th November:

> 'In a very short time they would have taught their young men to resist Home Rule and also to handle arms. He thought there was no hope for them except the hope of using arms'.

I do not think for a moment he has not a perfect right to say that, just as much as Mr Tom Mann had a perfect right to make his speech, just as much as the *Syndicalist* has a perfect right to publish the Open Letter. It would be very difficult for the Attorney-General to be able to distinguish between the Rev. William Wright and Mr Tom Mann.

Marquess of Tullibardine: Is it right that Mr Tom Mann's name should be brought in? He is under trial.

Mr Wedgwood: The Noble Lord must really understand that Mr Tom Mann and Frederick Crowsley are made of the same material as the hon. and gallant Gentleman (Captain Craig). They are quite willing to stand the racket. They are out to fight for freedom just as much as the hon. and gallant Gentleman.

Sir Rufus Isaacs: The hon. Gentleman is under a misapprehension. He has several times stated that Mr Tom Mann was being prosecuted for a speech that he made. That is not a point in the prosecution at all. The only use that is made of the speech is that therein he stated emphatically that he was, according to our view, responsible for the publication of the *Syndicalist*, and he made other statements of that character. The speech in itself, however violent, is not the subject of the prosecution.

Mr Wedgwood: I am very glad of the right hon. Gentleman's interruption. That means to say, I take it, that it is only printed words which are prosecutable, and that a man may say what he likes. It seems to me that there are three courses open to the Government. They may stop where they are and leave the prosecution at the *Syndicalist*, in which case they will incur, justly, the charge of partiality. It will be said of them that they are afraid to prosecute the *Labour Leader* on account of the Labour vote, and that they are afraid to prosecute hon. Members opposite because of arousing the fury of Ulster. These accusations will be made and will have, at least in the public mind, something of the savour of truth about them. Or else the other course open to the Government is to prosecute in every case, to proceed against every newspaper, and to see that they all get six months' and nine months' hard labour, and in order to carry out their policy to the logical conclusion, they should include speeches as well as publications in newspapers. Or else the other course open to them – the course which I think they ought to adopt – is to amnesty the prisoners, Messrs Bowman and Buck, and to cease prosecuting Tom Mann. Let them fairly recognize that they have made a mistake. Let them fairly recognize that on no principle of English tradition ought these prosecutions ever to have taken place, that a man is still able in a free country to express freely his opinions, however detrimental they may be considered to be by the vast majority of mankind. Let them recognize the position, and cease these prosecutions. Let them amnesty the prisoners, and then at last we shall have put an end to all those prosecutions of the Press and all this interference with the liberty of Englishmen, which we have fought for in past generations and which we pride ourselves upon still. Class feeling is strong enough in this country. You may embitter it. There is no sign of the bitterness wearing down. Are you going to embitter it by having the working classes smarting under an obvious injustice? Put that matter right, and start afresh with the clean slate which you are so often talking about. I plead with the Government not in the interests of these men – they do not ask mercy – they do not want mercy – I plead with the Government in the interests of Liberal tradition and in the interests of the traditions of our country, of which we all, on whichever side of the House we sit, are justly and rightly proud.

CHAPTER XXI

TRIAL FOR INCITEMENT TO MUTINY
1912

At the Salford Petty Sessions on 28th March, I was brought up on remand and committed to the Assizes, bail being allowed in £200 and two sureties of £100 each.

The Assizes were held in Manchester, and my trial came on 9th May. The following report is from the *Weekly Citizen* of 11 May, 1912.

'Tom Mann!'

Thus bellowed the stentorian voice of a Manchester Assize Court official on Thursday, in the officious way these functionaries have.

The sprightly, well-knit figure of the great agitator stepped forward. Tom was smiling just as if it was a mere part in a comedy he was playing, instead of being the chief figure in a drama – a drama which at best was converted into a farce by the very nature of the absurd charge.

Tom was ushered into the dock – a very uncommon prisoner placed in the spot wherein common and sordid felons often stand. In that one incident the dignity of the workers was lowered to the ground. It was an indirect insult to Britain's millions of workers that one of their leaders should have to undergo this humiliation. Tom Mann, however, took the insult quite coolly.

Wigged and robed counsel were there for the 'Crown', to make the most damage they could against the prisoner. Mann was his own barrister, and he was quite competent to defend himself. To assist him in any legal points which might arise was his solicitor, Mr Quilliam, of Liverpool, well-known and highly appreciated in Socialist circles.

The Judge, Mr Justice Bankes, in his gaudy robes, sat in solemn state upon the Bench, and out and in popped idle barristers to get a peep at the 'terrible man who told the soldiers not to shoot, don'tcherknow'. In the body of the court were a few prominent trade-union leaders and friends of Tom Mann's, but there were more outside who had been refused admission for some unknown reason by the officers.

Not Guilty

The list of indictments was read first of all, and then Tom was asked if he was guilty or not.

'Not guilty' came his prompt answer.

The question was put from the Bench as to who appeared for the defence – the prosecuting counsel had already announced that they were for the 'Crown' – and on Tom saying that he would defend himself, the Judge looked in his direction a moment.

Mr Justice Bankes, noting something amiss, asked if the prisoner would like to have some facilties for taking notes. Tom assented, and a small table was placed in the dock.

Tom sat down beside it, opened a notebook, and began taking notes of the 'allegations' the prosecution raised.

'May I have the witnesses out of the court?' he asked as soon as the proceedings had started.

'Certainly,' replied his Lordship, and the witnesses were ordered to retire.

Mr Langdon, KC, then addressed the jury. There had been an endeavour, he said, on the part of the prisoner to get the soldiers enrolled in the army to disobey the lawful orders which they might receive or to commit acts of disobedience to their officers in a way that would amount to mutiny and disobedience to the Crown.

Soldiers' Duties

Next Mr Langdon defined the duties of the soldiers. There were certain important obligations on military subjects of the Crown. The soldier really had a double duty.

He owed a duty both as a citizen and as a soldier, as much of one, perhaps, as the other. They differed little in character and extent, but in substance they even overlapped.

Clad though he is in uniform the soldier remains invested with the duties which everyone of us owes to the State of which he is a member.

Over and above his civil duties, which were no less than those of the civilians, the soldier by virtue of his military oath, had duties arising from his position as a soldier. Those duties were great and important, and subject to heavy punishment in case of disobedience.

Where the military were called in to preserve peace the duties he was called upon to discharge were of the gravest importance and required the utmost discretion in their exercise.

The 'Open Letter'

The endeavour to incite to mutiny and disobedience was contained, counsel added, in a couple of columns printed in the *Syndicalist* and was in language of great power, well chosen to the end in view, and addressed – the prosecution submitted with a deliberate intent – to soldiers in order to get them to violate their duty, and that at a time when the discharge of their duty was a matter of the gravest moment.

Mr Langdon read the whole of the 'Open Letter'.

Terrible Contingencies

Expressions in the letter were directed to the terrible contingencies which sometimes arose, and which had arisen in recent times, when industrial struggles trouble the country – struggles carried on generally with self-restraint, but sometimes accompanied with violence, riot, and pillage.

That document contemplated a time when the police were helpless, and the last resource of organized authority had to be brought into play to control the forces of disorder.

Subject to the orders of the magistrates, whose duty it is to maintain order and to protect property, these forces had to be employed, and if the riot and pillage and violence continued – if the appearance of the military forces alone was not sufficient – then, he regretted to say, those forces had to be employed, under the law, with effect, in order to achieve the ends of Society in the maintenance of peace, and the protection of proprety.

The language, Mr Langdon continued, was well chosen to influence the minds of those to whom it was addressed, men who, as they were told, might be out of the colours some day and liable to be shot at themselves.

They could not get away from the inevitable conclusion that it was intended to seduce soldiers from their duty, and to incite them to mutiny when orders were given them which they ought to obey.

Questionable

Counsel then dealt with the question of Tom Mann's responsibility for the publication. Mr Langdon said the *Syndicalist* was published in January of this year by the Industrial Syndicalist Education League.

Of that League a Mr Bowman was secretary, and the prisoner Mann was chairman. It was printed at Walthamstow by two men named Buck.

The Judge: How can we admit this evidence?

Counsel contended that it was quite an admissible statement, and an argument ensued upon that point. Finally the Judge addressed Tom thus:

'I presume that you would desire the whole of the occurrence at Salford to be in the knowledge of the jury?'

'Quite so,' promptly answered Tom.

Counsel then went on with his argument, and said that the editor of the paper and the secretary of the League had been arrested for the publication of the Letter.

On 15th February a man was arrested at Aldershot for endeavouring to distribute copies of the Letter to soldiers in camp, and on 13th March there was a meeting at Salford at which a speech was made by the prisoner, while on March 14th there was another meeting, and it was in respect to publication at that meeting that the indictment was drawn up, and to that publication he desired to call attention.

Alleged Offence

Mr Langdon read extracts from the speech made by the prisoner on that occasion as follows:

'They (the Government) have already prepared the hotel and barracks for the military, and they have appointed men in charge of this, right in this very district, in this town, and all around. What are they doing it for? To bring them here to shoot you down. That is what for. That is their intention. They are trying to close the mouths of any of us that dare to talk freely and interchange opinions with some degree of courage. Therefore it is that they have arrested the man that our chairman has referred to.

'There are two brothers who are printers of this little paper; they have printed it on behalf of the committee of which I was chairman. The secretary of that committee, a comrade of mine, Guy Bowman, was arrested after leaving my house last Friday evening on his way to his own at Walthamstow.

'The detectives went there, searched every room, and confiscated all they could get hold of in the way of copies of the paper and also new matter prepared for the next issue. They took him to the police station, charged him with treason, felony, or some other rot, landed him in Brixton Gaol and refused him bail, and he has been there this week. What has he done? He has made no remarks whatever; he is simply identified with the issue of this little paper.

'Now I will read you a paragraph or two. It contains an open letter to British Socialists – no! I beg pardon, British soldiers:'

Built of Different Stuff

After that Mann, said Crown counsel, read extracts from the 'Open Letter', and continued:

'Now I will ask you is there anything wrong there? Is it not true? They are called upon to murder us. (*A voice:* "Yes.") We know they were called upon to murder in Liverpool ... and if these soldiers be ordered to fire and to murder, to fire and to kill – for that is how they have been told to fire – and then to tell us we dare not, and shall not, on pain of imprisonment, raise our voices, utter a sentiment, or dare to address them, and urge them not to do so, then if we obey, we are indeed cowards and mean things.

'But we are built of different stuff, and by all the gods and devils I will let them know that I am fearless in the matter. I do not know to what extent there are detectives or plain-clothes police in this hall, but at each meeting I have been at for a long time there have been men sent by the police for the express purpose of taking notes. It may be just as our comrade Bowman has been charged with treason, felony, and what not, for being identified with the paper he has issued; if he is punished for that, and it is an offence and so serious they will not allow him to come out on bail, I do not see how I shall escape as chairman of that committee. You must not be surprised if I, too, am arrested, and find myself in court, but because of that possibility I am not going to cease from denouncing these tactics'.

Counsel said that this meant that the prisoner fully understood what the letter was aimed at, that he realized that it was an endeavour to penetrate into the allegiance of the soldiers and seduce them from their duty and incite them to disobey the lawful orders of their officers.

Nearly in Camera

A strange incident marked the commencement of the evidence. The first witness, Herbert Fitch, of Scotland Yard, was giving his story of what had happened at meetings prior to Salford, when the Judge, interposing, said:

Someone has sent me a telegram asking me whether I have given orders that the public should be excluded from the court. I have given no orders. I have made inquiries, and I have ascertained that the officers are not excluding any particular individuals at all. They have allowed as large a number of people to come in without distinction or selection as the court will comfortably hold, and that is the only exclusion that has been in any way carried out. I have ordered some more to be allowed to come in, and I think the court is now reasonably full.

Mann: I was personally wondering when we came into court why so few were in.

Judge: Do you wish to make some application to me?

Mann: I don't.

His Lordship next raised the question as to whether evidence could be admitted with regard to what took place on 14th January, the indictment being in respect to what occurred on 14th March. He asked the prisoner if he had any objection.

Mann: I have no objection, my lord; none whatever.

Quite Indifferent

Judge: Do you wish it introduced?

Mann: I do not wish it; but I am quite indifferent. I would prefer that you decided.

Judge (to Mr Langdon): Then you must satisfy me.

After some legal argument his lordship decided to exclude all evidence as to what occurred on other dates than 14th March.

He pointed out that the indictment might have been framed in a different way, and it might have alleged a continuous endeavour, but it had been limited to a particular endeavour on a particular date, and by particular means.

Mr Langdon: As your lordship pleases.

Detective-Sergeant William Markland of the Salford police, spoke as to Mann speaking at Pendleton Town Hall on 14th March, when between 600 and 700 people were present. Mann read out the three opening paragraphs of the 'Open Letter to Soldiers' finishing up with the words, 'Don't do it'.

Prisoner added he was pleased to take responsibility for that, and said two brothers had been locked up for printing that paper, but they only printed it for a committee, of which he (Mann) was the chairman. He saw Sergeant Clarke buy a copy of the paper in the hall. On 20th March last, witness received accused into custody at New Scotland Yard. Mann made no reply to the charge read over on that occasion.

Other police witnesses corroborated.

Fearless of Consequences

The clerk of the Court then read the following statement taken from Tom Mann by the police:

I plead not guilty. At the same time, as regards the evidence given concerning some of the things I have said, particularly that of identifying myself with the chairmanship of the Industrial Syndicalist Education League, that is perfectly correct, and it was that league that was responsible for the paper called *The Syndicalist* being brought into existence, and as chairman I am quite prepared to share all necessary responsibility. Some of that which has been given as evidence against me is contrary to fact and at the Assizes I shall give evidence to that effect.

The statement that I used the words 'Don't shoot your comrades; turn your rifles round and shoot the other people', is absolutely untrue. Neither have I personally been identified with the writing, the publishing or issuing of that Open Letter to Soldiers, beyond what I have already stated in my capacity as chairman. I did not know of the existence of the Open Letter until several days after the issue of *The* January number of *The Syndicalist*. I do not say that because I have any reluctance to go to prison or endure any other punishment imposed, but as friends and comrades of mine have already been convicted in connection therewith I fail to understand why further conviction should be called for.

I am advised by my counsel that the matter immediately at issue is my personal culpability or otherwise in connection with the Open Letter to Soldiers. I am quite fearless of the consequences. It is true what I said at the meetings, as given in evidence, and I unhesitatingly repeat, that I agree entirely with the spirit and object of that letter. I would like to make one remark concerning that extract quoted from the reporter's notebook. I believe it to be absolutely correct, and I stand by it in every particular. Tom Mann.

TOM MANN'S SPEECH
RIOTS DELIBERATELY CAUSED

The police evidence being ended, the Judge asked: Do you wish to give evidence on oath?

No, answered the prisoner, but I wish to make a statement from the dock. The Judge assented, and Tom Mann, speaking clearly and deliberately, said:

I wish to raise one point which will have a direct bearing upon the statement I wish to make, on a point of law, and that is that while soldiers are engaged on active service they are certainly covered by the military law, but while they are engaged assisting a civil authority, they are then covered by the civil law, and differ in no respect from ordinary citizens, and any commands given to them which they are bound to obey must be lawful commands.

The word lawful is of vital importance here. I am indicted with having endeavoured to seduce soldiers as soldiers from their duty, from the obeying of lawful commands. I plead that I have not done any such thing.

I shall endeavour to show what the soldier's position is as a soldier, and when he is engaged in assisting a civil authority, then he is a citizen and should be treated as such in all respects.

Even the authority quoted by the learned counsel for the prosecution makes that admission. I do not think learned counsel named it: I think it is Lord Justice Stephen, vol. 1, *History of Criminal Law*.

Liable for Murder
It was because the citizen might be called upon to do certain things, so therefore might the soldier be called upon to do the same thing in his capacity as a citizen. If one might employ arms for the purpose of maintaining order, so might the soldier do the same.

If one could not do it the other could not. It was not sufficient for an officer to order soldiers to do a certain thing for them to do it; they must not do it if there was no justification for it.

If there was no justification for the soldier firing, no justification for officers ordering them to fire, and no justification for the magistrate asking the officers to give the order – each and all of these were liable to stand for trial for murder or manslaughter as the case might be.

He mentioned this to show it was permissible for a man to address soldiers in their capacity as citizens, to urge them to comply with, not to exceed, that which the law would approve of.

Soldiers when at work in their capacities as citizens were covered by the civil law, and amenable to it in all respects.

He had addressed nothing directly or indirectly to soldiers serving King and Country in their capacity as soldiers, and it was quite another matter to address something to soldiers when they were called upon to aid the civil authority.

He then quoted the result of the Featherstone Riots Inquiry, and contended that the report of that inquiry supported his contention in full.

Not Responsible
This Open Letter that has been read so carefully, so effectively, Mann proceeded, I am not the author of.

I did not write it. I didn't cause it to be printed. I was not directly or indirectly connected with it being issued.

I didn't know that it existed until I saw it in the paper called *The Syndicalist*. *The Syndicalist* is issued under the supervision of a committee, the Industrial Syndicalist Education League, of which I am chairman.

I am quite prepared to be saddled with all responsibility in connection therewith, irrespective of my not having been identified with the production of the letter.

It is known that that Open Letter addressed to British Soldiers was in existence in leaflet form six months before it was printed in *The Syndicalist*. It was printed in several papers.

No Evasion

I am not asking to be allowed to escape any punishment that ought to attach to me, if punishment ought to attach to anyone at all, for I deliberately declare I am the chairman of the committee that authorized it, but I did not know of its actual existence until I saw it in *The Syndicalist*.

This letter is an appeal to soldiers when called upon to engage in industrial disputes on behalf of the civil authority and when they are bound by civil law. Surely then it is permissible for us to ask them not to murder.

Such is my opinion, he determinedly declared, and if it is wrong – well, I am prepared to stand by it.

I have only said what the authorities have already said, that even rioters are not enemies unless they are armed in a warlike manner.

Therefore, when we ask them not to murder us, it means not to do some things that have been done in the past by the soldiers; for in the past soldiers have, in obedience to their officers, fired and killed, and have had to stand their trial.

Riots Deliberately Caused

I know – and this is what I put in for my defence – I know that riots or disturbances are deliberately caused by those occupying responsible positions. In making my statement I desire to illustrate it.

I am justified in this statement by the events of last August in Liverpool. Then the men on strike were perfectly orderly, and my own efforts, as the Chief Constable has stated, were directed entirely towards the maintenance of the peace.

The public, had, of course, to suffer a certain amount of inconvenience on account of the number of men who were out of work, but there was no need for calling out the military or the navy.

Mann then gave an account of what happened in the struggle on St George's Plateau on Sunday, 13 August, 1911.

The matter had been raised in the House of Commons, when the Attorney-General stated that Mann was not being prosecuted for his speeches.

The Judge: Yes, but I don't think we will go into that. We must confine ourselves to the evidence which has been produced to-day.

Mann: Quite so, my lord. Your ruling all the time.

Prisoner added that if the military had been called upon to fire on the crowd at that gathering it would have been murder, and he thought he was justified in advising soldiers not to do that.

Prosecution's Motives

Mann added that he was compelled to come to the conclusion that these proceedings had been taken because of his connection with the Syndicalist movement.

Others had written and spoken as he had, but they were not identified with the particular movement with which he had been identified.

He knew no other reason why action was being taken to prevent an ordinary person of his stamp from having the free exercise of speech.

He had urged people to organize and to use their power to escape from the poverty they were in, and he had criticized the action of the local authorities in preparing for the use of the military in times of trade disturbance.

I am not asking your mercy in any respect, added the prisoner, but I am claiming the right, as a man, as a citizen, as a native of this country, and as a workman, to organize for the removal of the worst evils which afflict this country.

I did not publish the letter, he concluded, but I don't differ from it. I don't wish to have my liberty curtailed, but I shall not ask for mercy in any shape or form, and I stand for the principles of the Open Letter.

SIX MONTHS AWARDED

THE JURY FOUND TOM MANN GUILTY

Asked whether he had anything to say why judgement should not be passed, Mann replied firmly, 'No, sir'.

In passing sentence, Mr Justice Bankes said:

So far I feel that I ought to follow the course that was taken with regard to the publisher of this newspaper.

I do not know what the effect of this trial may be, but I hope it has brought home to your mind that the law is not what you suggested to the jury it was, and that at any rate in the future you will refrain from bringing yourself within the provisions of the statute which forbids this conduct, which seems to me to be unworthy of anybody who realizes what he is doing because it is an inducement to people to do something which must bring grave punishment upon them.

The suggestion that the law might be altered is, of course, a suggestion which is quite lawful to be made by those who think there ought to be any alteration, but to do what the jury have found that you have done is mischievous in my opinion in the highest degree.

All I have to do is to pass a sentence which the publisher of this newspaper is already undergoing, and my sentence is that you be imprisoned without hard labour in the second division for six months.

Mann, on receiving the sentence, asked if he might be allowed to see his wife and his solicitor, and this permission was accorded.

As Tom Mann was about to be taken to the prison of Strangeways he was for a moment able to pass a brief message to our special representative. It was:

There must be no apologies for me, and there must be no petition.

This is the message he asks the paper to give his friends and supporters.

Tom went cheerfully into his six months' humiliation and imprisonment.

Guy Bowman was imprisoned in Wormwood Scrubs, and I was at Strangeways, Manchester. It might have been difficult to find anyone willing to accept responsibility for *The Syndicalist*, had not Comrade Gaylord Wilshire, editor of *Wilshire's Magazine*, stepped into the breach and kept the paper going till Guy Bowman was released. Also an Italian comrade, Odin Por, an ardent Syndicalist, contributed articles and encouraged others to do the same. Many friends in and out of Parliament at once commenced vigorous propaganda, holding protest meetings on a large scale, and demanding our release. It was particularly interesting to me on getting released to find who had been specially active in organizing the meetings, putting questions in Parliament, and in a variety of ways taking action to bring pressure to bear on the Government. My thanks were given in the best way I could give them on my release, but I desire here to express my gratitude and sincere appreciation for the good and effective work that obtained our release long before the sentences expired. I was out after seven weeks in gaol instead of six months, to which I was sentenced, and this undoubtedly was in consequence of the many meetings held and resolutions carried, and sending them to the right quarter, plus the determination manifested to take further action, if necessary. Whatever the cause, the prison gates were opened, and we were able to take up the work again.

CHAPTER XXII

CONCLUSION AND FAREWELL

TEN years have passed since the incidents just related. No detailed account of my life during this period will be attempted in the present volume. Some day, perhaps, I shall write a sequel. Meanwhile I shall close with a brief sketch of the intervening decade, and a summary of present outlooks. First of all, and in this connection, I want (subject to certain reservations to be explained towards the close of this chapter) to reiterate my belief in the general truth of the Syndicalist theory of ten or twelve years ago.

Notwithstanding the eclipse of the term Syndicalism, the theories and methods advocated by the Industrial Syndicalist Education League (confirmed by the experience of the great strikes of ten years back, and further substantiated by the results of the railwaymen's strike and the coal stoppage since the war), still hold the field as against the theories and methods of the Labour parliamentarians. I cannot today express my outlook more forcibly than it was expressed in an article I wrote when under remand in Strangeways Prison. It appeared in *The Syndicalist* for April 1912. I reproduce it in full.

> The exceptional trade-union activity, the increase in volume and variety of the various phases of Labour unrest, and the recent application of Syndicalist principles and methods in the industrial world, is simply so much evidence that the efforts of the working class to obtain improved conditions are not flagging, but multiplying; and all who recognize the existence of the Social Problem have cause for satisfaction that this stimulating force is apparently in the ascendant and destined to produce great results in the near future.
>
> Syndicalism means the control of industry by 'Syndicates' or Unions of Workers, in the interest of the entire community; this necessarily pre-supposes the relatively perfect industrial organization of all who work, and the right relationship to each other of every

section. Robert Owen, over eighty years ago, advocated the necessity for such a method of organization, and made a very good start at putting it into practice; but, as it proved, the workers were not equal to resorting to such relatively highly-trained methods; and they have had to spend twice forty years in the industrial wilderness because they were neither mentally nor physically qualified to enter the Promised Land. Since Owen's time, several other methods have been resorted to by the workers to escape from their industrial bondage, but none of them have proved really effective, parliamentary action least of all.

In Robert Owen's vigorous days the workers of England had no political rights, and it would appear that Owen set small store by the possession of any such 'rights'. He saw and taught that the workers' difficulties arose as a consequence of their industrial subjugation to the capitalist class – in other words, that the members of the employing class had no concern for the members of the working class, except to control and exploit their labour force for the specific purpose of using them as profit-making machines for themselves.

The Syndicalist of today has learned that all-important fact, and so refuses to play at attempts at social reform through and by means of Parliaments, these institutions being entirely under the control of the plutocracy, and never tolerating any modification of conditions in the interest of the working class, save with the ulterior motive of more firmly entrenching themselves as the ruling class.

All this is admitted by most Socialists as regards the motive and object of the capitalist class, but the typical Socialist retains an abiding faith in the 'wisdom and power' of Parliament, and seeks to achieve revolutionary changes by means of Parliament. And yet he also fully admits that all the really serious grievances of the workers are economic or industrial and not political in character. Many of them can also see clearly enough that Parliament cannot manage or control an industry, or really rectify industrial wrongs; but still the glamour of this imposing bourgeois institution commands their obeisance and subjection.

The Syndicalist, that is, the trade and labour unionist of the revolutionary type, recognizes not only that all changes favourable to the workers must be brought about by the workers, but also that the only correct method of doing this is through and by the workers' own industrial organizations. Organized labour means the

Conclusion and Farewell

control of labour power by the labourers organized, and this means the control of wealth production to the extent to which Labour is organized.

It is only while Labour is partially organized that recourse to strikes is necessary; not even the general strike will be necessary when Labour is universally organized. Universal organization must carry with it industrial solidarity, i.e. universal agreement upon the object to be attained, for otherwise the capitalists will still triumph. With solidarity on the industrial field the workers become all-powerful.

There is nothing but a little reflection wanted to enable anyone to see that such is really the case. All students of social economics, who recognize the operation of the law of wages, know that, irrespective of what the worker produces, all that the worker on the average receives is a subsistence wage; but we also know that, in order to get that subsistence wage, there are some who work but six hours a day, whilst others work twice and even three times as long. The most effective means of securing social betterment is by reducing the working hours. It is better to get the subsistence wage for relatively few hours than for many hours of work.

Syndicalism will do this, and by so doing will solve the problem of unemployment, and by the same means will kill excessive working hours; and by the same methods will wipe out all low wages. A further application of the same principle will secure to the workers the full reward of their labour. All will come in a perfectly natural manner as the direct outcome of industrial solidarity guided intelligently and applied courageously.

The State Socialist, confronted with the unemployed problem, admits the necessity for trying to cure the evil, and proposes a 'Right to Work' Bill. This proposal has been in the forefront of the State Socialists' programme for fully twenty years, and it has never yet reached the stage of serious discussion – that is, it has not yet been considered of sufficiently urgent importance to be classed by the average parliamentarian as being within the region of practical politics. Nor is there any valid reason for supposing it is likely to be seriously dealt with by those who claim to attach importance to it.

The Syndicalist says: 'Apply direct action and reduce working hours up to the point of absorbing all available workers in the ranks of the actively employed, and quite as rapidly as labour-saving devices are applied still further reduce working hours, so that there will never be any unemployed'.

'But,' says the parliamentarian, 'in order to reduce hours we must have an Act of Parliament'. *The Syndicalist* says: 'Such reduction of working hours can be far better brought about by industrial organization. Nothing is wanted but the organization of the workers, and agreement to use the organization for such a purpose'.

The trade unionists themselves, having had their minds so fully occupied with the idea that Parliament is the all-important institution, and never having even hoped to see all workers organized industrially, have failed to realize what enormous power lies in industrial solidarity.

The nearest approach to any one industry exhibiting solidarity was that of the late great strike of the miners in March 1912; but even here it was not complete, for many colliery enginemen and others did not give in their notices at the same time as the colliers, and no arrangement at all was made with other organized workers to secure their co-operation in an active and warlike manner.

The armchair discussions that took place for several weeks before the miner's notices expired, and the ready acceptance of the intervention of the Government, showed how childishly simple were many of those responsible on the men's side. They did not view it as a national battle to be fought by the organized workers engaged in the class struggle. Unfortunately, a large percentage of the 'miners' leaders' had no conception that there was or that there is a 'class struggle'; and, indeed, they had done their utmost to prevent the national claim for a minimum wage coming along as forcefully as it did.

Some of the capitalist papers charged these same leaders with being 'Syndicalists'! The fact is that many of them had never pronounced the word in their lives, and not five per cent. of them knew what the term meant. But they made an excellent fight, and were truer Syndicalists in fact than in theory. Nevertheless, if the Syndicalist principle of brotherly solidarity in all industries had been understood and resorted to, the whole pressure of the transport workers, including railwaymen, would have been applied at the end of the first week, and no power on earth could have prevailed against them.

Once again, the object aimed at by the Syndicalists is the control of each industry by those engaged in it in the interests of the entire

Conclusion and Farewell

community. This will be followed by the ownership of the tools and other means of production and transportation jointly by the industrial community. Strikes are mere incidents in the march towards control of industry and ownership of the tools of production. 'Sabotage', 'Ca'Canny', and irritation strikes are mere incidentals in the progress onwards. The master key to the entire problem is INDUSTRIAL SOLIDARITY.

Naturally, much absurd criticism has been directed against 'Syndicalism', and quite a host of Labour men have hastened to declare not only that they are not Syndicalists, but, indeed, that they have pronounced opinions against it – which, upon analysis, amounts to this: they are obsessed with the plutocratic institution of Parliament and are also fearful lest identification with the workers' real movement should debar them from sharing the contents of the Egyptian fleshpots. But they need not fear, timid souls! They may still propitiate plutocratic opinion by disclaiming identification with the virile fighting force that is already lifting the working class out of the bogs and quagmires of mugwumpish parliamentarism.

The watchwords are INDUSTRIAL SOLIDARITY and DIRECT ACTION. By these means we can and will solve unemployment, cure poverty, and secure to the worker the full reward of his labour.

Now, before presenting a brief statement of my present outlook on the matters discussed in the foregoing article, it will be well to give a summary account of my doings since it was written.

In 1913, I went to the United States on a lecturing tour, travelling from Boston in the east to San Francisco in the west. I visited seventy cities, and lectured under various auspices. For instance, some of the meetings I addressed were organized by the IWW (Industrial Workers of the World), others by the AFL (American Federation of Labour), others by the Socialist Party of America and by various trade unions. The editorial committee of *Justice*, the Socialist paper of Pittsburg and district, arranged meetings for me. I also lectured to the economic section of Chicago University, and gave addresses in Seattle, and at the Labour Temples of various cities. It was an intensely interesting experience, giving me opportunities of coming into contact with all kinds of working-class organizations, more particularly the trade unions, and also enabling me to learn essential facts concerning conditions of labour, rates of wages, and the workers' standard of life. Of great value to me personally were the opportunities I had of meeting representative persons engaged in public work, and of learning from them at first hand their views and methods.

One friend in particular gave me much assistance in arranging meetings. This was W. Z. Foster, of Chicago, who shortly afterwards took so prominent a part in the successful organization of the stockyard workers of Chicago. A description of the conditions under which, prior to their organization, these workers carried on their occupations, was one of the main themes of Upton Sinclair's famous book *The Jungle*.

To return for a moment, before quitting the US, to Comrade Foster, I should mention his close connection with two recent and notable developments in the American Labour movement.

In the first place he is the historian of the great steelworkers' strike. In the close of 1919, more than 365,000 steelworkers put up a spirited fight against the Steel Trust, but were defeated after the stoppage had lasted three and a half months. The workers were beaten by the Iron Heel, by the organized forces of capitalism assisted by all the repressive powers at the disposal of the State and Federal authorities. I cannot recommend too highly, to earnest students of the contemporary Labour movement, William Z. Foster's account of the affair in his book *The Great Steel Strike and its Lessons*, published by Huebsch, New York, 1920.

Secondly, in August 1922, Foster became closely identified with one of the most promising of recent developments in the US, the Trade Union Educational League. This is a remarkably live body, which aims at exercising a revolutionary influence within the AFL. It is destined, I think, to help greatly in lifting the reproach that the United States is the most backward land in the world as regards Labour organization.

Early in 1914 the South African Government deported to England nine men who had been actively connected with the trade-union movement on the Rand in the Transvaal. I was sent to South Africa to endeavour to weld working-class forces together, and was enthusiastically received by the miners, the railwaymen, and others. To my pleasurable surprise the foremost contingent in a procession of ten thousand people who met me at Johannesburg station, was a couple of hundred young Dutchmen with their trade-union banner. This was a great advance on anything I had seen when I was in the same district in 1910. At that date, very few of the Dutch Africanders were working in the mines, and those few would have no truck with the Britishers. In the interval between my two visits, economic pressure, and fraternization, had brought the young Dutchmen into the industrial field, and they had learned the necessity for industrial organization.

At the present time eighty per cent of the white workers at the gold mines on the Rand are Dutchmen. The recent labour dispute on the Rand had helped to consolidate working-class feeling yet further. In the 1922 strike, the forces of capitalist and governmental repression were ruthlessly used. Large numbers of the workers were shot down, and there is ample evidence to show that some of those who were killed had no direct connection with the dispute. Upwards of five thousand arrests were made, and fourteen hundred persons were prosecuted. A number of the strikers have been sentenced to death.

At the date when I pen this concluding chapter of my memoirs I have received an urgent invitation from the trade unionists and communists of South Africa to revisit that country at once. The heavy sentences inflicted upon the strikers have had a depressing effect, and the unions need to be reorganized. I have agreed to put my hand to this work, and am to sail by the next boat on 15 September, 1922.

Thus we see, in the new and the old countries alike, the same domination of the ruling class, and the fight to the death by that class when resistance is shown by the workers. The class struggle is being waged in every country; and, since the great World War, more fiercely than before.

In recent years all my reflections and my experience have led me to recognize more clearly than ever the correctness of the revolutionary attitude. By this I mean that there is no possible hope of establishing a satisfactory condition of society so long as ownership of the means of production and the control of industry remain vested in the capitalist class. There is no possibility of abolishing wage slavery so long as the wages system obtains. There is no hope of abolishing the wages system, and therefore the profit-making system, through friendly collaboration with the capitalist class, or through relying upon the institutions of that class. The capitalists are savagely fighting the workers in every country. All the recent inventions and the most perfected methods of warfare are utilized against the workers. They are used without scruple in Western Europe, America, and throughout the British Empire.

Trade unionism is of no value unless the members of the unions are clear as to their objective – the overthrow of the capitalist system – and are prepared to use the unions for that purpose. Political action is of no value unless all political effort is used definitely and avowedly for the same end, the abolition of the profit-making system.

Last year I was sent to Moscow by London trade unionists, as their red delegate to the first congress of the Red Trade Union International (now named the Red International of Labour Unions – RILU). In Russia I had the opportunity of conferring with the delegates of over forty nationalities. I was confirmed in the conviction that the Russian Revolution has taught us many things. Perhaps the most important of these is that the administration or management of industry must be by councils of workers and not by parliament. Whilst it may be possible by parliamentary action to prevent the capitalist class from using force to block the workers' movement, this negative advantage is the utmost we can hope to achieve by parliamentary methods. Parliament can never become the instrument through which the workers can secure and exercise the control of industry. I am, therefore, strongly in favour of the universal establishment of Workers' Councils, and the universal formation of Shops' Committees. These institutions are indispensable instruments for achieving the complete overthrow of capitalism and the full control of all forms of industry by the workers. Such control will be secured, and the administration of industry will be effected, through industrial organizations, through our present trade unions when they have shed their narrowness and absurdities, have broadened their bases, and have welded themselves together so as to become equal to all industrial requirements.

This is the essence of Syndicalism. The outlook for the future is not that of a centralized official bureaucracy giving instructions and commands to servile subordinates; I look for the coming of associations of equals, working co-operatively to produce with the highest efficiency, and simultaneously to care for the physical and mental wellbeing of all. This is precisely what we advocated as Syndicalists. But we are undoubtedly approaching the day when we must be ready to avail ourselves of any and every opportunity. With the experience of Russia to guide us, I entirely agree that there will be a period, short or long, when the dictatorship of the proletariat must be resorted to. The effective working of such a dictatorship would not be promoted by ignoring the existence of the plutocratic State machine, or by indifference to its functioning in a manner hostile to the workers. Reluctantly, therefore, I differ from the Syndicalists in various countries who do not recognize the desirability and necessity of collaborating with the Third International. I know full well that to rely upon parliamentary action to achieve our emancipation is futile; but I admit that, when the hour is approaching for getting to grips with essentials, it would be impolitic to leave the forces of the State machine in the hands of our plutocratic enemies.

As far back as 1886, I took an active part in celebrating the Commune of 1871, and have continued to participate in the anniversary celebration down to the present time. I gladly accepted the name of Communist from the date of my first reading of *The Communist Manifesto*, and have ever since been favourable to Communist ideals and principles.

I find that the yearnings and strivings of earlier years, becoming more and more definite and precise in later years, are in accord with the elemental urge of the working class towards real freedom. All the activities of my adult life have been a participation in the revolutionary working-class movement – that movement which, though at times unconsciously, makes ever for the one true goal. The philosophy of all this is clearly set forth in what I regard as an invaluable book, *Creative Revolution*, by Eden and Cedar Paul. In my judgement, if this volume could be broadcasted amongst the workers, it would do inestimable service. Such a book could not have been written a dozen years ago, when I was an enthusiastic advocate of Syndicalism. The experiences of the World War, and the Russian Revolution, were essential to the clarification of our ideas. As a result of that clarification, we have drawn much nearer to the real thing than was possible before. No longer do we 'see men as trees walking', for now we 'see every man clearly'. Or at least we have gained a clear vision of the next step and the next, to carry us to the desired goal. I make an excerpt from *Creative Revolution* as summing up one phase of the situation.

'In so far as socialist propaganda has been truly effective, it has not – such is our contention, based on our reading of modern psychological science quite as much as on our adhesion to Marxist economics and sociology – been effective mainly because of rhetorical appeals to reason and justice, but mainly because it has, wittingly or unwittingly, pursued the tactic of the class struggle: because it has, designedly or undesignedly, aroused a revolutionary impulse among the mass of the workers to secure improved conditions of life and labour; among a large number, to achieve self-government in industry; and, among the peculiarly intelligent minority, to throw off for ever the yoke of Capitalism, to abolish wage-slavery, and to make an end of ownership rule. *Creative Revolution*, Page 41.

'If those who are animated with this revolutionary will, endeavour to achieve their ends through direct action, if they are convinced that to reach the land of Canaan they must take a short cut out of the parliamentary desert in which they have been wandering for forty years, it is not for would-be leaders to gainsay them. That is their vision, and they will follow it to the end, undismayed by the fact that many of those who have helped them thus far on the road now shrink back with horror from the contemplation of the forms which the final struggle is assuming.

'Marx and Engels, seventy years ago, had Pisgah-sights of the promised land. Today Lenin, Trotsky, and the Russian proletariat and poorer peasantry occupy the outlying regions. Here, we shall not follow blindly in their footsteps, for in Britain, in France, in Italy, in Germany, in America, each proletariat has its own peculiar problems to face. But, broadly speaking, the left-wing socialists in all lands are agreed upon two points at least. They hold that parliament is outworn, and that the growing economic power of the workers must fashion new forms of political expression. And they are confident that the main impetus of advance must be the vital impetus of the class struggle'.

I am aware that numerous books upon the coming revolution

have recently issued from the press, but amongst many really good books the one I would advise the student to turn to without delay is *Creative Revolution*.

Here, for the time being, I must bring my memoirs to a close. When I resume my pen, it will not merely be to give a more detailed account of my experiences during the last ten years, but also (I hope), to relate some further activities worth recording as the outcome of the unceasing urge towards the one thing worth working for at this juncture in the history of mankind – THE SOCIAL REVOLUTION.

INDEX

Abraham, William, 51, 74, 77.
Agricultural Labourers' Union, 9, 278.
Amalgamated Association of Coal Porters (Winchmen), 109.
Amalgamated Engineering Union, 19, 120, 278.
Amalgamated Engineers (New South Wales), 185.
Amalgamated Miners' Association (New South Wales), 185, 186.
Amalgamated Society of Engineers, 17, 18, 21, 22, 26, 28, 29, 32, 71, 73, 88–90, 119, 125, 133, 152, 163, 177, 182, 228, 278.
Amalgamated Society of Railway Servants, 70, 210, 213, 228.
American Federation of Labour, 267, 268.
Arbitration Act, New Zealand, 134, 135, 136, 183.
Arbitration Act, Federal, 187.
Arbitration Acts, 181.
Arbitration Courts, 154, 182, 183.
Arbitration Courts, Federal, 189, 190.
Aveling, Eleanor Marx, 31, 67–8.

Bakers' Strike in New Zealand, 183.
Battersea Progressive League, 29.
Besant, Annie, 8, 16, 38, 51, 58.
Bijou Theatre, 155, 157, 165.
Black Friday, 278.
Blacksmiths' Union (New South Wales), 185.
Boilermakers' Union (New South Wales), 185.
Boot and Shoe Operatives' Union, 71.
Bowman, Guy, 203, 205, 230, 233, 236, 241, 248, 253, 254, 261

Bradlaugh, Charles, 7, 8, 11, 16, 26
Broadhurst, Henry, 10, 51, 71.
Broken Hill Dispute, 185–96.
Buck, 230, 233, 248, 253.
Building Trades' Operatives, 278.
Burns, John, 25, 26, 28, 33, 34, 39, 42, 43, 44, 50, 51, 58, 59, 61, 63, 64, 73, 89, 94.
Burrows, Herbert, 29, 40, 58, 68.
Burt, T., 11, 51, 75, 77.
Butchers' Strike in New Zealand, 182.

Carpenters' and Joiners' Union (New South Wales), 185.
Carters' Strike in Liverpool, 210–13.
Carters' Union, 216, 219.
Chambers, Tom, 119, 217, 219, 228.
Champion, H. H., 25, 27, 28, 40, 42, 54, 56, 64, 159.
Churches and the Labour Movement, 85–97.
Churchill, Winston, 223.
Class War, 162, 165, 269, 272.
Combination Laws, 37, 277.
Combined Trade Union Committee (Broken Hill), 185, 190, 194.
Conciliation Board (New Zealand), 183.
Conciliation Boards (Liverpool, 1911), 210.
Connell, Jim (author of *The Red Flag*), 68–9.
Cotton Spinners' Union, 77.
'Country without Strikes', 129, 183.
County Council (London), 79, 91.
Crowsley, Fred, 230, 243, 244, 248.
Cunninghame Graham, R. B., 44, 64, 123, 124.
Curtin, Jack, 158.

Index

Davidson, J. M., 121, 122, 123, 124.
Deportations from South Africa, 199, 268.
Direct Action, 230, 267; *see also* Syndicalism.
Disputes Committee (Broken Hill), 190.
Ditchfield, T., 216, 219, 228.
Dock House Joint Committee, 77.
Dock Labourers, National Union of, 109.
Dock Strike of 1889, 60–69, 278; Sequel thereto, 70–84.
Dock, Wharf, and Riverside Labourers' Union, 70, 109, 227.
'Don't Shoot', Leaflet, 230–49.

East London Labour Emancipation League, 32.
'Economic and Social Justice', 96.
Education Act, 4, 278.
Education, Independent Working-class, 278.
Eight-Hour Demonstration (Sydney), 142.
Eight-Hour Working Day, 38, 42–59, 77.
Eight-Hour Working Day in Australia, 146, 147.
Eight-Hour Working Day in New Zealand, 183.
Eight-Hours League, 44.
Engine Drivers' and Firemen's Association (New South Wales), 185.
Engineering Employers' Federation, 89, 90.
Engineers, *see* Amalgamated Engineers.
'Engineers' Journal', 52.

Federal Arbitration Court, 189–90.
Foster, W. Z., author of *The Great Steel Strike and its Lessons*, 268.
Free Speech Fight, 168–76.
Furniture Trades' Association, 207.
Furniture Trades' Union, 51.

Gardiner, the Rev. T., 86, 91, 92.
Gasworkers' and General Workers' Union, 120.
Gasworkers' Union, 70, 278.
General Confederation of Labour, 205.
General Railway Workers' Union, 70, 213.
General Workers' Union, 49, 120.
George, Henry, 16, 17, 21.

Hardie, Keir, 51, 52, 98, 99, 104, 234.
Home Rule all round, 123.
Hull, 108, 225, 228.
Hyett, Frank, 158, 171.
Hyndman, H. M., 25, 26, 27, 28, 29, 31, 40, 42, 104.

Independent Labour Party, 41, 98–105.
Industrial Disputes' Act, 179, 195.
Industrial Federation (South Africa), 198.
Industrial League, 195.
Industrial Solidarity, 203–13, 267.
'Industrial Solidarity', 224–28.
'Industrial Syndicalist', 206.
Industrial Syndicalist Conference, 207.
Industrial Syndicalist Education League, 207, 230, 233, 234, 235, 253, 256, 258, 263.
Industrial Unionism, 161, 194–6.
Industrial Workers of the World, 196, 203, 267.
International Conference of Trade Unionists, 51, 53.
International Federation of Ship, Dock, and River Workers, 106, 119, 278.
International Labour Organisation, 106–17.
International Socialist Congress—
Paris (1889), 103.
Brussels (1891), 103.
London (1896), 103, 104.

International Shipping Federation, 208, 209, 226, 227.
International, First, 278.
International, Second, 278.
International, Third, 271, 278.
International Transport Workers' Conference, 109.
International Workingmen's Association, 278.
Irish Republic, 193.
Irish Transport Workers' Union, 229.
Iron Moulders' Union (New South Wales), 185.
Iron Workers' Association, 77.
Ironfounders' Union, 80.
Isaacs, Rufus, 232, 233, 244, 248.

'Joe Miller', 57, 115.
Jones, J. P., 156, 159, 175.
Jones, W. H., 216, 219, 228.
'Justice' (London), 25, 33, 68, 239.

'Labour Leader', 103, 239, 246, 248.
Labour Movement and the Churches, 85–97.
Labour Party (Australia), 159, 185.
Labour Party (South Africa), 199.
Labour Party (Victoria), 143, 144, 146, 147, 150, 157.
Labour Protection League, 64, 109.
Labour Representation League, 10.
Labour, Royal Commission on, 74–9.
Labour Troubles in South Africa, 1914, 199.
Labour, Union of, 109.
Langdon, Mr. K. C., 251, 252, 253, 255, 256.
Larkin, James, 228, 278.
London Co-operative Wholesale, 80.
London and India Docks Joint Committee, 61, 77.
London Dock Strike of 1889, 60–69; sequel thereto, 70–84.

London Reform Union, 92.
London School Board, 58.
London Tailors' Union, 28.
London Trades' Council, 51.

Mabon, *see* Abraham.
Malthus, 9, 14, 15, 16.
Man with the Red Flag (John Burns), 42.
Mann, Mrs. 175.
Manning, Cardinal L., 65, 85–6, 92, 93.
Maritime Strike of Australasia, 74, 278.
Marx, Karl, 10, 67, 101, 272, 277.
Masons' and Bricklayers' Union (New South Wales), 185.
Melbourne, 28, 136, 142, 146–7, 149–51, 155–6, 158–60, 162–5, 167–9, 171, 174, 175, 177–81, 185, 190, 192, 196–7.
Mersey Carters' Union, 228.
'Miller, Joe', 57, 115.
Millwall Docks' Company, 77–8.
Miners' Association (Victoria), 147.
Miners' Association (New South Wales), 186.
Miners' Federation of Great Britain, 47, 278.
Miners' Strike of 1912, 230, 266, 278.
Miners' Union (New South Wales), 178–9.
Morris, William, 29–33.
Minting Act, 235, 239, 246.

National Amalgamated Coal Porters' Union, 109.
National Amalgamated Sailors' and Firemen's Union, 70, 109.
National Amalgamated Union of Labour, 109.
National Council of Labour Colleges, 278.
National Democratic League, 125.
National Sailors' and Firemen's Union, 70, 109, 207–9, 226, 228.

National Transport Workers' Federation, 207, 215, 227.
National Union of Dock Labourers, 109.
National Union of General Workers, 49.
National Union of Railwaymen, 213, 278.
Nationalisation of Means of Production, Distribution, and Exchange, 43.
New Unionist Movement, 71–3, 79–81.
Nine-Hour Day, 5, 29.
No-Conscription Campaign, 160.
Northumberland Coal-Strike, 46–7.
Northumberland Miners' Association, 47, 51, 77.
Northumberland Miners' Union, 46.

Old Bailey, 28, 42, 232–3, 241/2.
Open Letter to British Soldiers, 230, 235–8, 242–3, 252–4, 256–60.
Operative Society of Bricklayers, 71.
Organisation of General Workers, 118–25.
Oxford Committee of the Universities' Settlement Association, 79–80.

Parliamentarism versus Direct Action, 263–7; see also Syndicalism.
Parliamentary Committee of Trade Union Congress, 51.
Paul, Cedar & Eden, authors of *Creative Revolution*, 271–3.
Plumbers' Union (New South Wales), 185.
Police Brutality, 214–29.
'Political Register', 241.
Port Workers of Antwerp, 109.
Port Workers of Marseilles, 109.
Port Workers of Rotterdam, 109.

Quilliam, W. B. (Carters' Union), 216, 219, 221, 228.
Quilliam (Solicitor), 231, 236, 250.

Railway Mens' Union (Scotland), 77.
Railway Servants, see Amalgamated Society of Railway Servants, and National Union of Railwaymen.
Railway Workers' Union (France), 110.
Railwaymens' Strike (1911), 210–13, 278.
Railways Union (Victoria), 158.
Red International of Labour Unions, 270, 278.
Red Trade Union International, 270, 278.
Right-to-Work Bill, 265.
Rogers, Thorold, 22, 36, 37.
Russian Revolution, 270, 271.

Sabotage, 267.
Sailor Gang (New South Wales), 185.
Sailors and Firemen's Union, 70, 109, 207, 208, 209, 226, 228.
St George's Plateau, 214, 215–19, 221–2, 224, 259.
Scottish Railway Strike, 74.
Seditious Meetings Act, 246.
Self-Government in Industry, 272.
Shakespeare Mutual Improvement Society, 19.
Shearers' Union, 144.
Ship, Dock, and River Workers, International Federation of, 106, 119, 278.
Shipping Federation, see International Shipping Federation.
Signalmen and Pointsmen's Union, 213.
Smillie, Bob, 52, 53.

Smith, E. M., 130–2, 135–6.
Social Democratic Federation, 24–33, 37–46, 49–51, 100–101, 120, 121.
Social Questions Committee, 155, 157.
Social Revolution, 273.
Socialist League, 30–33, 38.
Socialist Party (America), 267.
Socialist Party (Victoria), 157–62, 164–7, 169, 171, 175, 181, 185.
'Socialist Party and Political Action', 161–2.
Socialist Workers, Writers, and Poets (Australia), 157–67.
South Africa, 146, 192, 197–9, 268–9.
South Australia, 146, 148, 186, 187, 190, 191, 192.
South Wales Miners' Federation, 52, 77.
Steelworkers' Strike in USA, 268.
Stone Masons' Union, 51.
'Story of the Dockers' Strike', 68.
Strangeways Prison, 261, 263.
Strike Committee (Liverpool, 1911), 210–14, 217–19, 228.
Sydney, 74, 142, 151, 178–80, 190, 191, 193.
Syndicalism, 196, 203–6, 263–7, 270, 271.
'Syndicalist, The', 230, 232, 234–6, 239, 246–8, 252, 253, 256–60, 261, 263.
Syndicalist Education League, *see* Industrial Syndicalist Education League.
Syndicalists, 110, 203–7, 230–62.

Tea Operatives' and General Labourers' Union, 64.
Thames Steamship Workers, 109.
Third International, 271, 278.
Tillet, Ben, 50, 61, 63–5, 72, 98, 107, 178, 207, 227, 275.
Tolstoy, Leo, 243, 246.
'Tom Mann Train', 192.

Tower Hill, 64, 67.
Trade Union Congress, Liverpool, 1890, 73.
Trade Union Educational League, 268.
Trade Unionism, New and Old, 71.
Trafalgar Square, 42, 45, 46.
'Transport Worker', 214, 215, 217, 224.
Transport Workers' Conference, International, 109.
Transport Workers' Federation, 207, 215, 227, 278.
Treasonable Practices Act, 246.
Trial for Incitement to Mutiny 250–262.
Trotsky, Leon, 272.
Tyneside and National Labour Union, 70.
Typographical Association, 77, 80.

Victoria Dock, 78, 82, 83.

Waiters' Union, 125.
Way to Win, The, 193–5, 275.
Wallace, Alfred Russell, 96.
Webb, Beatrice, 37, 70.
Webb, Sidney, 37, 70, 76.
Wedgwood, J. C., 233, 238, 244, 247, 248.
Wellington Bakers' Union, 183.
Western Australia, 146.
Westinghouse Automatic Brake, 12, 13.
White Star Line, 76, 210, 224.
Williams, John, 25, 28, 39, 42.
Wilson, Havelock, 107, 109, 207, 208, 218, 219, 226.
'Work of the Socialist Party', 164–7.
Workers' Union, 51, 119, 120, 125, 230, 234.
World War, 269, 271.
Wormwood Scrubbs Prison, 261.

Young Ireland Society, 121.